One for Another

Golden's Rules and Tools for
Creating Healthy Relationships

One for Another

*Golden's Rules and Tools for
Creating Healthy Relationships*

Douglas B. Golden, Ph.D.

www.GoldenPathPublishing.com

To Aaron and Rachel, Leah, and Michelle

Designed and text composition by Steve Rachwal
Edited by Charity Heller
Manufactured in the United States of America

ISBN: 978-0-9859993-0-8

Library of Congress Control Number: 2012921342

Golden Path Publishing
www.GoldenPathPublishing.com

Contents

Section III. *Bridging Differences*

Acknowledgments

This book has taken me a long time to write and I have many people to thank. On my sixtieth birthday, six years ago, and after I had been working on it off and on, my wife and my three children wrote me a birthday card encouraging me to double my writing efforts. I had been thinking that, in part, I wanted to leave this book as a legacy to my children, so knowing that they also had an investment in my finishing the writing was motivating.

When I completed my first draft in 2009 I had several readers, my brother Bob and his wife Minna, my friend and colleague Linda Grounds, and, of course, my wife. I am most grateful for their initial read and wonderful suggestions. Linda read the entire book giving me detailed feedback that I found invaluable. My second draft was completed in 2011 and I again ask Linda to be a reader along with two other friends and colleagues, Richard Coleman and Lisa Maas. This time Rich read it from cover to cover making great commentary and Lisa had important overview ideas that were helpful. Linda again helped me in all aspects of this process, from the title to the nuts and bolts of publishing. My friends David Morganstern and Martha Rothstein also read for me making significant contributions. When I sent a copy to my brother-in-law, Steve Rachwal, for an initial review for the layout and design, my sister Karen picked up the draft and started reading it. Her support and enthusiasm really helped. I also sent a copy to my son, Aaron, to ask him technical advise for digital publication and on his own he read the entire book giving me very insightful feedback in many long telephone calls. All of my readers have busy lives so I am particularly appreciative that they found time to help me with my project. Unless you have done writing yourself, it may be difficult to understand the enormity of the contribution by one's spouse. There are an extraordinary number of times that Rhoda served as my consultant. "Do you like it better like this or like that?" And her constant encouragement and support were staple for the completion of this project.

Charity Heller from a Mighty Pen did an outstanding job as my editor. At this very moment Steve Rachwal is designing the book and laying it out for publication. His highly creative and expert skills, and thoughtfulness are already coming together to produce an attractive and accessible finished project. Many thanks.

I want to also acknowledge my many clients over the years who have allowed me into their lives in such a personal way. A huge number of my ideas have sprung forth directly from the work that I have done with them. Many of the exercises were developed in an effort to help them solve their relationship difficulties. Others, who have known of my efforts in writing this book, have been very supportive which has felt wonderful.

I particularly want to acknowledge some people who have been a source of inspiration in addition to my friends and family. For twenty years or so we lived next door to our friends and neighbors, Dick and Arlene Dyke. They were twenty years our seniors and Dick was always calling Arlene his bride. Their loving relationship has served as a model for Rhoda and me and I feel so lucky that they just happened to be next door when we moved in. I also want to acknowledge my parents, Hy and Evelyn Golden (Grandma Golden). I feel so blessed that their relationship gave me life and that I was nurtured and guided by them. Mom's ceaseless energy in the service of others, particularly for the last twenty years after dad died, was not only an inspiration to me, but to countless others as well. And finally, this year, Rhoda and I will be married 39 years. That is a long time and I wear it like a badge of honor. I am so grateful to her as my constant companion and partner for these many years.

Preface

One for Another. Grandma rarely came to the beach anymore

to join her large extended family at the family reunion. She was eighty-five, and coming down the long wooden stairs from the boardwalk to the beach, trudging through the sand, and sitting in the sun was difficult at her age. But she always liked to come down to the beach at least once over that six-day stretch, even if it was only to say hello for a few minutes. I picked her up at the beach house and luckily we found a parking spot, not too far from the boardwalk.

It was hot. The temperature was in the mid nineties, without much of a breeze. Grandma was walking slowly and I held her hand. She was stooped over from years of osteoporosis, so sometimes she had difficulty holding up her head. About halfway down the stairs, we both saw a somewhat overweight woman struggling to get her beach bag back on her shoulder. She had stopped climbing the stairs and was a little pooped out. "May I help you?" Grandma asked. The woman nodded and Grandma slowly proceeded to help readjust the bag on the woman's arm. The woman seemed a little bewildered at first that this perfect stranger, older than herself, had stopped to help her. Her facial expression then changed, and with soft and appreciative eyes she thanked Grandma. With some effort, Grandma raised her head and looked at the woman. The eye contact was but for a brief moment. "One for another," Grandma said. She lowered her head, took my hand, and continued down the stairs. Not another word was said. It was a precious exchange.

I'm sure that Grandma never remembered the incident or thought that it was anything special. The same sort of thing probably repeated itself again and again over the years for Grandma. However, for me, it was powerful. I was dumbstruck by that little moment of caring and Grandma's humanity. "One for another." Those three words that came off Grandma's lips so effortlessly became seared in my memory. I thought those three words, that simple phrase, carried a message that could benefit us all. "One for another" was Grandma Golden's Rule.

Introduction

"The polis (city-state) precedes the family" (Aristotle 384–322 BCE). For many, this statement strikes at the very heart of the notion of individual freedom, one of the greatest achievements of modern Western culture. However, it can be argued that this very quest for individual freedom has created a preoccupation with the self that has been the undoing of the institution of marriage. Aristotle was wary of individual freedom; when he wrote *Politics*, he stated that the rules of order as generated by the state are necessary for family and individual happiness. He believed that becoming a virtuous person required education and training in subjects like ethics, self-discipline and rationality. Successful societies have always lived by rules of order, be they the Ten Commandments, the *Magna Carta*, the U.S. Constitution or the many unwritten rules defined by customs, mores, and manners. Successful relationships require a set of rules that may vary from culture to culture and from relationship to relationship. The breakdown of these rules can easily lead to the deterioration of the relationship.

I believe that Western culture is now experiencing this breakdown. Thus, I am proposing Golden's Rules for creating healthy relationships.

"Do unto others as you would have them do unto you." This is *the* Golden Rule. It has origins in many ancient cultures and it is an ethical cornerstone for many religions. Long before Aristotle it was recognized that societies are strengthened when people get along. The Golden Rule has breadth, good common sense, and a seeming simplicity for helping to create good relationships. Many components of this rule serve as a foundation for Golden's Rules so I will begin by analyzing some of those elements. It's not quite as simple as it appears.

The Golden Rule points out several things:

1. This rule is for *you*. In an eleven-word sentence, the word *you* appears twice. So this is a rule that is referencing what *you* can do to have good relationships with others.

2. The subject matter of this rule is *good relationships with others*.

3. This rule presumes that you *want* to have good relationships with others.

4. There is an assumption that there are things that you *should* do in order for those relationships to be better; thus it is called the Golden **Rule**.

5. It is a plan of *action*. It starts with the word *do*—*Do* unto others.

6. You should take action and *treat others like you want to be treated*.

7. It is presumed that you *know* how it is that you want to be treated.

These components of the Golden Rule are also important for *Golden's Rules*. However, while it is assumed that people *know* how they want to be treated (point 7), many people only vaguely know and they have difficulty articulating what they know. This is one reason for writing this book. Most people don't spend a lot of time thinking about the specifics of how they want to be treated and even if they do, it might be difficult for them to put those specifics into words or actions. I've spent over thirty years as a psychologist in private practice thinking about how people ought to treat one another and I'm putting some of that thinking into words for you. My goal, however, is to not only present compelling ideas but also to help you create action plans for improving your relationship. Throughout this book, I am going to guide, direct, encourage and motivate you so that improvement actually occurs.

Part of the title of this book is *Rules and Tools* for creating a healthy relationship. All of the section headings are *Rules* and many of the statements in boxes are *Tools*. While these Rules and Tools could also be called *pointers, guidelines, suggestions* or *advice*, the words *rules* and *tools* were chosen for a particular reason. The word *rule* was chosen to emphasize that this is something you should do, even if you don't want to, and it should be done with intention and commitment. *Tools* are suggestions for behaving or thinking, that have practical utility for implementing the Rules to help you have a more fulfilling personal life and healthier relationships.

Acquiring these Rules and Tools necessitates having an attitude for personal growth. All growth involves change. Making changes means that you have to think differently, feel differently, or act differently. You might feel awkward or mildly uncomfortable doing something different and that is why it is important to have an attitude for personal growth. Here are four components to this attitude:

1. Embrace new **ideas** or new concepts that guide you.

2. Have an **intention** to act in new ways.

3. **Motivate** your intention.

4. Make a **commitment** to follow through with your intentions.

1. All of the Rules and Tools in this book are **ideas** or cognitions. They are based on my years of practice, intense study and mindful living for most of my sixty-six years of life. In addition to making good common sense, they are reasonable and they are rational. Rationality is an important part of being healthy. These Rules and Tools are ideas that can help you create healthy relationships.

2. If these ideas make sense to you and you want them to improve your life, then you need to create a goal and have a sense of purpose. A self-statement about wanting to do something in particular is your **intention.** Clear, unencumbered intentions are an important component of growth.

3. Once your direction is set and you are positive that you want to go in that direction, you need some fuel in the gas tank. In physics, that fuel or energy is called potential energy. In humans, we can call that energy passion, motivation or willpower. There are four forces that shape your adult life: your genetic inheritance or your nature; your upbringing or your nurture; ongoing things that happen to you through the forces of nature or by the will of others; and things that you make happen by way of your own will. We can control only one of these four forces and that is our will. It is our most powerful personal change agent.

Passion is energy that arises almost without effort. It is motivating and it is essential for good relationships. Willpower is different. It is the energy that you use to get yourself to do things even when you may not feel like doing them. Willpower is the energy of self-discipline. It is very easy for us to do things in the same way that we have always done them, to have habitual behavior and not rock our own boat. The force that pushes us out of our comfort zone is our willpower.

If we liken willpower to fuel in a gas tank it becomes a bit mysterious. First, at different times we seem to have more or less fuel in the tank. How does that happen? Second, we seem to play a role in filling our own tanks. How do we do that? We are able to summon up more willpower at different times, even if it is a mystery exactly how we do it. We can make a choice and we can have initiative. Sometimes we "just do it." There may be some physical or psychological discomfort that we experience when we push ourselves hard and perhaps that can be called our *determination.* Suffice it to say, as long as you're headed in the right direction, the harder you push, the more likely it is that you will get there.

4. When you make an agreement with yourself to follow through with your intentions, it becomes more likely that you will be successful. That agreement to follow through is your **commitment.** A strong commitment increases your motivation to follow through, even if, at any given moment, you may not feel like it.

I wish that improving our relationships could boil down to just one rule, like the Golden Rule or even just a few rules but I just don't think that it's possible. There are over sixty Rules in this book and at the onset that may seem like a lot; but actually some of them overlap and repeat common themes. For example, some of the Rules in the chapter called "Healthy self" are repeated as they apply to relationships:

- being joyous and enjoying your partner's company

- having gratitude and showing appreciation to your partner

- knowing how to be accepting and being able to accept your partner's shortcomings

- developing the construct of relative right and wrong and being able to have that attitude when negative feedback is being given

Sometimes the same concept is approached from different perspectives. I have discovered that people sometimes are more able to understand a concept if it is delivered in one way and not in another, in one context and not in another. And if it is a new concept, repetition helps. Thus, while this may seem like a lot of Rules, I'm sure that they could be synthesized down to fewer themes. However, my goal for this book is not to simply present my ideas; it is to help you learn them.

So, here we go.

Let's get started with *One for Another: Golden's Rules and Tools for Creating Healthy Relationships.*

How to use this book

This book can be used in two distinctly different ways. It can be used in the traditional way as most books and be read from beginning to end. Each chapter builds on the previous chapter, moving from individual health to developing relational bonds to bridging differences to solving problems. Rules and Tools that are developed early in the book support Rules given later in the book. The book is comprehensive and covers a lot of ground.

This book can also be used as a reference, a sort of encyclopedia of skills and guidelines for creating healthy relationships. Each Rule can stand on its own in helping to build a particular skill. Thus you can peruse the Table of Contents and pick out a section that addresses a particular area of concern, without necessarily reading the entire book. Many sections are cross-referenced, so upon completion of one section, another related section can be read to further address your concern. The book can therefore be read in a hop-scotch fashion and not all at once and still give you valuable information for improving your relationships.

One of the primary goals of this book is to give you useful ideas that can be implemented immediately to produce positive results. Thus, all of the Rules and the Tools in this book are action-oriented. Some of them may be self-explanatory and easy to implement; others will require concentrated practice. I have written exercises at the end of each section to assist you in implementing the specific Rule to which it relates. To get the most out of this book, take the extra time to do the exercises. There are a lot of exercises, and doing them all will likely take many months—so be sure to focus on those that are most important to *you*.

Some of the exercises are meant to be done individually and some are meant to be done together with your partner. Finding time to do the exercises with your partner will contribute a great deal in helping you improve your relationship. Finding that time may be easier said than done. **I would like to strongly encourage you to set a regular time or times each week to do these exercises and work on your relationship.** The more effort and time you put in, the more progress and results you will accomplish. I'm often reminded of an old advertisement for changing your oil: *Change your oil now; change your engine later.* I'm sure you get my point.

Many of these exercises are done on an individual level and most of them ask you to develop new thoughts about how to feel, think and act. This requires heightened awareness. It is not likely that any of the ideas in this book will have any impact on you unless they have greater duration and frequency in your consciousness. This means that the ideas need to stay in your mind for an extended period of time and with repetition. One methodology for doing this is keeping a **personal growth notebook.** This is a notebook in which you can write down the ideas that are most important for you to remember and apply. If there are Rules or Tools that are particularly important for you to remember, write them down in your notebook. It will help you to develop new habits for personal and relational growth if you spend a little bit of time looking at your notebook every day. I have consolidated all of the Tools to go with their respective Rule and put them in a "Toolbox."

In addition to reviewing your personal growth notebook and the Toolbox, I would like to make some other **suggestions for how you can heighten your awareness.**

- Read about a topic that is important to you in the morning when you first get up.
- Think about that topic at different times throughout the day.
- Review the topic again before drifting off to sleep.
- Discuss the topic with your partner or with a friend.
- Read about the topic out loud with your partner.
- Write a paragraph or two about the topic.
- Put sticky notes on your mirror with words or phrases that you want on the tip of your consciousness.
- Program software to periodically bring up words or phrases related to the topic.
- Read other self-help books on related topics of interest.
- Chart your progress on a specific plan of action.
- Ask for feedback from others about a behavioral change.
- Take a class or go on a retreat that relates to personal growth.
- Utilize songs or verse as a means of focusing attention on a topic of importance.
- Go to a place of worship while reflecting on some aspect of growth.
- Call on a higher power through prayer.
- Meditate.

Another powerful way to gain awareness and create change is through psychotherapy. If you are already engaged in psychotherapy and are using this book to support that work, thank-you. However, if you find that after developing awareness and doing the exercises you are still not making the kind of progress you would like to make, you might want to consider marital and/or individual therapy. If you are involved in individual therapy and want to improve your relationship, then one of your therapeutic goals should focus on making your own personal changes that will help to improve that relationship. If your therapy turns into a means to support your negative feelings about your partner, it is not likely that you will see any substantial change in your relationship. This book can help you to identify the personal changes that you need to make.

You will notice that some of the Rules in this book require explanations that are many pages, while other Rules are only a couple of pages long. The length of the explanation does not connote the importance of the Rule. Some ideas may be easy to explain and easy to understand but hard to implement.

I would like to make one final point about this book. Having a healthy relationship is not about crisis management; it is about maintenance. Many of the people that I see in my practice come when their relationships are already in a lot of trouble. The Rules and Tools in this book are not only to be used when things are going badly; they are to be used all the time. Balance is one of the keys to life, and finding a balance for maintaining your personal and relational health is essential.

Section I
Healthy Self

Introduction

While this book is a guide for creating strong relationships, you cannot assume that a strong relationship will guarantee happiness. In fact, it is probably best to consider it the other way around; that is, having strong relationships starts with a sense of inner well-being. So I am going to start by discussing personal mental health.

The first four Rules for a healthy self relate to attitudes: a combination of thoughts, beliefs and feelings. They are the attitudes of:

1. Joy
2. Gratitude
3. Loving spirit
4. Lightness/humor

There is often a reciprocal relationship between attitudes and actions. That is, the stronger the attitude, the more likely it is that a behavior will result from that attitude; and the more we act in ways that are associated with the attitude, the stronger the attitude becomes. While there may be many activities that can strengthen these four attitudes—joyful activities, acts of appreciation, acts of loving-kindness, and laughter—there are other pathways for strengthening these attitudes such as contemplation, meditation and prayer. Through the ages, some of the most beautiful prose and poetry ever written are in the form of prayers and many of those prayers contain elements of these four attitudes. I encourage the use of any form of contemplation, meditation or prayer that might be of assistance in achieving these attitudes. Some meditations will be included in the Exercise sections for each of these attitudes. Like changing any habit, the best results for changing or acquiring a new attitude will be achieved by intentional repetition of actions and thoughts daily.

Rules for physical health and a variety of other important rules for achieving good personal mental health will follow the four attitudes.

RULE #01: **Be present with a joyful spirit.**

The first attitude is the attitude of *joyfulness*. I believe that one of the best ways to build and strengthen this attitude is by having joyful experiences in the present moment. **Being present with joyfulness is taking delight in what is going on right now, in this moment.**

- enjoyment that comes through the senses: seeing, hearing, smelling, tasting and touching something that gives us a positive feeling
- enjoyment that arises out of our interests and curiosity
- enjoyment that results from the satisfaction we experience by something that we are doing
- enjoyment from the personal connection that we experience between our self and others

One of the most significant aspects of our intellect is our sense of time. It is often in our consciousness, either in the forefront of our minds or in the background. This sense guides us through our day, from the time we get up till the time we go to sleep. Remembering the past and anticipating the future strengthens survival and adaptation. At any given moment, our attention can be on the past, on the present or on the future. Unfortunately, we can become consumed with regrets about the past and with worries about the future; replacing regret and worry with fond memories and joyous anticipation helps. However, I am also suggesting and encouraging you to have a different kind of joy—a joy that is steeped in the experiences of the moment, the here and now, and not on thoughts that are rooted in time. **Being joyful requires that we not be so captivated by the dimension of time that we are unable to be conscious of the moment. Being mindful of the moment is sometimes called having "presence."**

> *Take delight in what is going on right now, in this moment.*

How we come to joyful feelings is a very individual matter. In the exercises following this section of the book, give some thought to how you bring joy into your life. I could make a list of the various ways that people bring joy into their lives but it would end up being a very long list and I think it would be too impersonal. So, by way of illustration, let me tell you some of the things that bring joy into my life:

I love to be in nature: walking, hiking, skiing, or being on or near the water. But the place that I spend most of my time in nature is in my garden. The beauty of plant life draws my attention to the outdoors and feels wonderful to me, no matter the season. Nurturing a seed or a sapling to a fully adult plant gives me enormous gratification. I feel the presence of the universe in nature.

I love playing the piano and singing. Making music gives me an incredible feeling of presence and music can propel me through a wide range of emotions that is restorative. As I gain mastery over a song, I feel a sense of accomplishment and my creativity unfolds in a way that gives me a strong sense of my uniqueness.

I love spending time with my wife, with my children, with my extended family and with my friends. Enjoying each other's company and having a sense of connectedness completes me. When my presence is reflected back through the presence of others and when I reflect their presence, I feel like a loving entity has been created. Each of these relationships has its own special properties that are dynamic and uplifting. Later is this book, I will discuss the "we." For me, it is powerful and in the moment has a sense of timelessness.

I love to read. It opens up the world to me. It stimulates my brain. It helps me to learn and grow. And it gives me a good laugh.

I love to write. Writing forces me to think and put my swirling thoughts and feelings into words. It unburdens me. I understand myself better by writing.

I love my work. I feel so honored that people share their private and personal stories and feelings with me. And I get great satisfaction from feeling like I have made a difference in people's lives by helping them with their difficulties. I feel blessed that I am able to do this work.

I love a lot of simple little nothings. It's a bit hard to explain but I think that it arises from sensations and interests.

These are some of the things that bring joy into my life.

But that's me. What about you? Is it important to you to have joy in your life? Does it give your life meaning? I suppose, in some ways, it is an existential question. **For the purposes of this book and for what I am saying about mental health, I am proposing that having joyful feelings within yourself and within your relationships is essential.**

As we cruise through life, starting from the moment of our birth, we encounter a multitude of sensations and stimuli. Some of those stimuli give rise to positive feelings and some stimuli give rise to negative feelings. Some people spend the better parts of their lives just trying to quiet the negatives, while others seek out the positives.

If you are twelve years old and you are going for a ride in the car, you can spend your time making sure that your siblings don't have a better seat than you; that the window isn't down and creating a draft; that your parents won't make you wait too long to go to the bathroom; that you won't get hungry; that you aren't going to be bored wherever it is that you are going; that your friends won't dump you while you are gone and that you remembered to pack everything that you need...

Or you can enjoy the car ride: play car games with your siblings, look out the window, listen to music, read, relax, plan some fun things to do or write a letter to a friend.

Life is kind of like that car trip. If you live life for the purpose of avoiding discomfort, any little disruption that has the smallest negative quality will command your attention. However, if you lead life in an uplifted way, minor negative things will roll off your back, and if your attention is on the positives, you will be preoccupied with them.

> *Actively bring positive thoughts and feelings into your mind so that little negative things can roll off your back.*

One of the goals for good mental health is living with an uplifted and joyful spirit. A great deal of psychotherapy serves the purpose of helping people remove the barriers that stand in the way of having that spirit. Many sections of this book serve the same purpose of helping to remove these barriers. Barriers have to come down but that is not the only thing to do to reach the goal of joyfulness. You have to actively try to create a joyous spirit in order to reach this goal. If it doesn't come naturally, then you have to make it happen. If you are traveling down the road and you get a flat tire, you have to get out and fix the flat. However, you need to get back in, once the flat is fixed and enjoy the ride!

I do think that some people have an easier time having a joyful spirit than others. Some are just born with more delight, more fascination or more curiosity than others. We assume there is some component in the human biochemical physiology, in the human DNA that makes it easier or harder.

Our upbringing further impacts our innate physiology and the biochemistry of our brain. As I mentioned in the introduction, these two forces, nature and nurture, are very powerful in shaping who we are, including whether or not we are delighted or distressed by the sensations all around us. The other force that I mentioned is called willpower. **It is that force, your willpower, your conscious choosing and the effort you expend, which helps you to reach the goal of having a joyful spirit.** It may be harder for some than others. If you tend towards being easily distressed rather than being delighted, it will be harder work for you. **You can spend a lot of time tearing down barriers, and that work can be hard, but without doing the work of creating a joyful spirit, you may end up feeling miserable because it will always seem like there is another barrier to bring down.**

> *If you spend all your time bringing down barriers, you will never experience the joy that you are trying to reach.*

You can do several things to create this joyous spirit. The first is to go back to your primary state of consciousness and begin to notice the sensations that impact you. Concentrate on the sensations that are pleasurable to your body and hold them in your awareness. Try to let the uncomfortable sensations pass in and out of your consciousness so that they get less of your attention.

For example, if you are sitting outside in a chair, try to notice the pleasantness of the sun, the wind against your skin, the variety of colors and shapes of objects around you, the sound of the wind in the trees, any pleasant smells, the steady beating of your heart, the rhythm of your breath. Hold those sensations in your consciousness.

If the chair is a bit uncomfortable, if the temperature changes while you are sitting and at times you feel too warm or too cold, if you happen to notice that a pigeon has pooped on the ground not far from where you are sitting, or if you feel a bit hungry, see if you can let those sensations come and go while still holding on to the pleasant sensations.

This state of consciousness can be taken anywhere and can always be used as a tool for creating joyfulness in your life.

> **1. Hold pleasurable sensations in your consciousness.**

A second thing to do for creating a joyful spirit is to develop your sense of curiosity and interest. One of the defining features of the human brain is the desire to know why and how things are the way they are. Our ability to build things, to create and to solve problems is on orders of magnitude higher than any other species. The human brain is also defined by our pursuit of knowledge. Your brain has all of these features; if they remain idle, your interest in life will slowly diminish. To grow this capacity of your mind is to ask questions like the young child asks: *Dad, why are apples red? Why are there little seeds inside the apple? Why do apples fall to the ground? Why do the leaves fall off the apple tree when the weather gets cold? How did the apple tree get there? Have there always been apple trees? Do apple trees die? Can I grow an apple tree? Who was Johnny Appleseed? Did Johnny Appleseed have a real job?*

...if you have ever spoken to a curious child, you know that these kinds of questions can go on forever. We also know there is a certain kind of joyfulness in curiosity. It is that kind of mental activity that can lead to great joy for you. **If life seems boring, start asking questions and be interested in the answers.**

---

2. *Develop your sense of curiosity and interest.*

A third way to create joy has to do with activity. Since we are mobile creatures who spend two-thirds of our days awake and active, we want to do things that we enjoy. There are many tasks that we do that we may not call enjoyable; however, on the list of all the things that we do in life, there needs to be a considerable number of activities that we can enjoy. If for some reason you don't do many things that you enjoy, then you need to begin to explore and pursue new activities that can accomplish this for you. These activities need to be pursued with the attitude of conscious enjoyment that I described above. But activities are not only about sensations; pursue activities that also promote your interest. Don't give up if you don't immediately take a liking to a particular activity. Practice steps one and two above to see if you can develop activities that are enjoyable.

---

3. *Do things that you enjoy.*

The fourth step is creating enjoyable relationships. If you can do the first three steps toward creating enjoyment in your life, this fourth step will be much easier to accomplish and it will feel better when you do. When you can hold pleasurable things in your consciousness, develop your sense of curiosity and interest, and do things that you enjoy—and if you do these with someone else—life can feel pretty wonderful. If you rely on others to do the first three steps for you, your relationships will be unbalanced and may become a burden for the other person. You have so much more to give when you bring a spirit of joyfulness to a relationship. Joy that is created in a relationship is almost addictive. This book is principally about relationships, so it's obvious that I believe that relationships are one of the finest kinds of joys that people can experience. For many, the absence of relationships and the resulting loneliness can be one of the lowest lows. With this in mind, I encourage you to journey down the path of creating joy in your life and taking your loved ones on that journey with you.

4. Create enjoyable relationships.

Many people use chemical substances to create a spirit of joyfulness and some caution needs to be exercised regarding this. Too often, these substances are used exclusively and addictively to feel joy. This comes at great cost to the individual and to relationships. In and of themselves, substances don't create joy. They may help a person to be less depressed or anxious, stop ruminating, cope better with stress, and even enhance some joyful aspect of experience but, on their own, they don't produce joy. Far worse than that, if used in excess or inappropriately, substances can hurt the body and become addictive in a way that interferes with a person's ability to have joy. When that happens, substances only end up producing pain and despair. In fact, if you are abusing substances, most of this book won't be of much help to you because you won't be sufficiently conscious to do the work that you might need to do. Denial is a key component of substance abuse; if you use substances regularly, ask yourself several questions that will help you realize if you are over using or abusing substances:

- Do I use substances almost every day?
- Are the substances I use prescription or non-prescription?
- Is the way in which I get the substances legal?
- Are the substances I use legal?
- Do I have habitual use of substances?
- Do I use them till they are gone?

- Do they prevent me from doing other activities that are constructive?
- Do I use them as a result of an acute need?
- Has anyone else told me that the substances I take make my behavior worse?
- Has my doctor told me to stop?
- Do the substances I take interfere with my sleep, eating, or any other aspect of my physical health?

While responding "yes" to any single question may not necessarily mean there is a problem, good judgment will likely be your guide. If you are unsure, ask yourself this question: *If I gave my answers to the above questions to someone I love and respect, would they think that I had a problem with substances?* If the answer is "yes," then you probably do. I started this paragraph by stating that this is a cautionary note; please, don't rely on substances to bring joy into your life. Expend the effort that is required for creating joy in more permanent and less destructive ways.

> ## *Be careful with the use of substances.*

Life is so short. Be aware that each day you live, you have one less day. Every day is precious. Don't waste them. You are blessed to have the gift of life. It is a journey and it will come to an end. Make the enjoyment of the trip one of your highest priorities. Don't wait! Seize the moment and turn it into joy. Don't wait to survive a heart attack to enjoy the beating of your heart. Don't wait to survive cancer to awaken with happiness that you are alive another day. Don't take too long after waking up to begin enjoying your day. Start by finding joy in the mundane, in all the little relatively inconsequential things of daily living. Find some bigger ways in which life can be joyful and orient yourself towards that. Don't dwell on the negatives. Let them pass by if you can. **Embrace life, create a positive and joyful outlook, make each day precious and enjoy the trip.**

> ## *Enjoy the trip.*

- *Take delight in what is going on right now, in this moment.*

- *Actively bring positive thoughts and feelings into your mind so that the little negative things can roll off your back.*

- *If you spend all your time bringing down barriers, you will never experience the joy that you are trying to reach.*

- *Hold pleasurable sensations in your consciousness.*

- *Develop your sense of curiosity and interest.*

- *Do things that you enjoy.*

- *Create enjoyable relationships.*

- *Be careful with the use of substances.*

- *Enjoy the trip.*

EXERCISES FOR BEING PRESENT WITH A JOYFUL SPIRIT

1. Spend some time by yourself and write down the kinds of things that bring you joy. Discuss what you think are the various components of those things that create joyful feelings.

2. Think about how you commonly spend your days and your weeks. Think about the amount of attention that is focused on the past, present and the future. Using a scale of 100 percent, roughly assign a percentage to the amount of attention that you give to each. Write it down.

3. When you think of what presence is for you, what words come to mind? Write down the descriptors of the variety of feelings that occupy presence for you. Using a scale of 100 percent, roughly assign a percentage to the amount of attention that you give to each. Was a feeling of joy on your list? What percentage did it get?

4. Think about whether you attempt to be happy more by taking down barriers or more by directly creating positive and joyful experiences for yourself.

5. Practice holding pleasurable sensations in your consciousness. You can do this in two ways:

a. Sit in a chair somewhere. Try to pay attention to the sensory information that you receive and try to distinguish between positive and negative sensations. Try to let the positive sensations occupy your consciousness and try to let the negative sensations pass through your consciousness.

b. Try to do this same exercise while you are walking down the street or while you are involved with some other activity. The more involved the activity, the harder this exercise will be; but try anyway. For example, if you are outside washing your car, try to be conscious of pleasurable sensations even while you are concentrating on doing a good job.

6. Write down ten things that interest you. Why do you suppose that you are interested in those ten things? Write down your answers.

7. Write down five things or five people about which or whom you know very little. Write down ten questions about those things or about those people that would help you to get to know about it or about them better.

8. Review your schedule for the past week and try to remember if you were engaged in activities that brought you joy. Write down what some of those things were. What percent of the entire week do you think you were involved in activities that you could call joyful? Consider whether or not you spend enough time devoted to joyful activities. If not, see if you can make a plan for spending more time on joyful activities. Implement that plan.

9. Write down five new things to do that might bring you joy. Consider whether or not you want to begin doing any of those activities. If so, create a plan for doing them. Implement that plan.

10. Think about the amount of time you spend interacting with people you like. Does this seem adequate? If not, create a plan for spending more time with people you like. Implement that plan.

11. Does it seem that you don't have enough people in your life with whom you spend enjoyable time? If so, why is that the case for you? Do you feel lonely? What else could you do to meet new people? Make a plan and implement the plan.

12. Are you overusing or abusing substances? Use the screening test above if you are unsure. If you are overusing or abusing substances, create a plan of action for diminishing your use.

RULE #02: **Have an attitude of gratitude.**

If you have joyful moments in your life, try developing gratitude for those moments. It has not been uncommon over the years for people to tell me that their mothers or fathers taught them not to expect "thanks" for things that they were supposed to do. Appreciation was given only in the rare occurrence of an event that was out of the ordinary and unusually special; giving thanks for common everyday occurrences was not done. I have also met people who feel like they deserve to have what they have. In fact, they sometimes feel entitled to have even more than what they have, as though they have a "manifest destiny" for wealth and good fortune. The trouble is, when that destiny is not fulfilled, they can feel pretty miserable.

I don't share any of those points of view. **I believe that it is entirely an act of good fortune that we are even alive.** If we could figure out the probability that a single egg and sperm would result in a specific individual, we would likely find that the probability to be astronomically low. Yet here we are. Life starts miraculously. And just think: You were born into life at *this* time in the existence of the human race, when technology is advanced and medical science and good nutrition allows us to live longer and with more ease. If you are reading this book, first, you can read; second, you had means to acquire a book. Considering the huge numbers of illiterate people in the world and the high degree of poverty, you're doing pretty well. You are not a slave, impoverished, illiterate or starving. You are likely not a victim of tyranny, pestilence or famine. And if, by chance, you have been victimized, it is likely that you are now seeing brighter days.

> *Raise your consciousness for all that you have and be grateful that you have it.*

If enjoying life is the first key to happiness, then being grateful for the life you have is the second key to happiness. This means noticing all the things that are going well for you and feeling good that they are going well. It means appreciating all the things you have rather than feeling envy and bitterness for those things you don't have. It means taking pleasure in people and what they add to your life rather than seeing them as insufficient, punishing or barriers to getting what you want. It means enjoying and appreciating nature in all its forms and particularly as nature manifests in your neighborhood.

Enjoy nature in **your** neighborhood.

Gratitude is different than pride. Pride is taking credit for our attributes or accomplishments. *Gratitude* is giving credit to forces outside of our personal control. Gratitude about our attributes and accomplishments is *humility;* it is knowing that they have many elements of causality outside of our control. Unlike entitlement, gratitude means treating what you have as though it is a gift. Even if what you have is the result of your own hard efforts, you can be grateful that you were blessed with the abilities to accomplish what you accomplished. Gratitude is an attitude that can be available at any given moment. It can be on the tip of your tongue. Just the thought of it and a breath of air can almost instantaneously begin to alter your mood. It is a powerful leveler. When people experience gratitude simultaneously, all other moods can more easily be resolved, leaving a wonderful sense of connectedness.

Have humility about your attributes and your accomplishments.

Often the question arises: *If I am grateful, to whom am I grateful? If I am thankful, to whom should I give thanks?* The answer is: to whomever or whatever you would like, as long as it comes with the feelings of gratitude. Over the years, I have been exposed to an enormous number of belief systems that speak to this issue. What seems to tie most of them together is a belief in a force or an entity over which there is no control and to which there is gratitude. Some people call that force *God,* some people call that force the *Power* and some people say that it is the force that has no name. For some people, this force is very personal; for others it is not. Some people pray to this force and some give homage to this force through meditation. It is a personal matter and it ought to be personal to you. You choose to whom or to what you are grateful. For the purposes of this book, I simply call this force the *force of the universe.*

- *Raise your consciousness for all that you have and be grateful that you have it.*
- *Enjoy nature in your neighborhood.*
- *Have humility about your attributes and your accomplishments.*

EXERCISES FOR HAVING AN ATTITUDE OF GRATITUDE:

1. Think about your upbringing and reflect on whether having an attitude of gratitude was a part of that upbringing. Did your parents have feelings of gratitude? Or did they teach you that "thanks" was only given for things that were unexpected?

2. Do you think you were raised with feelings of entitlement? Were you raised to believe that you deserved to have what you have? Were you raised to believe that you should have more than what you have?

3. Do you think that you are a grateful person? How often does gratitude occur to you? Do the kind of thoughts that you have on Thanksgiving only come on Thanksgiving?

4. Do thoughts of gratitude come to you only by way of things that people do for you or are you grateful for who you are or what you have regardless of who was involved in giving it to you?

5. Write a list of at least ten things for which you are grateful that are the direct results of someone else's efforts.

6. Write a list of at least ten things for which you are grateful and which are not the direct result of someone else's efforts.

7. If you haven't done so already, see if you can develop a time for morning contemplation. Use some of that time to contemplate thoughts and feelings of gratitude. Try to gather readings, meditations or prayers that have been written on the topic and use them as part of your morning contemplation. Write something yourself, if you are so inclined.

I wrote a morning meditation for a friend of mine a few years ago who was struggling. I was empathic to his struggles but I wanted him to try connecting with a feeling of gratitude for the many things he had. Perhaps you could adopt it for yourself as a way to count your own blessings. Here it is:

A Meditation on Gratefulness

Good morning, universe
    and thank you.
Thank you for the darkness that is followed
    by the light.
And thank you for the cleansing rain,
    the warming sun
    and the cooling breezes.

And thank you for creating me:
    my brain that gives me understanding,
    my heart that can feel the pain in others,
    my hands for building and for planting,
    my legs for wandering,
    my eyes to see your majesty,
    my ears to hear your glory.

You have given me
    health,
    wakefulness,
    self-awareness,
    curiosity,
    memory,
    compassion,
    generosity,
    playfulness,
    resilience,
    perseverance,
    ingenuity,
    acceptance,
    holiness,
    and love.

I have been blessed with your abundance:
> *ample (and delicious) food,*
> *a beautiful and secure home,*
> *lush gardens,*
> *layers for withstanding the elements,*
> *beautiful children,*
> *loyal pets,*
> *caring friends,*
> *devoted teachers,*
> *colorful acquaintances,*
> *places to exercise my spirituality,*
> *work and study that sustains my interest,*
> *travels to breathtaking places,*
> *music that I can both make and enjoy,*
> *great toys,*
> *and wonderful spots to sit and lay down*

I started with less and now I have more.

I have been given many abilities and talents
so that I might enjoy my life in such a profound fashion.

For all of this I am so grateful.
I bow my head in solemn reverence
> *and praise the benevolence of the universe.*

RULE #03: **Be generous and loving.**

If you enjoy life and have a grateful attitude, being generous and loving comes with greater ease. People are generous in so many different ways. Some people give back by making charitable financial contributions, some give their time through volunteerism, some give their talents, some give with listening and compassion. We usually think of generosity as being extended to other people but generosity can also be extended to animals or even to the planet. There are people who volunteer by working in animal shelters and others who volunteer by helping fight forest fires or picking up debris in public areas. All of these acts of generosity have one thing in common: **In the moment of generosity, there is a suspension of personal needs in the service of another.** For that time, be it brief or extended, there is not a need to get something in return. It is as if to say, *I feel that I have enough right now, so I want to do something for you.*

> ### *There are many ways to be generous.*

Generosity is a continuum of planned and spontaneous generosity. *Planned generosity* is thought out in advance and delivered in a prescribed fashion. Giving gifts is planned generosity. Making something for someone else is planned generosity. *Spontaneous generosity* occurs when a person is not necessarily thinking about someone else and then a moment occurs in which giving seems important. This can be the act of a good Samaritan who comes upon someone who is injured or in distress. It could be sharing food that was just about to be eaten alone. There are many types of generosity somewhere in between these two polarities. Many types of volunteerism are planned in advance but knowing exactly what is going to be encountered may not be apparent until the last moment. Shoveling snow for an elderly neighbor may be planned a day in advance but it can also be spontaneously done.

This distinction is made because it calls upon a different mindset to be prepared for generosity at a moment's notice. To have this mindset, you have to be able to be interrupted. You have to be able to switch gears and direct your attention to the needs of others, no matter what else you are doing, as if to say, *Right now somebody else is more important than me.* While all generosity is wonderful, spontaneous generosity is harder to achieve. The more gratitude that you have and the more you feel like your own needs are satisfied, the easier spontaneous generosity is to achieve.

Develop both planned and spontaneous generosity.

There is an old expression and a title of a song that says, "Love makes the world go 'round." I believe that romantic love does make the world go 'round and so do other kinds of love. Thousands of songs and poems have been written about romantic love, infatuation and broken hearts. Whether it is the "Songs of Solomon," "The Song Angels Sing" or "Your Song," the theme is one of romantic love. Affection and romance are deserving of a thousand songs and a thousand more, however, it is not this meaning of love that I am now discussing. Romantic love is filled with passion. It also contains the expectation that love will be returned. **Romantic love is not selfless.**

The love of attachment is another wonderful form of love but it is typically not selfless love, either. There is some aspect of mutual need fulfillment in attachment, even in the parent-child relationship. A particular type of attachment is called *unconditional love*. Those words quite literally mean *love without conditions*. It is the kind of love that is best exemplified in the parent-child relationship and in some other family relationships. It is the notion that whatever the child does and whoever the child is, the parent will love her nonetheless. Love will not be withdrawn. Most other relationships are typically not unconditional. Most relationships have boundaries and limits and if those boundaries are crossed, love is withdrawn. In marriage, love is not unconditional; sometimes love just diminishes and if boundaries are violated, love may be withdrawn. **Among the many types of loving attachments, unconditional love is closest to selfless love and the loving spirit.** Unconditional love is not the same as selfless love because it typically manifests in ways in which love is returned. A child responds to his parents' hugs by hugging back and there is a big payoff in that returned hug. Without a doubt, unconditional love can certainly spring forth more readily from the loving heart.

Romantic love and attachment love are not selfless love.

The English language uses but one word to describe all different kinds of love. Selfless love is a feeling of care and concern for fellow human beings, animals or the planet, without regard to getting something in return. It may be described as having a "loving spirit," and it is exemplified by acts of loving-kindness. The loving spirit is its own reward; it is satisfying in its own right. Having a loving spirit connotes a gentle, attentive and nurturing quality. It means extending ourselves with an open heart, tenderness and with our shoulders down so as to invite and encourage the loving spirit in others. I believe that some of the finest qualities of human beings are contained in acts of loving-kindness: care, compassion, concern, empathy and generosity. These are all qualities of a person with a loving spirit. A person can feel passionate about having a loving spirit without the passion of romantic love. It is not a feeling that comes and goes, based on a particular individual or individuals. *The loving spirit, once achieved, can be constant, enduring and ever present.* Particularly during times of stress, it may be necessary to remind ourselves to be conscious of having a loving heart, but the more we practice, the easier and more omnipresent having a loving spirit becomes.

> ### *Have presence with caring, compassion, concern, empathy and generosity.*

One of the best examples I can give you of someone with a loving heart is a woman I met some years ago. Her name was Effie. Effie was a good nurturing mom who looked after all of her children, making sure that they were all fed, clothed, sheltered, tucked in at night, supported, and unconditionally loved. However, it was how she related to her community that defined the essence of her loving spirit. Effie had very little preoccupation with her own personal needs. Food wasn't that important to her; she always slept easily and well; she exercised enough to keep fit (even ice-skating into her late eighties); she didn't have materialistic concerns; clothes were for keeping warm and cars were for transportation. What was important to her was the health and welfare of people in her community. She was a great believer in the old adage: *The love in your heart wasn't put there to stay; love isn't love till you give it away.* Effie lived that adage and gave away her love every day of her life by participating in every sort of community volunteer effort. She served on boards for people with disabilities, the disadvantaged and those who were sick and dying. She worked in the schools and helped to promote adult educational programs. She cooked for people who couldn't cook for themselves. She worked with the elderly, help-ing them to stay fit. **Her acts of loving-kindness were personal and were direct.** People felt her impact in the way she said good morning because she really wanted them to have a good morning. Everyone's story was important, so she made time to listen. While Effie had boundaries around what she wanted and needed to do to be a good mother and wife, she said "yes" many more times than she said "no" to a request for her help. I heard her talk once about how she modeled her life after her father, whom she called a humanitarian. It is wonderful word to describe people who work in the service of others. It is a way to translate the loving spirit into acts of loving-kindness, particularly as it relates to other humans. There are many humanitarians among us. You can be a *humanitarian*. Effie lived by another code that is written on her tombstone. It says, *It is not what you get but what you give that measures the worth of the life you live.* I mention Effie to illustrate what it means to have a loving spirit. We cannot all give in the way that Effie gave but we can all have a loving spirit that compels us towards acts of loving-kindness, no matter how big or small.

> • *Develop both planned and spontaneous generosity.*
>
> • *Have presence with caring, compassion, concern, empathy, and generosity.*

EXERCISES FOR BEING GENEROUS AND LOVING:

1. Do you consider yourself to be a generous person? How are you generous? Write down five to ten ways that you show generosity.

2. Do you think that your generosity is more planned or spontaneous? Go over the examples that you listed above and designate whether your generosity is more planned or spontaneous.

3. What could you do to have a mindset of spontaneous generosity? Write it down.

4. Write down ways in which you have the three different kinds of love: romantic love, relational/attachment love and a loving spirit.

5. Think about the five qualities of the loving spirit mentioned in the text: caring, compassion, concern, empathy and generosity. Write a sentence or two on what each one of these words mean to you. They will all be discussed as you read through this book and you might come back and look at your definition after you have read something else about it.

6. Consider whether these are qualities you wish to have. Think about how you currently manifest these qualities and how wish to manifest these qualities. Bring attention to these qualities during some of your morning meditations.

7. Gather any poems, prayers, or writings on the subject of loving spirit and make them a part of your morning meditation/contemplation. Write something of your own if you wish. After Grandma passed away, I wrote a prayer/meditation in her memory that I would like to share. It starts and ends with feelings of gratitude, because I believe that having a loving spirit is founded on gratitude. I gave it the same title as I gave this book.

One for Another

Oh, Great Universe,
Thank you for giving me another day
> *so that I might see your majesty.*

You bring me such abundance,
> *sustenance, joy, pleasures,*
> *and the warm presence of the human spirit*
> *that surrounds me.*
I want not.

Today I mirror
> *your glory*
> *by finding the loving part of me*
> *that honors you.*

As I have been given so much,
> *today, lead me to be the giver.*
Let me use my senses
> *not only to delight in your beauty,*
> *but also to hear the suffering,*
> *see the afflicted,*
> *and feel the broken heart.*

As you grace me with shade
> when I am warm,
> and give me warm clothes
> when I am cold,
> so, too, help me to be discerning,
> so that I can give what is needed
> rather than what I need to give.

Give me a gentle hand
> so that I can feed
> even the most timid,
> and outstretched arms
> that I can embrace
> all of your creatures.

Awaken me from routine
> so that I don't become complacent.
Let me not be obsessed
> by ambition.
Give me awareness of pride
> so that my service to you
> is not muted by service to myself.

Help me to have confidence
> that love is expressed
> in small daily acts of devotion
> and not grand acts or displays.

Help me to heal quickly
> from all forms of hurts,
> sufferings, and indignations,
> so that I might move
> from my self-involvement
> to caring for others.

And help me to stay humble
>   so that I can clearly feel the need
>   of those who are in my immediate reach
>   so that I might extend to them
>   my deepest love.

For all this
>   I give thanks.

RULE #04: **Have a lightness of being and a sense of humor.**

This section is not about how to be funny. I don't know the first thing to tell somebody how to be funny. I know that sometimes I'm funny, but I couldn't tell you how I get there. Comedians probably know how to talk about it, but I don't. What I can talk about is how to enjoy humor and how to have a light-hearted attitude. That's what this section is about.

So many things in life are unbelievable or absurd or just don't make sense. If you try to make sense of them, you can't. If you get too bummed out, you'll be miserable. So you may as well laugh about it. I'll give you a couple of examples from my own life.

About six weeks before my wife was supposed to deliver, we were at the obstetrician's office. There he told us that my wife was going directly from his office to the hospital because she was going to be having a baby—likely in several hours. I ran home to get all of our gear for the delivery. I figured I'd better clean my contact lenses one last time because I didn't know how long I would be at the hospital (dumb idea). I typically rinsed my lenses over the sink so that any excess saline would just go down the drain…and I usually put in the stopper, but I was in a hurry (another dumb idea). You can probably guess, while I was rinsing, one of the lenses slipped out of my fingers and washed down the drain. I figured that I *had* to have my contacts (I don't even remember why I had *that* dumb idea) so I went down to the basement and found a pipe wrench so I could take off the trap of the sink drain. When I dumped out the water into a colander, sure enough, there was my contact. I washed it again, this time not over the sink, and headed over to the hospital. I had my own quiet little drama while my wife was staring down an early delivery. To me, this story is so absurd it is funny. I laugh every time I think about it now.

Here is another example. This was probably twenty years ago. Our kids were quite little and we were all headed to the Oregon coast for an overnight trip. As you can imagine, it is always a bit of an ordeal to get children ready and out the door for an overnight, and we were likely running a little behind our ideal departure time. It was a Saturday morning and my wife wanted to stop at Starbucks for a coffee to go. She thought it would take but a few minutes. It turned out there was quite a line, and what we originally thought might be five minutes was turning into fifteen minutes. As the minutes ticked by, I become increasingly more frustrated and inpatient. I left the parking spot that we were in and started driving around the parking lot. By the time my wife got into the car, I was in a noticeably quiet mood. You know—the type you can cut with a knife. It took about five minutes to get from the Starbucks to the freeway, and nobody said a word. I can remember it as though it were yesterday. Just as I was about to make the left-hand turn to get onto the freeway, the thought came into my mind: *Doug, you're going to the beach. You're not going to catch a plane. We aren't going to be late to the show. You're going to the beach.* The absurdity of the whole thing got to me and I just started laughing. Of course, that broke the ice for everyone, and we were able to get onto the road with Dad in much better humor. The disaster was averted by the mere thought of the absurdity of it all.

There are tons and tons of these kinds of events in our lives. **We have to be able to laugh at ourselves.** We can't take things too seriously. Now I know that there can be a fine line between when it is time to laugh and when it isn't, but **you have to be ready to laugh, just in case you're well within the bounds that laughter is appropriate.** You have to be ready to put a smile on your face, to draw up your lips and let out a roar.

> *Don't be too serious! Be able to laugh at the absurd and at yourself.*

Some things are foolish and even goofy. We can be goofy ourselves. It's fun. We can be playful. Many people like to be playful, but sometimes the heaviness of adult living bears down on our shoulders so heavily that we get stuck and can't see humor in anything. If you are one of these people, develop a willingness to laugh and try to focus on something funny. You can be in the mood for humor long before the comedy show ever starts. That's the goal. It's having the attitude. Who knows? If you get into the mood well enough, you may end up being humorous yourself.

> *Be in a mood for humor before the comedy show begins!*

My dad could be very funny. He had that Jack-Benny type of delivery, with the pause and the look. Some of you know what I mean. Johnny Carson had it, too.

It makes me smile just to think of those three men. Well, anyway, Dad used to tell the same joke over and over at our dinner table when we were growing up. It always made Mom slightly uncomfortable because it was a bit off color, and I hope that I don't offend you, because I'm going to tell it now. (I can almost hear my siblings now, saying to themselves, *I can't believe that he is going to put that dumb joke in his book!* But I am.) Not because it is all that funny, because it isn't. It is about laughing at the ridiculous. Well, here goes:

Two rather proper Englishmen were sitting silently on a park bench for what seemed like an indeterminable amount of time, when one of them turned to other and said (Dad used the thickest British accent he could muster at this point), "I say, old chap, did you just s__t?" To which the other gentleman replied, "Well, of course I did. You don't think I smell like this *all* the time."

That is when my father would roar in laugher, and although we kids had heard that same old tired joke a hundred times, we would roar in laughter as well. Mom would go and sort of tidy up the dishes about the time we were all laughing, and say, "Oh, Dad!" And we would all laugh a bit more. It was sweet, funny, and light-hearted. It was about not taking life too seriously.

> **Be able to laugh at dumb jokes.**

Many years ago, Norman Cousins wrote a book called *The Anatomy of an Illness*. It was essentially an autobiographical book about how he survived a very serious illness. Part of his cure was watching old humorous TV shows so he could get a good belly laugh. He believed that this was an integral part of his healing process. I have since gathered together all my funniest DVDs and put them right on the top shelf of my bookcase. They are part of my hospital gear should I ever be hospitalized with a serious illness. My wife will know right where to find them—I just hope she doesn't drop her contacts in the sink on her way out the door.

> - **Don't be too serious. Be able to laugh at the absurd and at yourself.**
> - **Be in a mood for humor before the comedy show begins.**
> - **Be able to laugh at dumb jokes.**

EXERCISES FOR HAVING A LIGHTNESS OF BEING AND A SENSE OF HUMOR:

1. Was there anything in this section that gave you a lightness of being? Do you have an idea why? If it did give you a sense of lightness, close your eyes to see if you can hold on to the feeling for a few minutes.

2. Do you know what kinds of things bring a smile to your face? Write down a few. Do you know what kinds of things make you laugh out loud? Write down a few of those as well.

3. See if you can remember any stories about yourself that make you smile now, or even make you laugh. Write down a sentence or two about a few of them, so you can remember what they are. Close your eyes and replay the situations in your mind; when the story stops, keep your eyes closed to see if you can hold on to the feeling for a little while longer.

4. Do you know any funny jokes? Put them in a file. Add other jokes when your find them. Look at your joke file from time to time and laugh to yourself.

5. Make a list of some of the most light-hearted or funny movies, TV shows, YouTube videos, or short stories that you can remember. Create a little stash of these gems for yourself that you can go to in a time of need.

Good physical health leads to good mental health.

Plain and simple, if you aren't physically healthy, all of the rest of the suggestions in this book will be more difficult to do. It is important to try to be as physically healthy as possible. **That means getting a good night sleep, eating properly, exercising and seeing a health practitioner when appropriate.** You already know this. So if you aren't living a healthier lifestyle, you probably have a good reason, like:

- not enough time
- too much stress
- too much availability of unhealthy choices
- not enough self-discipline

My clients tell me that their number one reason for not exercising or shopping for fresh food and preparing it is they are too busy. Making a living creates tremendous time demands, and typically both members of a partnership are working. Times have really changed from when at least one parent was home to do most of the domestic jobs. My clients report typical daily schedules that are dominated by work leaving little time for anything else. Weekends are often packed with a multitude of domestic responsibilities. However, with careful scheduling and cooperation, they often find extra time for health-related activities. If exercise is done from home, it is less time consuming. Many people resist the degree of structure that may be required to squeeze in everything, but there may not be any other choice. It's a real commitment.

> *Try to find time in your schedule for doing health related activities.*

Life today is stressful. No longer do people say their current circumstances are easier than when they were growing up. For many it is the opposite: current circumstances seem harder than when they were growing up. Given our current economic conditions, stress is higher for many people than ever before. People just want to escape from the difficult realities of life. It is totally understandable. Unfortunately, many of the choices that people make to relieve stress are unhealthy:

- smoking
- excessive use of alcohol
- excessive use of caffeine
- using drugs
- over eating
- excessive fast food and sweets
- excessive time playing video games or watching television
- excessive time on the internet

It is ironic that these unhealthy activities which reduce stress momentarily lead to poor health, which creates even more stress.

> ### Don't slip into using unhealthy stress relievers.

Finding healthy ways to reduce stress is a challenge that we all face. Some healthy stress relievers are:

- exercise
- good sleep
- good nutrition
- talking to your partner about your day
- getting together with friends and family
- playing with the family pet
- doing something recreational
- going for a walk
- listening to recorded music
- making music
- doing arts and crafts
- puttering around the house
- engaging in a hobby
- building something

- reading a book
- watching some type of entertainment
- writing
- learning a new skill
- meditating

Having healthy stress relievers reduces the temptation of unhealthy stress relievers.

Develop healthy stress relievers.

Our American culture does not make it easy for us to be healthy. Food-processing technologies have made it very easy for us to curb our appetites with food that requires very little preparation. Television runs all night long, keeping us from going to sleep. Having two-plus cars keeps us from walking. Power tools reduce the need for muscle power. Tweeting keeps us from writing letters, and text messaging keeps us from talking. It really is a dilemma: **Easier often becomes unhealthier.** We automatically want to do what is easiest, fastest, tastiest and most pleasurable. Hopefully a small voice can say, *Maybe that choice isn't good for you.* That's the voice to make louder.

Easiest isn't necessarily best.

That voice is the voice of self-discipline. By definition, self-discipline means getting yourself to do something that you don't feel like doing. With the constraints we have on our time, easy access to unhealthy stress relievers and a culture that offers so many ways to avoid doing things that help us to be physically fit, living a healthy lifestyle requires increasingly greater self-discipline. It can take self-discipline to:

- exercise in the morning when you don't feel like it;
- exercise in the evening when you are tired;
- take the time to prepare healthy food when you are hungry;
- abstain from smoking, drinking too much alcohol, or using drugs;
- go to bed when you want to stay up, and
- not take the easiest path when doing something harder is better for you.

> ## *Improving your physical health may require increased self-discipline.*

I can't over emphasize the importance of exercise for a healthy body and a healthy mind. **There is no question that exercise decreases both depression and anxiety, two of the biggest mental health problems.** Over the past hundred years, our culture has experienced a seismic shift from a largely agrarian, rural society to an industrialized, urban society, which has changed our lifestyles from being more active to more sedentary. It is a huge shift psychologically, too, from thinking that the normal activities of the day keep us strong to thinking that we have to engage in special activities to keep ourselves strong. Jack LaLanne is often credited with starting the fitness movement only sixty years ago. Today if you want to be healthy, you may have to plan and motivate yourself into physical activity and exercise. **There are three types of exercise that I think are important: aerobic exercise, stretching and resistance training.**

- Keep your circulatory system strong with aerobic exercise.
- Maintain your flexibility with stretching.
- Keep your muscles strong with resistance.

All of these exercises become increasingly more important as you age. However, establishing the discipline of exercise early in life vastly increases the chance that you will continue to exercise throughout your life. But it is never too late. You just have to do it. Start now if you haven't already.

> ## *Exercise improves mental health.*

While exercise is a concentrated activity, a non-specific and generally active life-style is another key to good health. Most of us spend a lot of time sitting and not enough time doing weight-bearing activities. We were meant to be on our feet, and walking is good for us. Try saying to yourself, *Come on, legs!* and just get going.

> ## *Develop an active lifestyle.*

Good eating habits are also very important. I will make just two suggestions: eat less and eat fresh.

> ### *Eat less and eat fresh.*

Many of us need more sleep. Five hours of sleep is not enough. Everything suffers from lack of sleep: mood, performance, mental activity and your relationships. The solution for most people is to go to bed on time. There are so many reasons why people don't go to bed on time: we want more time to relax, have fun, or get things done, or we think that it might be difficult to fall asleep. One very big challenge is getting children to go to sleep. You can find solutions to all of these problems if you are motivated and if you make sleep a priority.

> ### *Make sleep a priority.*

There may be some debate about whether "seeing a health professional when appropriate" is an activity that increases physical health. There is no doubt that going to a physician or a healer of some type can help you if you have hurt yourself or if you are ill. If you don't see a health professional, depending on how badly you are hurt or how ill you are, you might die. Dying isn't unhealthy. Death is a fact of life. You can be healthy and die at age thirty-five or at age ninety-five. Going to a health professional might help you to live longer, but that is not the same thing as being healthy. On the other hand, if you hurt yourself or get ill, and you don't die and you don't get better, you might have chronic health problems for the rest of your life—and that's not healthy. That is why seeing a health professional when appropriate is important. As an added bonus, if your health professional also practices health maintenance and disease prevention, they are absolutely helping you to live in a healthier way.

> ### *Use health professionals when necessary.*

- *Try to find time in your schedule for doing health related activities.*
- *Don't slip into using unhealthy stress relievers.*
- *Develop healthy stress relievers.*
- *Easiest isn't necessarily best.*
- *Improving your physical health may require increased self-discipline.*
- *Exercise improves mental health.*
- *Develop an active life style.*
- *Eat less and eat fresh.*
- *Make sleep a priority.*
- *Use health professionals when necessary.*

EXERCISES FOR INCREASING AND MAINTAINING GOOD PHYSICAL HEALTH:

1. Review your schedule. See if you can find a time to exercise at least three to four times a week. Be concrete about it and work it out with your partner if necessary.

2. See if you can implement this plan for the next month and reevaluate.

3. Conduct a personal evaluation of the following habits and write down what is okay and not okay, for you:

	okay	not okay
Smoking:	☐	☐
Alcohol use	☐	☐
Caffeine use:	☐	☐
Drug use:	☐	☐
Food proportions:	☐	☐
Eating fast food and sweets:	☐	☐
Time spent on video games or television:	☐	☐

4. What are some of your healthy stress relievers? Write them down. How often do you engage in those activities? Would you like to do them more often? What is a practical and useful goal for you regarding these activities?

5. Discuss practical and useful goals for engaging in these activities with your partner. See if you can come to an agreement. See if you can make a plan for reaching these goals.

6. What are some areas of physical health where you think you need to be more self-disciplined? Write them down. Be specific about what you would actually be doing to show greater self-discipline.

7. Are you engaged in exercise, aerobic, stretching, and resistance? If not, what could you do more of, and when?

8. Have a conversation with your partner about how you can have good nutrition. Make a plan for shopping for healthy food and preparing it. Do some menu planning for a month to see if you can get yourself on a better track for good nutrition, if you aren't already.

9. Count up the average number of hours of sleep you get each night. What is your goal? When do you need to go to sleep to reach that goal?

10. Do you have a health professional that you can see to help you if you are hurt or sick? If not, see if you can do a little research and find someone. Make an appointment so you can get to know one another. If it has been a long time since you have seen your regular practitioner, make an appointment just to check in.

RULE #06: **Know thyself.**

We do not exist independently from our environment, and thus we are constantly trying to achieve a satisfying state of coexistence with the environment. One of the most important ways to create this state of satisfaction is by filling our **NEEDS, WANTS,** and **DESIRES**. When we are babies, our needs, wants, and desires (NWDs) are filled without our having any verbal awareness of them. However, as adults, awareness of our NWDs increases the likelihood that they will be satisfied.

Become aware of your needs, wants, and desires.

Awareness of feelings is also very important. Feelings can serve as an indicator of your NWDs. Your body might need food, but if you never feel hunger you might starve to death. Some feelings simply let you know about your state of being, like sadness. At any given moment, you may feel, to name a few: joyful, grateful, loving, humorous, anxious, aroused, fearful, defensive, prepared, frustrated, angry, combative, avoidant, tired, hungry, sad, happy, exhilarated, satisfied, dissatisfied, guilty, remorseful, ashamed, or a multitude of other feelings.

Become aware of your feelings.

In my work, I have discovered that many adult men and women don't know what or how they are feeling. They might know if they are upset, but that is about it. They may not recognize it if they are scared, anxious, sad, hurt, guilty or embarrassed. They may be defensive because of those feelings and not recognize their defensiveness. Even if they were aware that they might be having these feelings, they are not sure that they really want to feel them, let alone express them. *Why bother?* they might think. *Why get in touch with a thought or a feeling that has the potential for either feeling bad or blowing up in my face?*

It may have to just be a leap of faith.

Knowing *how* we feel enables us to more easily process those feelings. We might say that feelings are a little bit like food moving through the digestive track. If there is an obstruction in the digestive track, a person can get very sick. Well, if there is an obstruction in the feelings track, a person can get mentally sick. Negative feelings are more likely to get stuck, and when they get stuck for a long time, they can create numerous emotional difficulties. When we experience a stuck feeling and become aware of it, we can apply particular kinds of thinking or actions that help feelings to get unstuck, get processed and dissipate. This results in a greater lightness of being and greater ease in navigating through life's experiences.

> ### *Having awareness of feelings allows them to be more easily processed.*

In addition to NWDs and feelings, we have other aspects of our selves:

- strengths and weaknesses
- limitations
- boundaries
- likes
- dislikes
- style
- temperament
- pace
- expectations
- values
- beliefs
- core beliefs
- priorities
- those things that we think we can change
- those things we think we cannot change

Awareness of these helps to create our identity and further define our relationship with the environment.

When we interact with the environment, we are either in a state of satisfaction or a state of dissatisfaction. While in this state of dissatisfaction, we are either trying to modify the environment to suit us or modify ourselves to suit the environment. I sometimes refer to this process as **NEGOTIATION.**

When we are in this process of negotiation, it is helpful if we know what we are willing and able to change and what we are not willing or unable to change. This is a continuum ranging from *easy to change* to *difficult to change.* When we understand this continuum, we are in a much better position for engaging in this negotiation process.

> *Knowing your capacity for changing the environment and changing yourself helps you to better adapt by means of negotiation.*

All of these aforementioned aspects of ourselves solidify during the developmental years. It is important to have a strong sense of self to create a foundation of security when moving away from the protected environment of the parental home, a process called *emancipation.* Often, during emancipation, self-characteristics take on greater rigidity when we feel like our well-being is at stake. However, over time and as adults, we begin to differentiate those things that are most important and that are we want to preserve from those things that are less important and that we are willing to change. Those aspects over which there is no compromise are called **BOUNDARIES.** Knowing our boundaries is really important for creating the best fit with the environment.

The same holds true when we are forming significant relationships. By knowing our boundaries and who we are, by understanding what is more or less important to us, and by knowing what is more or less changeable, we can make the best choice for continuing in a particular relationship and then creating the best fit possible. This is the process as we begin to mold ourselves to one another and create intimacy. Intimacy is the objective, and knowing ourselves is critical.

- *Know your boundaries. Become aware of your needs, wants, and desires.*
- *Become aware of your feelings.*
- *Having awareness of feelings allows them to be processed with thoughts.*
- *Knowing your capacities for changing the environment and for changing yourself helps you to better adapt by means of negotiation.*
- *Know your boundaries.*
- *Know your strengths and weaknesses, limitations, likes and dislikes, style, temperament, pace, expectations, values, beliefs, and priorities.*

EXERCISES FOR KNOWING THYSELF:

1. Write down ten of your most important NWDs. On a scale from one to ten (one being unimportant and ten being very important), how important is each NWD to you?

2. If this NWD goes unmet, what happens to your state of being? What feelings come up? If the feeling that comes up is anger, are you aware of any other feelings that might be behind the anger?

3. Review the list above of feeling states. Go through each one and think about conditions that might give rise to each of those feelings.

4. Review the list of personal characteristics above. Write each one in your notebook. Next to each one, write down aspects of that characteristic in yourself.

5. Write down any NWDs that have been reshaped as a result of being in the relationship with your partner.

6. What are some of your boundaries? Write them down.

RULE #07: **Learn how to be accepting.**

One of the great dilemmas of human existence has to do with how we cope with matters over which we have no control. Over the long span of evolution, Homo sapiens have survived and thrived principally as a result of their control over the environment. We didn't come to rule the animal kingdom by throwing in the towel and giving up. Some public figures advise us to "never give up," "persevere to the end" or "don't accept 'no' for an answer." It might sound good for certain situations, like playing on a sports team, but it doesn't really work in the real world. The universe presents us with many matters over which we have no control: less daylight in the winter, the changing tides, seasons of the year, the need for oxygen to live, aging, death, etc. We might prefer that the universe not operate in this fashion. You might like seventy-five-degree temperatures every day and being young forever, but it isn't going to happen, at least not any time soon. When things are not going well, a very strong desire arises in us to change something so we will feel better. This desire to change current circumstances is powerful, and it is reinforced by the positive outcomes of our efforts to relieve stress and promote enjoyment.

> *It is instinctual to want to act on the environment to reduce discomfort.*

The desire to bring about change in our circumstances is such a powerful and useful feeling that it often won't shut off, even when our actions don't or can't bring about change. When we are unable to effect change in our circumstances, that desire isn't so useful. Nonetheless, people can hold on to the desire for change tenaciously. Whatever is the strength and nature of our desire, there are times when, no matter how hard we try, we will not get what we want. It is at these times that we are pressed to stop beating our heads against the wall and let go of the desire to change the environment. It may be very difficult to do but it can be done. And it is very important that it be done.

> *When it looks like you are not able to change the environment, stop trying.*

One of the most important mental mechanisms that we have for coping with the inability to change a particular situation is *acceptance*. Acceptance means letting go of the desire to make things different from how they are right now, in this moment. Acceptance is a shift in thoughts, feelings and attitude. Letting go of the desire to change things from how they are strikes at the very biology of our being; it can be psychologically painful at first and is often associated with feelings of anger, frustration, and loss. Acceptance can be a difficult attitudinal change. Western cultures do not train their children in how to have attitudes of acceptance to the same degree that Eastern cultures have traditionally done. Consequently, many people in Western cultures may not even know where to begin in creating an attitude of acceptance. Here are some of the components that acceptance may involve:

- a feeling of letting go
- changing priorities of importance
- forgiveness
- moving through grief
- detachment
- changing expectations, needs, wants and desires
- changing negative thoughts
- shifting to positive thoughts

> *Acceptance means letting go of the desire to make things different from the way they are right now.*

An overall approach for developing acceptance is to become less preoccupied with unmet needs while becoming more conscious of needs that are currently being met or that can be met. When we can be preoccupied with notions of the universe that feel full, rich, rewarding, caring, joyful, sustaining, protective, just and/or loving; and when our senses are positively activated; and when we feel the divine spirit of the universe; then acceptance is easier, because the desire for that which we cannot have gives way to these other thoughts and feelings that are filling our consciousness.

Acceptance is opening or expanding our consciousness, beyond the immediate desire to change things, with positive thoughts and feelings.

Here are some helpful thoughts:

They didn't think that what they were doing would hurt me.

I see now that it wasn't her fault.

I know he won't change. It's just the way he is.

Some things just aren't fair.

I think I perceived things differently than what occurred.

I think I was just being too sensitive.

This is just what happened to me.

I can't always get what I want.

It is what it is.

Bad things sometimes happen (S__t happens).

Acceptance means that we come to a place of calm in ourselves and are okay with things being the way they are. We are no longer trying to change things. We are no longer upset or sad about the way things are. While we remain attached to the world and to people in the world, we are no longer attached to whatever was causing us difficulty. We are at peace with ourselves.

Acceptance means that we are okay with things being the way they are.

We all have the ability to create this type of consciousness. You have this ability. It may require some practice both in letting go and filling your consciousness in a different way. You will find that this word *acceptance* appears many times throughout this book. It is a concept that has far reaching implications for achieving health and I invite you to consider its importance. The more you use this Rule, the easier it will be to use.

> - *When it looks like you are not able to change the environment, stop trying.*
> - *Acceptance means letting go of the desire to make things different from the way they are right now.*
> - *Acceptance is opening or expanding our consciousness, beyond the immediate desire to change things, with positive thoughts and feelings.*
> - *Acceptance means that we are okay with things being the way they are.*

EXERCISES FOR LEARNING TO BE ACCEPTING:

1. Spend some time by yourself and write down five situations or circumstances that have upset you and in which you feel like no matter what you do, the situations won't change.

2. Be willing to experience the feelings that are associated with your inability to change these situations. They might be feelings of helplessness, frustration, sadness, or fear. Write down the feelings.

3. Become clear within yourself that there is nothing you can do to bring about change in these situations. Become clear that someone else is not likely going to make change happen and change is not likely to happen by chance.

4. Review the list from Exercise 1 and write down what you might need to do for each of the situations above. Use this phrase: *In order to be accepting regarding this situation, I need to…*

   - *let go.*
   - *change my priorities of importance.*
   - *be forgiving.*
   - *move through grief.*
   - *detach.*

- *change my expectations, needs, wants and desires.*

- *change my negative thoughts.*

- *shift to positive thoughts.*

5. See if you have thoughts of blame, unfairness and righteous indignation associated with these situations. Try to shift away from those thoughts. Try to shifts to thoughts of understanding and simply acknowledge what has occurred in each situation. Try some of the suggestions from above.

6. For each situation, focus your attention on something related or unrelated over which you *do* have mastery. For example:

    "What I can do is this _____."

    "I can treat him this way instead."

    "I can go out for a run."

    "I can turn to someone else."

    "We can always enjoy _____ instead."

    "If it happens again I'm going to _____."

7. If any of your situations includes a feeling of loss, focus your attention on what you do have. Write it down.

8. Focus your attention on anything that gives you a pleasant sensation or good feeling in the present moment. Try to expand your awareness of the aspects of your life that feel full, rich, rewarding, caring, joyful, sustaining, protective, just and/or loving.

RULE #08: **You can't always get what you want.**

This might seem a little cliché after the Rolling Stones immortalized these words in one of their most famous songs of the same title. Who doesn't want what they want when they want it? For the purposes of this conversation and throughout this book, minimal distinction is made between needs, wants and desires (NWDs). One might argue that needs unsatisfied create more difficulty for a person than an unsatisfied want or desire. However, they are all on the same continuum. **The difficulty associated with an unmet NWD is not necessarily tied to the original strength of the NWD.** For the most part, if you want something, try to get it. If you run into roadblocks, try to overcome. I believe in perseverance, trying hard, self-discipline, dedication, staying focused on goals, planning, strategizing, being creative and—short of hurting others, hurting yourself or breaking laws or your ethical standards—utilizing whatever means you can to get what you want. This section of the book deals with how people deal psychologically and behaviorally with not getting what they want.

Preliminary exercise:
Spend a few minutes by yourself and write down five needs, wants or desires that seem to go unfulfilled on a regular basis.

Your needs, wants and desires are your personal responsibility.

It is the human condition to have needs, wants and desires. It is not your fault that you were born, but once you take possession of your life, you have to take responsibility for your genetic makeup; that means all your strengths and weaknesses, your appetite, how much sleep you need, your sex drive, your interests, your extroversion or introversion, your fears…the whole kit and kaboodle. While we are not blank slates on which development is recorded, development plays a very big role in further shaping our NWDs. Taking responsibility for the results of your development may be more difficult than taking responsibility for your genetic makeup, but ultimately, you have to do that as well. This is hard for many people who spend a lifetime blaming their parents or their difficult childhood. They often feel like victims, complain incessantly and are frequently miserable. Your NWDs, whether they are the result of genetics or development, are yours and nobody else's.

When you take responsibility for your needs, wants and desires, you also have to accept the associated risk of not getting what you want and the possible disappointment. That is your vulnerability. **Part of being an adult is recognizing that your having a need does not require the world to fill it.** This Rule is not about others' responsibilities resulting from their explicit or implicit agreements to fill your needs. Rather, it is about a point of view concerning your attitude when your needs are not met, no matter whether others have agreed to fill them or not. At the end of the day, they are still your needs, no matter how they got there or whether or not you were told that your need would be filled sometime in the future. Your needs, wants and desires are a condition of the present regardless of the past and the future and they are all yours.

> ### *You are responsible for your needs, wants and desires.*

Your needs, wants and desires can change.
It would make sense to say that our ability to let go of an NWD is relative to the strength of that NWD. Yet many people have trouble letting go of an NWD of any strength. In order to let go of an NWD, we have to first entertain the idea that it is possible. Second, we have to try. People change their NWDs all the time: smoking, drinking, sexuality, food needs, relationship needs, housekeeping needs, consumer needs, etc. It is possible. One good example is the compulsive desire to drink alcohol. Many alcoholics join one of the largest mental-health organizations of all time, Alcoholics Anonymous. This organization attempts to help alcoholics reduce their desire to drink alcohol. Hundreds of thousands of people have reported that their desire to drink alcohol is reduced as a result of being part of AA. It may not be easy, but it can be done. AA helps people believe that they can change, it helps to motivate them to change and it gives them a plan of action for that change. **Belief, motivation and a plan of action can help you to change NWDs that you may have previously thought were unchangeable.**

> ### *You can change your needs, wants and desires.*

Recognize and accept the limitations of yourself and others.
We all have limitations and those limitations impact the fulfillment of our

needs. Some parents teach their children that they can be whatever they want when they grow up. That's not true. If you are 5'4" tall, you are not going to be center on the basketball team. If you are terrible at math, it is not likely that you will be a nuclear physicist. If you want your spouse to wake you up in the morning and he has trouble waking up himself, it's not likely to happen. If you want your spouse to help select the color for painting the rooms and she is almost color blind—hey, good luck. While it is true that pushing yourself and encouraging others to do more than they currently do can yield very positive results, it is important to know when you have reached a limit. And limits do exist. An important part of accepting limitations is suspending judgment. That means not ridiculing, defaming, criticizing, condemning or finding fault with yourself or someone else because of limitations. **One of the reasons you can't always get what you want is because you or your partner *can't* fulfill your need.** That's just part of how things are. Everyone has limitations.

Accept limitations in yourself and others.

Know when to let go.

I believe in perseverance, trying hard, self-discipline, dedication, staying focused on goals, planning, strategizing, being creative and—short of hurting others, hurting yourself or breaking laws or your ethical standards—utilizing whatever means you can to get what you want. (Didn't I just say that?) **But as important as it is to proceed forward towards a goal, it is equally as important to know when to stop.** For some people, the need to get what they want is so great that letting go, even at the risk of harm to themselves and others, is not a viable option for them. So many disastrous outcomes have occurred as a result of an inability to accept the non-fulfillment of an NWD. Many people equate this with failure, defeat, deprivation, scarcity, loss of status or not being good enough. If you have some of these thoughts, you need to work on changing them when conditions warrant letting go. Having the willingness to let go of an NWD when appropriate can save your life, actually and figuratively.

Have the willingness to let go.

Once you establish a willingness to let go, you need to establish criteria for letting go in specific situations. Anyone who has done on-line dating knows about the need for establishing criteria for finding a significant partner. Many people establish criteria in the early stages of a relationship but fail to establish criteria after they begin to get attached. They stay in unhealthy relationships for way too long, as a result of a lack of willingness, a lack of criteria or both. Criteria need to be established for turning around if you are an adventurer, selling if you are in the stock market (know when to hold 'em; know when to fold 'em), when to speak if you are overly emotional, when to talk to your partner if you want to buy something expensive, etc. One of the exercises below will help you to begin to establish criteria.

Create criteria for letting go.

Get rid of feelings of entitlement. Don't blame others when you don't get what you want.

If you want a ham sandwich, you may just go to the refrigerator to get it. If it isn't there, you are not likely to blame the refrigerator for not having your sandwich. If you want something from somebody else and they don't give it to you, that's when trouble can begin. It all has to do with how you think about not getting what you want, particularly from others. If you think, *I'm supposed to have what I want, I deserve it,* or *It's my right,* you might get upset at whomever you thought was supposed fill your need. You might start having angry thoughts like: *What's wrong with him? Why can't she do what I ask? He doesn't care about me,* or *Why is she is so self-centered?* Do any of those thoughts sound like something that goes through your head? It is very easy to start blaming others when you don't get what you want, if you have feelings of entitlement.

Anger and blame often result from feelings of entitlement.

Feelings of entitlement are different than feelings of expectation that you will receive what has been promised to you or agreed upon. If a person has feelings of entitlement, that feeling typically supersedes any conversations or negotiations with somebody else.

Expectations based on feelings of entitlement are different from expectations based on commitments.

Differing sets of beliefs give rise to differing feelings of entitlement. **You can believe that, while you might want something, others may not be prepared or able to give it to you. You can believe that others aren't required to fill your needs just because you have them.** You may have to find an alternative or accept that you are not going to get what you want from them, right then or perhaps ever. While you may be disappointed or upset by not getting what you want, you are not apt to blame anybody, particularly if you don't start with a "supposed to" premise.

> ### *Learn how to be disappointed without blame.*

Learn how to deal with the upset or disappointment that may result from an unmet need, want or desire.

Okay, so you didn't get the ham sandwich. Now what? Well, you can keep scrounging around for one elsewhere, but you may not find one. So you are back to square one: no ham sandwich. How are you going to feel, and what can you do about it? As stated previously, your needs, wants and desires can change, but now we are down to brass tacks: no ham sandwich. Two feelings often arise with an unmet NWD: disappointment and upset. The strength of those feelings is dependent on the strength of the physiological and psychological arousal that arises when the NWD isn't satisfied. In the case of the ham sandwich, the physiological arousal has first to do with hunger. If you can't get anything to eat and you are pretty hungry, your arousal may be quite high. If you get something else to eat, that may pretty much resolve the problem. You may be a little disappointed that it wasn't a *ham* sandwich, but all in all, you're pretty okay. However, if you were intent on getting a *ham* sandwich and no *ham* sandwich is to be found, you may solve the physiological problem, but the psychological arousal may remain pretty high.

> *The degree of upset and disappointment is dependent on the physiological and psychological arousal that is associated with the unmet need, want or desire.*

While you may think that the physiological arousal from hunger would surely be stronger than the psychological arousal associated with wanting a ham sandwich, this is not necessarily the case. Often, psychological arousal far exceeds physiological arousal. However, what is most important is how to decrease that arousal. **As it turns out, the physiological arousal is often much easier to decrease than the psychological arousal.** If you ask any addict who has been in a treatment program, he will tell you that the physiological detoxification from drugs, alcohol or nicotine is not the toughest part. The toughest part is getting through the psychological desire and cravings. **The hardest part of those cravings is the anxiety, agitation and overall psychological arousal.** Many suggestions are available to help you with anxiety (see Rule 14, "Letting go of worry").

> *Decrease the arousal associated with an unmet need by decreasing the anxiety and agitation.*

However, most of our unmet NWDs don't give rise to high levels of arousal. We just have to wrap our minds around the idea that it isn't going to happen. When we do that, up pops disappointment. As long as the feeling of disappointment doesn't come with lots of agitation, there can be a pretty straightforward way of dealing with it. **Disappointment is another form of loss and learning how to deal with loss and disappointment is a huge part of taking responsibility for your unmet needs, wants and desires.** If you have NWDs, sometime you are going to have disappointments. It goes with the territory.

Four parts of disappointment:

1. ADMIT THAT THERE IS A LOSS. Often people try to find another way out so that they can still get what they want. Waiting for the ham sandwich to somehow magically appear in the refrigerator is just not going to happen, and you have to admit it.

2. GRIEVE THE LOSS. This means experiencing the sad feelings that you have that are associated with your loss and disappointment. Have a sense of compassion towards yourself about it, and don't be afraid of showing those feelings to your loved ones.

3. HAVE PERSPECTIVE. Balance what you don't have with what you do have. While there may not be a ham sandwich in the refrigerator, there is a turkey sandwich there.

4. BE ACCEPTING. You are okay with things being the way they are. Turkey will be just fine.

> *Decrease the arousal associated with an unmet need by decreasing the anxiety and agitation.*

Some final thoughts on not getting what you want.

In these last few paragraphs, a ham sandwich has been used to help illustrate these concepts. This is a light-hearted effort to simplify the concepts and is by no means intended to minimize the seriousness and the difficulty that this effort entails. There are other more serious examples. Young people have to accept rejection when they are dating. In sports, you may have to deal with getting cut from the team. In school, you may get a lower grade than you want. In business you may not get the promotion. You may have financial goals that you will never achieve. You might not be loved in quite the way you want to be loved. You may not get pregnant, and if you do, your children may not turn out just the way you wanted. Two very difficult desires are wanting to live in perfect health and wanting to live forever. Most people have to ultimately work through the loss associated with not being able to do something as well as they used to. Acceptance is a process, and one of the ultimate acceptances is of death itself. This may not be easy, particularly for someone who loves being alive. The continuous process of decline and death of parents helps us face this ultimate reality within ourselves. I think that the younger we are, the harder it is to do this. **I also think that we are never too young to begin to learn that you can't always get what you want.**

> *Work through disappointment to help with acceptance of an unmet need.*

- *You are responsible for your needs, wants and desires.*
- *You can change your needs, wants and desires.*
- *Accept limitations in yourself and others.*
- *Have the willingness to let go.*
- *Create criteria for letting go.*
- *Get rid of feelings of entitlement.*
- *Stop blaming others for not getting what you want.*
- *Learn how to be disappointed without blame.*
- *Decrease the arousal associated with an unmet need by decreasing the anxiety and agitation.*
- *Work through disappointment to help with acceptance of an unmet need.*
  1. *Admit that it is a loss.*
  2. *Grieve the loss.*
  3. *Have perspective.*
  4. *Be accepting.*

EXERCISES FOR NOT ALWAYS GETTING WHAT YOU WANT:

1. Spend about twenty minutes by yourself. Review your five unfulfilled needs, wants or desires from the Preliminary Exercise. Now write this sentence and fill in the blanks for each of these needs:

    I know that I want/need _____. The reason I have this need is because _____ (I was born this way; during development, X happened). In spite of the reason for having this need, in this moment I want to accept that I am who I am without blame. I am going to try to let go of all bitterness towards my parents or anyone else that may have caused me to be who I am. By accepting this need, I also accept that there is some risk that this need will go unfulfilled. It is what it is and I am who I am.

2. Take twenty minutes and write down five NWDs that you wish you didn't have. Now write this sentence and fill in the blanks for each of these needs: *It is possible that my need for _____ doesn't have to be with me forever. I am going to try to reduce the strength of this need. I am going to do this by doing the following: _____*
_____.

3. Take twenty minutes to write down five things that you want (or a goal). For each one of things that you want, write down what your thoughts and feeling might be if you don't get it (or reach that goal). Now for each one, write down several conditions for discontinuing your pursuit of what you want.

4. Review the five unfulfilled NWDs from above.

    a. For each one, write down any thoughts or feelings that you have that sound like "supposed-tos" or entitlements.

    b. For each one, write down new thoughts that you can have that might help you to not blame anyone for your unmet NWD.

    c. For each one, write down any feelings that you have had related to not getting what you want. If you have feelings of disappointment or loss, review the steps I have listed above and write down where you are in the process. Write down any statements that might give you perspective.

    d. If you have feelings of anxiety or agitation review the section, "Letting go of worry," particularly the part on meditation and relaxation.

5. Review the five unfulfilled NWDs from above. For each one of those NWDs, write down several reasons why it might be difficult for you or someone else to fill those needs. Think in terms of limitations. You can use the following as a guide:
    My need for _____ has not been satisfied because of me/my partner's inability/difficulty to _____.

RULE #09: **Accept uncertainty. Differing perceptions may be equally valid.**

> **Preliminary exercise:**
> *Write down five behaviors that you consider "right" and five behaviors that you consider "wrong." Don't write down any behaviors that are defined by the law as right and wrong. Try to write down the first things that come to your mind.*

You aren't always right. Thinking that you are always right can be a destructive way of thinking and certainly problematic in relationships. Within the context of relationships, we usually think this way in an effort to get what we want or to feel good about ourselves.

Attempting to resolve conflict by determining who is right and who is wrong is a pervasive problem-solving approach. It is largely learned. From the earliest moments in our lives, we are instructed by our parents in how to do things "correctly." We are told that there are right and wrong ways of doing things, right and wrong ways to behave. "What works," (that is, what pleases our parents, what gets us what we want, or what prevents bad things from happening) may not be distinguished from "what's right." **Many of us are raised in this absolutist way of thinking:** *Johnny, there are two ways to do something: the right way and the wrong way, and you're going to learn the right way.* **Our frame of reference can become steeped in this binary way of thinking.** We may not have learned that what works at home may not work in other environments or that what is right for our parents may not be right for somebody else.

It is important to recognize that there *are* absolutes. For example, there are many principals by which we live that can be called absolutes. **Some of these can be described as laws of cause and effect.**

- If you turn the water on in your tub and you don't turn it off, the tub will overflow.

- If you drive too close to the edge of a cliff, you raise the risk of an accident.
- If you spend more money than you have, you will be in debt.
- If you smoke cigarettes, you raise the risk of having health problems.

These are facts, important facts. And there are consequences when we don't adhere to them.

Laws of cause and effect are absolute.

The hard sciences provide many truths that help us to better understand the universe. But things begin to break down when we introduce the human factor of perception. Even when we think that hard science is yielding the truth, we may later find a better construct to describe the same phenomenon. At one time, and as a result of human perception and our egocentricity, it was thought that the earth was the center of the universe and that the sun circled the earth. It was heretical to believe that the earth circled the sun. Of course, with better means of observation, it was determined that, in fact, the earth did circle the sun. **How we see the universe is not the same as what the universe actually is.** In courts of law, eyewitness accounts are constantly being debunked. **Perceptions of the same phenomenon can differ.** So don't be so sure of yourself. Allow for the possibility that you might be incorrect—or even better, and particularly when dealing with relationships, there likely is not a "correct."

Perceptions are not absolute.

When it comes to social behavior, absolutist thinking becomes questionable. (Of course, there are some kinds of behavior that our society defines as right and wrong and they become our city, state and federal laws. Relative to the society in which we live, they are absolute.)

The laws of the land, by definition, are absolute.

Things begin to fall apart when we start thinking about customs and mores. Not only are these radically different from culture to culture, but, within a single culture, they change over time. At one time it was considered wrong to address a teacher by her first name, have a same-sex partner or get a divorce. And it was perfectly acceptable to smoke in any location, throw garbage out the window of your car and use heroine to treat pain. These things have all changed. What was wrong became okay and what was okay became wrong.

> ### *Customs and mores change.*

Most of the problems that we face on a daily basis don't have a clear right or wrong, good or bad.

- When is it best to wean the baby, pay your bills or do your exercise?
- How much should you give to charity, put into savings and spend on home improvements, vacations and food?
- Will you go to hell if you miss your morning prayers, eat the wrong food or not bow your head?
- Will you spread disease if you don't wash your hands after going to the bathroom, if you don't change the hand towels daily, if you use someone else's sheets or if you use a wooden cutting board?
- Does butter taste better if it is soft or hard?
- Is it better to start a race off slow or fast?
- Which is better, to cut the grass in a circle or back and forth?
- Is it proper to have your salad at the beginning of the meal or at the end of the meal?

> ### *Most of the problems that we face on a daily basis cannot be defined by being right and wrong.*

We need to be able to shift from absolutist thinking to relative thinking when dealing with relationships. Relative thinking is:

- what is best for me
- what is right for me
- what works for me
- what is comfortable for me

When it comes to what you observe, describe your observations as:

- what you saw
- what you heard
- what you felt
- what you experienced

…rather than what was absolutely said or what absolutely occurred. Allow for an element of uncertainty or two equally valid points of view, and you'll find that your arguments with others will rapidly decrease and your ability to reach mutual understanding will increase.

> *Develop relative thinking.*

- *Laws of cause and effect are absolute.*
- *Perceptions are not absolute.*
- *The laws of the land, by definition, are absolute.*
- *Customs and mores change.*
- *Most of the problems that we face on a daily basis cannot be defined by being right and wrong.*
- *Develop relative thinking.*

EXERCISES IN ACCEPTING UNCERTAINTY:

Review your list from the Preliminary Exercise.

1. Spend a little time with your list of ten items to see if you can make your definitions more relative based on circumstances.

2. Write down several ways in which your partner has engaged in "bad" behavior. Write down what she did using the word "bad" as part of your description.

3. Rewrite the same behaviors using language that is less absolute.

4. Practice rewriting the following sentences in less judgmental language.
   Try several rewrites for each sentence.

   - *You don't wash the dishes right.*

   - *That's the wrong way to make spaghetti.*

   - *I'm bad at talking to my customers.*

   - *I'm just no good at making friends.*

5. See if you can remember any situations in which you have experienced
   differences in perception with your partner. Try to remember if absolutist
   thinking on your part or his part was part of the problem. Consider how
   thinking about this in less absolute terms may have helped. See if you
   can come up with ways in which this could have been discussed differently.

RULE #10: **Don't be a victim.**

Preliminary exercise:

Write down 5 things that have been bothering you for a while. This might be something that has happened to you, something that your partner has done or hasn't done, or some situation that you don't like.

Just so there is no confusion here, victims do exist. There are victims of poverty, bigotry, rape, famine, pestilence, murder, and disease. All of these things occur that create great challenges for humanity and the need for understanding and compassion. However, far too often, when we experience situations of turmoil and stress, there are things that we can do to reduce our difficulties. **As I have discussed previously, there are matters over which we have control, matters over which we don't have control and many matters that are somewhere in between. It is a continuum.** This continuum may be different for each of us; let me give you an example of what I mean, starting with some examples of things over which we have less control and moving to examples of things over which we have more control:

Things that relate to the metaphysical > energy > matter > animals > people/close relationships > our own bodies > our feelings > our thoughts > our behavior.

We can reduce the sense of being victimized
1. *by promoting change in people and in situations,*

2. *by changing our attitudes, feelings or focus of attention, or*

3. *by leaving the situations that are causing us stress.*

Learning to not be a victim can start at an early age. Some toddlers learn early that when their needs aren't met through crying, they can shift their attention to something else or go to sleep. Others just remain upset. Some adolescents learn that when their needs aren't met by talking, fussing or arguing with their parents, they can decide that whatever they wanted wasn't that important, or they can go on to do something else. Others just remain upset. In the social arena, adolescents focus on how relationships are "supposed" to work; what is right and what is wrong and what is "fair." **If a need isn't met, the more adolescents think that something is unfair, the greater becomes their sense of victimization.** Remaining stuck on feelings of unfairness maintains upset and misery.

Don't let feelings of unfairness dominate your consciousness.

As adults we are also faced with similar choices when something happens to us that we don't like. We can try to do something about it, we can adjust our attitudes, or we can leave the situation. We also have that fourth choice: we can be miserable and feel like a victim. You are much more likely to feel like a victim if you are passive in the way you lead your life. All of the ways to keep from feeling victimized are active approaches to living. Bringing about change may require perseverance, self-discipline, dedication and utilizing your strength. Effecting change in your situations with other people typically requires conversation. Many sections of this book discuss this in detail. **Two skills in particular are important for helping you avoid feeling victimized:** *speaking up* **and** *having boundaries.*

Passivity increases feelings of victimization.

Making changes in relationships typically requires conversation. Perhaps some things change when one partner observes the discomforts of another without words being spoken, but it is not a reliable method for change. **Failing to speak up is one of the most sure-fired ways for a person to feel like a victim.** If you have this difficulty, perhaps it is because you are unsure of what to say, or because you're afraid of getting into an argument. Figuring out what to say and facing the risk of getting into an argument will help you avoid the victim role. An active approach often begins by using your voice.

Use your voice.

A second important skill to avoid feeling like a victim is having limits and boundaries, and asserting them so they aren't crossed. Compromises may be necessary for problem-solving; however, it is not a good idea to make a compromise that goes beyond your boundaries. Good negotiation depends on knowing what is most important, what is least important and what is somewhere in between (see graphic below). Things that are most important should not be given away solely for the purpose of getting along. Those things are called your *limits* or your *boundaries,* and many people have difficulty knowing them, let alone asserting them. You need to be able to do both.

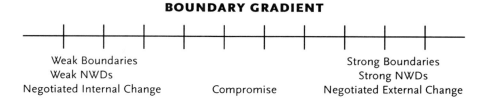

BOUNDARY GRADIENT

Weak Boundaries
Weak NWDs
Negotiated Internal Change   Compromise   Strong Boundaries
Strong NWDs
Negotiated External Change

Know your limits and boundaries and assert them.

There can be risks in asserting your boundaries, and one risk is that your partner may also have boundaries or not be able to make the compromises that you want him to make. It is possible that you can be at a stalemate regarding whatever is bothering you or your partner. You have probably heard people use the expression *Let's just agree to disagree.* If an issue is relatively unimportant, that might work. However, when things are critically important, a lack of agreement may mean no deal and no relationship. That is a pretty harsh reality but associated with setting limits is the possibility that a relationship might not be viable. Setting limits under these circumstances might be called the willingness to walk. Having the *willingness to walk* is particularly important when starting a new relationship. Many people make the mistake of not asserting this willingness early in the relationship and only assert it after years of misery, children, a mortgage, a lifestyle and many friends and family in common. **The earlier you begin to talk about boundaries in a relationship and have a willingness to walk, the less likely it is that you will ever have to walk, as time goes on.**

Have the **willingness to walk** *early in the formation of a relationship.*

Most of this book is devoted to suggesting ways in which you can try to bring about changes in your relationships *(external changes)* or changes in your attitudes and feelings *(internal changes)*. The internal changes are often the toughest to make because we tend to think of our attitudes, and, particularly, our feelings, as being unchangeable. I have heard statements like:

It's just the way I feel.

I can't take her talking to me that way.

I'm going to go nuts if he doesn't start doing more work around here.

I don't think that I can even get over what she did.

It just isn't fair.

These are common phrases that are a part of many people's everyday language. **The first measure of whether or not you can change an attitude or a feeling is whether or not you want to.** This may depend on the strength of your feelings, the importance of your NWDs, your values, your limitations and how basic that attitude or feeling is to who you are as a person. This is part of knowing yourself.

If you have the desire to change, a second criterion is whether or not your reactions *can* change. In relationships, this may be somewhat dependant on what another person does to you. If your partner steps on your foot, that is one thing; if he tells you that he doesn't like you...well, that's different.

There is something to the old kindergarten saying, *Sticks and stones will break your bones, but words will never hurt you.* While someone's words may serve as a stimulus or catalyst for your thoughts and feelings, and though they may feel automatic, your thoughts and feelings arise in *your* body and in *your* brain and are dependent on *your* sensitivities. That makes you ultimately responsible for your reactions.

Not everyone is the same. One person's reactions are not necessarily the same as another's. There is no one-to-one correlation between what someone else does and how everyone else will feel and think regarding his behavior. There is tremendous individual variation. One person may have very little reaction to what another does, while others may have a very strong response to the same behavior. Those differences have to be attributed to the reactor. If that reactor is you, then it is you who has to ultimately take responsibility for the feelings and the reactions that you have. Not taking this responsibility is just another way of thinking and feeling like a victim. (Please refer to the Appendix in this section for a more technical discussion of causality.)

Take responsibility for your own thoughts, feelings and attitudes.

If you become very upset by something someone else does, you can carry a grudge for years, or you can let it go. Fears can go away. Sadness can pass. Anger can subside. You can actively bring about changes in your own thoughts and feelings with some effort. In addition to changing your reactive thoughts and feelings, you can also change your preexisting negative attitudes. **Learning to change both reactive thoughts and feelings and preexisting negative attitudes keeps you out of the victim role—a role that just keeps you down, depressed and feeling miserable.**

Your inner experience is not immutable.

One thing that can't change is the past. Whatever has occurred is now over; however, the feelings you have associated with those past events can change. Anger, hurt, frustration, outrage, vengeful feelings and sadness can all change. They might change as a result of something you do with the person that hurt you. That person might apologize and you might forgive them. However, if those things don't work, then the feelings will remain unless you do something else. Some people feel like they can just wait it out and time will make the negative feelings go away. Sometimes is does. But sometimes the feelings seem to have gone away but just pop up again when you start thinking about what occurred. Another thing that you can do to change those feelings is *accept that what is past is past, and there is nothing more you can do to right a wrong or repair the damage.* As previously discussed in Rule 7, "Learn how to be accepting," acceptance is letting go of the desire to change things from how they currently exist. The experiential part of acceptance is often grieving the loss that things aren't the way you might like. That needs to be an active process. Perhaps you already have a way of dealing with not getting what you want. You might say:

- *I just turn the page.*
- *I just do something else.*
- *I just have a good cry.*
- *I just let it go.*
- *I just think to myself that things aren't always fair, and that's just the way it is.*

This is all the same thing as acceptance. If you already do this easily, that's great. If not, it will require some practice, and you may want to review the exercises from the section on acceptance.

Be able to have an attitude of acceptance.

Escape from feelings of victimization by becoming skillful in creating plans of action.

PLANS OF ACTION (POA)

I = Internal changes
E = External changes

Goal	Strategies (Internal/External)	Desired Outcome
Get sufficient Sleep	I: Go to bed by 10 p.m. E: Partner will use a reading light not the overhead	7 hrs of sleep/night
Have a pleasant dinner	I: Do not get angry about unexpected delays of twenty min. or less. Be accepting E: Partner agrees to call by noon if delayed by more than twenty min.	Kiss each other hello at the door Positive eye contact throughout dinner

---

Learn how to create Plans of Action (POAs).

- We can exercise control and reduce stress and the sense of being victimized:
    1. By promoting change in people and in situations
    2. By changing our attitudes, feelings or attention
    3. By leaving the situations that are causing us stress
- Don't let feelings of unfairness dominate your consciousness.
- Passivity increases feelings of victimization.
- Use your voice.
- Know your limits and boundaries and assert them.
- Have the "willingness to walk" early in the formation of a relationship.
- Take responsibility for your own thoughts, feelings and attitudes.
- Your inner experience is not immutable.
- Be able to have an attitude of acceptance.
- Learn how to create Plans of Action (POA's).
    1. Conduct an evaluation in which you try and determine what type of change is possible, external or internal, that will help you to feel better.
    2. Specifically clarify what those changes are.
    3. Develop a plan of action for bringing about that change.

EXERCISES FOR NOT BEING A VICTIM:

1. Review the Preliminary Exercise, five things that have been bothering you for a while.

2. For each of these five things ask yourself these questions:

    - *Is there anything that I can do to bring about a change in that circumstance or situation?*
    - *How can I behave differently in order to get my need met?*
    - *Have I been too passive?*
    - *Have I used my voice?*
    - *Have I asserted my boundaries?*

3. If you can do something differently to bring about a change in your circumstance, write down what some of the things that you can do to bring about this change. Create a plan of action for making this happen.

4. If you don't think that you can do something differently to bring about a change in your circumstance, ask yourself:

    - *Have I been stuck in feelings of injustice and unfairness?*
    - *Have I felt like my feelings are someone else's fault?*
    - *Have I felt like there isn't anything I can do or I want to do to change my feelings?*

5. If so, reread the sections above that are related to see if you can get yourself unstuck.

6. Write down things that you can do to bring about a change in your attitude or feelings. Create a plan of action for making these internal changes.

7. Think about whether or not acceptance is part of what you need to bring about a change in your thoughts and feelings. Review the exercises in the section on acceptance if you need more help.

8. If you need a combination of external and internal changes, write down both plans.

9. Over the next few weeks make a concerted effort on a daily basis to implement your plan of action. Develop a method of accountability for accessing whether or not this plan of action is working.

APPENDIX 10, "DON'T BE A VICTIM."
TECHNICAL DISCUSSION ON CAUSALITY AND BLAME

Psychological jargon often introduces new language without introducing new concepts, and thus I have tried to not use it. However, regarding the issue of blame or causality, new language is useful as it does introduce new concepts. In psychology, we often talk about the *stimulus-response chain* when describing observable behavior. In other words, when we observe behavior between two individuals, we notice one person's behavior and then the other person's reaction to the first person's behavior. The first person's behavior is called the *stimulus* and the second person's behavior is called the *response*. The second person's response then becomes the stimulus for the first person's counter response.

This continuous coupling of dyadic sequences is called the *stimulus-response chain.*

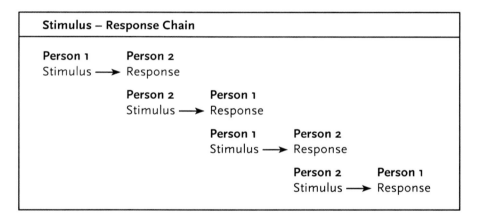

Stimulus – Response Chain

| **Person 1** | **Person 2** |
| Stimulus ⟶ | Response |

| **Person 2** | **Person 1** |
| Stimulus ⟶ | Response |

| **Person 1** | **Person 2** |
| Stimulus ⟶ | Response |

| **Person 2** | **Person 1** |
| Stimulus ⟶ | Response |

Sometimes the term *catalyst* is used to describe the stimulus and connotes that the stimulus serves the function of getting the response in the second person started. For our purposes, the question that is most important about the stimulus-response chain is the question of causality.

Does the stimulus cause the response?

More often than not, people tend to make this attribution, believing that the stimulus *does* cause the response. Common expressions are, *You made me so mad! You hurt my feelings,* or *You made me cry.*

> ***People commonly attribute causality to the stimulus.***

But let's think a little bit about what causality means.

Causality Example 1:
A car is driven into a brick wall at 40 miles an hour, and the car is damaged.
    We could say that the driver "caused" the damage by driving his car into the wall. **Several parameters are important in determining this idea of causality:**

1. There is **repeatability;** that is, if the car is driven into the wall multiple times, damage will occur multiple times.

2. There is **interchangeability;** that is, if there are different drivers, the car will still be damaged. If there are different cars, the car will be damaged even if there are different degrees of damage depending on the make and model of the car.

3. There is **consistency of time and place;** that is, if the car is driven into a wall in one location verses another location, damage will still occur. If the car is driven into a wall at different times of the day or during different times of the year, damage will occur.

I propose that these are criteria to use in determining that the stimulus "caused" the response.

Causality Example 2:
Jane slaps John across the face in the kitchen this morning and now he has a red cheek.
    Using the criteria above let's determine whether or not we could say there is causality:

1. It is likely that if Jane slaps John in the face with the same amount of force in the future, he would likely get another red cheek. Thus there is **repeatability.**

2. If Jane slaps Pete in the face with the same amount of force, Pete would likely get a red cheek as well. Likewise, if Sue slaps John, there would be the same outcome. Thus there is **interchangeability.**

3. If Jane slaps John in the bedroom tomorrow night, he is likely to get another red cheek. Thus there is **consistency of time and place.**

According to this criteria, I think that we are safe to say that Jane caused John's red cheek. She is to blame.

Causality Example 3:
John tells Jane that he doesn't like the coffee that she just made in the kitchen that morning, and she starts to cry.

1. Jane may not cry every time John tells her he doesn't like the coffee so there is not **repeatability.**

2. Since different people drinking coffee will yield very different results, there probably isn't **interchangeability.**

3. Since different times of day and different rooms may produce different results, there isn't **consistency of time and place.**

Clear causality is not established.

Jane tells John that she can't have sex for a week per doctor's orders, so every night for the next week, John gets drunk. Is Jane to blame for John getting drunk? If we apply the same criteria above we again see the inconsistencies and the inability to assign blame.

Most human interactions do not meet the criteria of causality as discussed in my first example of the car driving into the brick wall, or even in the example of Jane slapping John. They do not meet the criteria of repeatability, interchangeability and/or consistency of time and place. **Most human interactions have many conditions that go into determining what has occurred between two people, and causality rests in the interaction rather than in any single person. While a feeling might be provoked in one person by another person, that feeling is not "caused" by the other person.**

This is the idea of a catalyst. Certainly the state of mind of the person who has been provoked has something to do with the feelings he is having. If he is already in a bad mood, it is more likely he will become upset when something is said to him with which he disagrees. If he is sad about something else, he may more easily cry. And if he is generally an easily aroused person, then a whole variety of stimuli might arouse him. Thus, some responsibility rests with the respondent regarding how he feels, no matter what the stimulus is. This is a radical shift away from the idea that the stimulus "causes" the response, which seems to be so readily accepted in human relations interactions.

> *Causality most often lies in the interaction between two people rather than in any one person.*

While most stimuli don't cause the response in human interactions, that by no means relieves the stimulus person from responsibility for modifying her behavior. If one's partner is hurt by her behavior, based on the outcome, consideration needs to be given to working on changing what she did, whether or not there was causality. Change that is motivated by care rather than by cause, typically has less defensiveness and less anger, and just feels better.

RULE #11: **Let go of anger, blame, and resentment.**

Of course we all have experienced our own anger and the anger of others. It is a common human feeling. **It is important to distinguish the "feeling" of anger from the "expression" of anger. The feeling of anger is a physiological and psychological activation inside our bodies and minds. The expression of anger is how we behave when we are angry.**

> *There are feelings and anger and expressions of anger.*

EXPRESSIONS OF ANGER. It is universally acknowledged that great harm can result from some expressions of anger. From a very early age, we are taught to not express anger in certain ways, and that it is bad and wrong. Unfortunately, those teachings are often communicated differently by what our parents say and what our parents *do*. We carry those teachings into our adult lives. As adults, it is up to each of us to form our own set of values around the expression of anger principally because of the harm that it might cause.

Expression of anger can be thought of in two ways: 1) **anger that is cathartic,** meaning anger that serves to create a physiological and psychological release; and 2) **anger that is instrumental,** meaning that it serves the purpose of attempting to change someone's behavior. Cathartic anger and instrumental anger are both on a continuum. *(Refer to the graphic on the next page.)*

> *There are two forms of expressed anger: **cathartic anger** and **instrumental anger.***

There are two polarities on the continuum of cathartic anger, *talking* and *raging*. When people talk about their anger within the construct of a give-and-take discussion, problems are often worked out. At the very least, when one feels like their anger has been heard and acknowledged, it often helps to diminish the feelings of anger. **If done in a non-harmful way, talking about anger can be good for both the individual and the couple. It can be both cathartic and instrumental.**

> *Talking can be both cathartic and instrumental.*

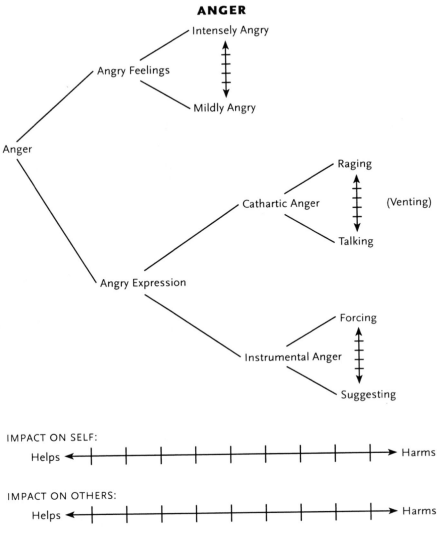

ANGER

TWO TYPES OF ANGER: Angry Feelings & Angry Expressions

TWO TYPES OF ANGRY EXPRESSIONS: Cathartic Anger & Instrumental Anger

The term *venting* is used to describe the release of expressive anger. You could also use the expression "getting it off your chest" to mean the same thing. Talking is mild venting, and raging is extreme venting. Many people believe that venting is helpful, that it gets rid of their anger, and that they feel better as a result. If others aren't hurt in the process, venting *may* be helpful. Research on anger paints a cloudy picture, particularly when the intensity of venting increases. Some people benefit from venting, but others do not. **Some people feel increased anger after venting and this increases the likelihood of harm to others.** Our jails are filled with people for whom angry venting turned into criminal behavior.

Whether or not angry expressions "cause" hurt feelings or harm in the strictest sense, as previously discussed, we need to take responsibility for our angry behavior. Some people don't care if someone is hurt or harmed, because they think it is deserved. This way of thinking can be very destructive to relationships. Nonetheless, we need to consider the degree of hurt that results from angry venting so that venting can be modified based on its impact. This could range from mild discomfort to significant harm. For example:

- discomfort
- mild guilt/remorse
- moderate concerns about one's character
- horrible thoughts about oneself
- inability to sleep
- breaking out in hives
- ruminating about it for days
- sick to one's stomach
- inability to stop crying
- fears of divorce
- loss of trust
- fear for one's personal safety
- fear for one's life
- suicidal thoughts
- red marks on the skin
- black and blue marks on the skin
- lacerations
- broken bones

Exercise 1 at the end of this section addresses the question of how much discomfort is okay for others to have as a result of your anger. Maybe you haven't thought much about this. This exercise will help you to create a guideline regarding what is okay and not okay in the expression of your anger. The laws of states and countries help to create these guidelines for the most egregious situations, but they certainly don't cover common everyday experiences of living with someone. This exercise is about heightening your awareness and modifying your behavior based on the amount of hurt that your partner has because you are mad and want to get something off your chest. If you wound a loved one, you have gone too far.

My position is this: Angry venting that results in harm is not okay. In addition to just being wrong, it can be destructive and it erodes intimacy. This is not just a suggestion like many of the Rules in this book. This is like the 11th commandment: **Thou shall not vent anger that harms others.**

Setting boundaries around the expression of anger has to start at the personal level. Later, you can discuss it with your partner and further decide where you have to draw the line, but it is up to you to enforce your own boundaries. Of all the human emotions, anger is one of the biggest culprits for causing harm to others; not the only culprit, but one of the biggest.

> ### *Cathartic anger that harms others is not okay.*

What about *instrumental anger?* This is anger that serves the purpose of getting someone to stop doing what you don't like, start doing what you do like, or change a pattern of behavior to comply with the way you want things to be done. Most of us are familiar with this because this is how we were raised. If our parents didn't like something about the way we were behaving, they got mad at us with the hope that getting mad would change our behavior. **Just because this was used to create behavior change by our parents doesn't mean that it is a good idea for us, as adults, to use with other adults.** One of the biggest problems with instrumental anger is that if often doesn't work. Often people are unreceptive to the message when anger is too intense. The second exercise at the end of this section addresses this. How much discomfort is okay for your partner to have because you are mad and want her to change? My position on this is the same as above: **Instrumental anger that harms our loved ones is not okay.**

> ### *Instrumental anger that harms others is not okay.*

One of the primary reasons people give for getting angry is because they are protecting themselves. They are defending themselves from someone's attack. If someone is legitimately being attacked—particularly physically attacked—this seems to be an acceptable use of anger. But exactly what is an "attack" in a primary relationship, and how much anger is required to defend yourself? *He started it,* is the domestic violence mantra. I remember growing up hearing the macho expression, *I didn't start it but I sure finished it.* He may have also *finished it* in jail. While there may be legitimate uses of anger if provoked, learning to bite your tongue or simply walking away before someone gets hurt is a preferred option.

These two exercises emphasize that **there are times when it is important to learn how to inhibit the harmful expression of anger.** That means neither saying nor doing harmful things. The lists you just created should be your guideline as to what is okay and what is not okay. You have several options for not saying or doing harmful things:

- Don't say anything.
- Keep your hands in your pockets.
- Replace your harmful verbal expressions with non-harmful verbal expressions.
- Replace your harmful actions with non-harmful actions.
- Leave the room.

Exercise 3 will be about developing things that you can say and do to replace harmful expressions and actions.

Find ways to express anger without causing harm.

ANGRY FEELINGS. While inhibiting angry behavior is very important, it may do nothing to decrease angry feelings. Is this something that you want to do? If you have already concluded that you don't want to have certain expressions of anger, you'll be more easily convinced to decrease angry feelings. This is because **angry behavior is driven by angry feelings.** Thus, if you decrease feelings of anger, inhibiting angry behavior with the methods above becomes less necessary. In addition to having an effect on angry behavior, decreasing feelings of anger is also helpful for our overall well-being. **People who are consumed with anger don't tend to be very happy,** and certainly when we are consumed with anger, we have less positive energy. You really have to be committed to decreasing feelings of anger, because it takes a lot of tough mental work.

> ### *If you stop feeling so angry, you'll stop being so angry.*

Eliminating angry feelings is not the same as "stuffing" angry feelings. When we "stuff" feelings, we simply cover them up by thinking about and doing other things. The angry feelings are still there, just bubbling beneath the surface. Sometimes this is called "holding a grudge," *(see Rule 57, "Be forgiving. Don't hold a grudge")*. Soon after the topic that made us angry is mentioned again, up pop those angry feelings. When we stuff feelings over a long period of time, they can be triggered very easily by events that may have nothing to do with the original difficulty. It is hard to be calm and relaxed and have a positive presence if we are all stuffed up with angry feelings. **If you really want to get rid of angry feelings, don't stuff them, get rid of them.**

> ### *Don't stuff your angry feelings; get rid of them.*

There are a number of ways to get rid of angry feelings. **One of the best ways to get rid of angry feelings is to express them.** Once you figure out what expressions are okay and what expressions are not okay, then talking your angry feelings over with someone else is one of the best ways to get rid of them. Timing, tone and language are all important for positive results. **Talking about angry feelings can be a constructive process, not a destructive process.**

> ### *Talking through angry feelings in a constructive way is one of the best ways to get rid of them.*

Another way to reduce angry feelings is by using our capacity for understanding another person's point of view or their circumstances and activating our empathy. We have many examples of this:

- You are walking down the street talking to a friend and a lady runs right into you. You might immediately get mad—until you see that she is walking with a white cane and visually impaired. Immediately your anger might change to helpfulness.

- Your husband is over an hour late for dinner, which he was supposed to pick up for the entire family, and he didn't call. Everyone is hungry. You might be mad—until you get a phone call from the hospital telling you that he was in an automobile accident.

- Your wife seemed to be engaged in behavior that seems rather suspicious—until you came home for dinner and all your friends are there, saying, "Surprise!"

These examples illustrate that an understanding of circumstances can change the way we feel. Sometimes we have to work at understanding and at not getting so stuck in our reasons for being angry that we won't even entertain the possibility of listening and trying to understand the other person's perspective. The fourth exercise at the end of this section is going to help you develop a greater capacity for understanding.

> *Understanding another person's perspective or circumstances can help get rid of angry feelings.*

Another way to get rid of angry feelings is to understand why you are so angry in the first place and nullify the reason for your anger with thoughts that you can believe. Some common reasons that we have for feeling angry are:

- Injustice
- Betrayal
- Humiliation
- Defamation
- Injury
- Insult
- Violation of agreement
- Unmet expectations

For each reason for being angry, we may need to tell ourselves something that helps to nullify our reason for being angry. For example:

Reason: I'm angry because what she did was not fair.
Counter: Much in life in not fair, and I have to learn to accept that.

Reason: I'm angry because he humiliated me.
Counter: He never even knew that I might be humiliated by what he did.

Reason: I'm angry because this is her third automobile accident.
Counter: She's really trying to be a good driver; she just has a hard time with driving. I'm glad no one was hurt.

In the fifth exercise, list some of the reasons why you get angry and then write counter arguments that might help to diffuse your anger.

Nullifying thoughts can help get rid of anger.

Often we are *self-righteous* about our anger, saying, *I have a right to be angry*, or *I have a good reason to be angry.* Unfortunately, strong self-righteous attitudes about being angry can quickly lead to hurting others. **We don't have the right to hurt others; that is one of the main reasons for writing this Rule.** What is more important than a "right" and a "reason" to feel angry is whether we want to feel angry. **If you don't *want* to feel angry, try to:**

1. Reconcile with the person with whom you are angry;

2. Look at the situation from the other person's point of view;

3. Bring to mind new ways to think about your reasons for being angry in the first place;

4. Practice letting go, forgiveness, and acceptance.

Sometimes letting go is the only way to reduce angry feelings, because the infraction is neither understandable nor okay at any level. This is hard, and the anger may end up being transformed into agitation and then sadness, as we go through this process. When an infraction is so bad, there may have to be forgiveness or letting go without reconciliation. Sometimes a relationship cannot survive the worst infractions. But more often than not, this is not the case and reconciliation can occur. In either case, it is important to find a pathway towards joyous living, and that is hard to accomplish when we are sitting on a lot of unresolved anger.

> *Letting go may end up being your only option for getting rid of anger.*

- *Cathartic anger that harms others is not okay.*

- *Instrumental anger that harms others is not okay.*

- *Find ways to express anger without causing harm.*

- *If you stop feeling so angry, you'll stop being so angry.*

- *Don't stuff your angry feelings; get rid of them.*

- *Talking through angry feelings in a constructive way is one of the best ways to get rid of them.*

- *Understanding another person's perspective or circumstances can help get rid of angry feelings.*

- *Nullifying thoughts can help get rid of anger.*

- *Letting go may end up being your only option for getting rid of anger.*

EXERCISES FOR LETTING GO OF ANGER:

Try to work through the following exercises spending a couple of days on each one. You can do more than one at the same time. The guidelines and the methodologies that you have created need to be reviewed every few weeks over a period of six months and then as needed.

1. How much discomfort is okay for your partner to have because you are mad and want to get something off your chest?

    a. Is there any type of physical pain or discomfort that is okay for your partner to have as a result of your anger? Bruises; Bleeding; Upset stomach; Headache; Other?

    b. How do you determine when it is okay and when it isn't okay?

c. Is there any type of psychological pain or discomfort that is okay for your partner to have as a result of your anger? Tears; Agitation; Worry; Rumination; Fear; Other?

d. How do you determine when it is okay and when it isn't okay?

2. How much discomfort is okay for your partner to have because you are mad and want her to change?

a. Is there any type of physical pain or discomfort that is okay for your partner to have as a result of your anger? Bruises, bleeding, upset stomach, headache, other?

b. How do you determine when it is okay and when it isn't okay?

c. Is there any type of psychological pain or discomfort that is okay for your partner to have as a result of your anger? Tears, agitation, worry, rumination, fear, other?

d. How do you determine when it is okay and when it isn't okay?

3. Replace harmful expressions and actions.

a. Write down five harmful ways you express anger verbally that can be changed to non-harmful expressions. Write down the five non-harmful expressions of your anger.

b. Write down five harmful ways you express anger by your actions that can be changed to non-harmful actions. Write down the five non-harmful actions.

4. Create understanding.

a. List five situations in which you were angry with your partner. State why you were angry from your point of view.

b. List five ways in which you can understand the situation from their point of view so that you will be less angry.

5. Reasons and counter reasons for getting angry.

a. List five reasons that you have for being angry.

b. List five counter reasons or nullifying thoughts that will help you to be less angry.

RULE #12: **You have more power to change yourself than to change others.**

One of the fundamental questions of life is how will we be taken care of. **To what degree are we responsible for our own wellbeing?** By the time most of us are done with school, we have come to the conclusion that we mainly have to take care of ourselves. However, if young adults don't learn this most basic lesson, they may have difficulty. Even after becoming part of an intimate relationship, taking care of oneself remains essential.

After childhood, self-care becomes essential.

Everyone has problems or some area for personal growth. But improvement doesn't occur all on its own. It takes some effort. For some people that effort seems like too much work so they sweep their problems under the carpet. Unfortunately, problems often fester and get worse when they are avoided. Problems need to be solved—and this is particularly true in relationships. If things are bothering you, think about it, talk about it, and try to arrive at a solution.

Don't sweep your problems under the carpet.

Primary intimate relationships present an interesting problem because of their close resemblance to the parent-child relationship. Consequently, **a partner may unconsciously think that her relationship has the same characteristics as the parent-child relationship and expect that her partner will take care of her like an idealized parent.** Thus, she may have unrealistic expectations that her partner is responsible for her happiness and that by complaining, her partner should change to satisfy her NWDs. The problem is, her partner probably doesn't want to parent her any more than she wants to parent her partner.

Your partner doesn't want to carry the primary responsibility for improving your relationship any more than you do.

In the adult relationship, couples try to develop a system of give and take. Both parties are working to make the relationship better. For you, as an individual in the relationship, it is necessary to think about what *you* can do to help in making things work better. You may want your partner:

- to think the way you do and to agree with you
- to share all the same values, child rearing practices and outlooks on life
- to go and do what you want to do
- to listen when you want to be heard
- to make love when you want to make love

More often than not, it doesn't always work out that way. Consequently, who makes the changes? Who makes the accommodations? Ideally, it is a combination of both people's efforts. However, since you are the one reading this book and your partner is elsewhere, at this moment it is useful to think about what you can do. While it is true that you can probably improve the way you articulate your needs, which may result in a change on your partner's part, you might want to start thinking about what else you can do to improve the relationship. It ultimately gets back to that same old thing: **change your behavior or change your attitude.** That's the "take away" that I ask my clients in couples therapy to think about at the end of each session. **The single greatest change starts with you!**

What can **you** do to improve your relationship?

Some people are a little surprised to find out that in therapy they have to actually ask themselves what *they* can do to improve. They think that it is a magical process, and if they just say what is bothering them everything will get better. That is rarely the case in couples therapy. Simply expressing feelings may actually cause more difficulty, particularly if, after the feelings are expressed, both parties feel like it is the other partner's responsibility to do the changing. Relationships don't improve with that premise. **When it comes to couples work, each person has to take responsibility for making changes.**

When it comes to *your* relationship, you have to take responsibility for making changes. The good news is that you *can* do it. You *can* change. *You have the power.* While you can't do all the work for your relationship on your own, it is the most productive thing that *you* can do to improve your relationship.

When you do the work you need to do, you will undoubtedly feel better about yourself. And, when you do the work you need to do, you significantly increase the likelihood of improving your relationship. Start with yourself.

- ***Don't sweep your problems under the carpet.***

- ***Your partner doesn't want to carry the primary responsibility for improving your relationship any more than you do.***

- ***What can you do to improve your relationship?***

EXERCISES FOR TAKING PERSONAL RESPONSIBILITY:

1. If you haven't done it already, get your **personal growth notebook** that I described in the Introduction, "How to use this book." Write down five problems that you think are significant in your relationship.

2. What do you think you can do to help fix each of these problems? Write it down in your notebook.

3. Try to come up with a plan of action for implementing these changes. Try to address variables like when, where, how often, and under what circumstances you will practices these changes. Write this plan of action in your notebook.

RULE #13: **Recognize the negative influence from the past.**

This is a very big topic and I am not suggesting by writing this Rule that you can bypass any need for psychotherapy or guided introspection. The purpose of this Rule is to remind you that one of the greatest barriers to attaining good mental health is old, unresolved negative influences from the past. **There is a process for resolving these negative influences:**

1. **The first step is acknowledging that such negative influences might exist for you and that it might be worthwhile to try to understand those influences, if they do exist.**

2. **The second step is sorting out the nature of those influences.**

3. **The third step is trying to quiet the mind and the body of these influences.**

Depending on one's individual history, this effort may be brief or it may last a long time. This Rule is simply suggesting that you start this process.

The way in which past influences manifest in the present may be easy to understand for those of you who have done personal growth work. However, for many "first timers" who come to my office, the concept that the past manifests in the present, in any fashion, is a new concept. Thus, **when they have very strong emotional responses to current situations, they do not understand that it may not be the current situations alone that are provoking the strength of those feelings. Past circumstances may also play a role.** For example:

- If John was frequently ridiculed for not doing well in grade school, he might easily feel demeaned by his wife, who didn't think her standards were met in house cleaning. John may not even be able to have a discussion about differing "standards" because of that sensitivity.

- If Jane grew up with an alcoholic father, she may be particularly more sensitive to the drinking habits of her husband.

- If Scott was told, "Don't you cry or I'll really give you something to cry about," he might have difficulty expressing sadness as an adult.

These are just a few of the tens of thousands of examples that I have heard as a psychotherapist over the years.

Be open to acknowledging that your past experiences may influence your current sensitivities.

Trying to understand your personal sensitivities is a very important part of not overly empowering others' behavior towards you. Along with your sensitivities are the ways in which you go about protecting yourself from being hurt. These are your *defenses*. There are many types of defenses, and I discuss this more fully in Rule 49, "Lower your defenses." Suffice it to say at this point that these defenses can cause a lot of trouble.

If you understand past influences on your emotions, you might be able to make better attributions regarding the cause of those emotions and work on the emotions internally rather than externally. This makes you less of a victim and reduces interpersonal tensions. It gives you more control over your own well-being. This delving into the past to understand these influences can be difficult because our memories of the past can sometimes be spotty. There is also the problem of what is called "constructive memory"; that is, believing that we remember something that didn't happen as though it did happen. This is why talking with a trained professional can be so useful. He can give you assistance in recognizing and illuminating some of these past influences. He can also help you reduce their current influence. Recognizing the negative influence from the past is actually more of a journey than a destination, and I encourage you to begin that journey.

- *Making better attributions improves your ability to resolve difficulties.*

- *Be open to acknowledging that your past experiences may influence your current sensitivities.*

- *Making better attributions improves your ability to resolve difficulties.*

EXERCISES FOR RECOGNIZING NEGATIVE INFLUENCE FROM THE PAST:

1. Write down five negative influences from the past that you think still have an influence on you currently.

2. See if you can identify specific situations in which you thought you were responding only to the current situation and now realize that past influences, and the sensitivities or defenses that arose from those influences, were part of the problem. Write down:

   - the situation
   - the past influence
   - the sensitivity or defense

3. Ask yourself if you would like to try to reduce that influence, and think about how you might go about doing that.

RULE #14: **Let go of useless worry.**

I believe that our success as a species, as Homo sapiens, rested in part, on our ability to anticipate circumstances that might hurt or harm us. We might say that this capacity to worry kept us alive during times of great peril. While some worries *are* useful, most people in industrialized countries don't live with the peril of their ancestors, yet many people worry excessively, have far too much anxiety, and/or live in fear. These three words are often used to describe the state of being that I am going to discuss in this section: *worry, anxiety,* and *fear.*

> **Preliminary exercise:**
> *Write down five to ten worries or fears that you have that wish you didn't have.*

Worry is a state mind in which we anticipate the possibility of a negative outcome for some future event. Worry can have a short duration, but often rumination persists for an excessively long period of time. Our thoughts can become perseverative; that is, they repeat themselves over and over. We can also become preoccupied with those thoughts. We usually think of worry as having a specific focus, worrying about something in particular. Sometimes people have generalized worries like general feelings of dread.

> *Worry is a negative anticipation about a future event.*

Anxiety adds more of a physiological state of being; the body can be tense and tight, and there is a feeling of unsettledness, unease or stress. When anxiety is situation-specific, a person may have very clear thoughts regarding why he is anxious. However, sometimes a person will feel anxious and won't know why and his thoughts are vague and unclear. This is sometimes called *generalized anxiety.* A person can be worried and feel anxious at the same time. Worries can have a gradient of anxiety from weak to strong. Worries with a lot of rumination and a lot of anxiety can be overwhelming.

> *Anxiety is a feeling of unsettledness, unease, and/or stress.*

Sometimes the word *fear* and *worry* are used interchangeably, and that may happen throughout this book. However, I don't think they exactly describe the same thing. *Worry* is a state of mind that often has only mild physiological arousal, and it projects into the future. *Fear* is heightened state of physiological arousal that can create a state of hyper alertness and vigilance right now. Fear gives rise to immediate thoughts and feelings about taking a course of action, doing something, like running away. Sometimes people are unable to act when they feel fear, and they describe being frozen in fear.

> ***Fear is an immediate state of distress with associated impulses to take action.***

Let me give you an example of how these words might be used:

Jane is afraid of crossing bridges and is **worried** about a car trip that is coming up in a few weeks because she is driving over a long bridge. As she gets closer and closer to the day of departure, her **anxiety** increases. On the day of her trip, the closer to the bridge she gets, the more **fearful** she becomes. When she is on the bridge, she becomes **frozen in fear.**

In the last chapter, I discussed recognizing negative influences from the past. One of those influences might be the development of excessive worry and fear that grows out of experiences. People have so many different kinds of worries and fears:

- having enough money
- getting hurt
- the children
- the pets
- love
- getting old
- being harmed
- when left alone
- embarrassment
- having to do something unpleasant
- dying

Some of these worries and fears are adaptive and some are not. **But whether adaptive or not, worries and fears often sit in the back of our minds influencing decision-making, keeping us uptight, and preventing us from enjoying life right now.** While avoiding disaster is important, you have to ask yourself if your want to live only to avoid disaster.

For those of you who seem to get preoccupied with worry and stress, try to sort out what is truly adaptive for you and what is needless rumination. If you find that you are afraid of being eaten by a tiger and there is no tiger anywhere for thousands of miles, don't go buy a tiger gun and sit by the door guarding the house from a tiger attack. See what you can do to quiet the churning of your mind.

> ### *Sort out what is adaptive and what is needless rumination.*

There are quite a variety of ways people go about quieting the mind from non-adaptive, excessive worries and fears, and quieting the body from anxiety. Here are some of the most common approaches. The first few techniques involve having awareness of specific troublesome worries. The later approaches may not require this awareness. Some of these techniques will work better than others, given particular individuals and the particular worries, anxiety, or fear they have. **All of these approaches take practice and repetition.**

1. **Replace unwanted or irrational thoughts with new rational thoughts.**
   For example, if you worry that the plane you are on is going to crash, you might think about the actual probability that the plane will crash.

   You might say to yourself, *Planes almost never crash. I am far more likely to get killed in a car wreck than a plane wreck, and I don't worry about getting in a car, even when I'm not driving.*

   Or you might think, *The pilots that fly these planes have been through rigorous training and thousands of hours of airtime. I'm sure they know what they are doing.*

   Or: *Most everybody else on this plane seems calm. If there was real danger wouldn't a lot more people be upset?*

   Or: *I don't see anything out of the ordinary that would lead me to believe that something is wrong.*

   Or: *I know that I typically get worried at a time like this. Just because I'm worried doesn't raise the real risk that something disastrous is going to happen.*

These are all rational thoughts, and by practicing this kind of thinking, particularly in advance of getting on the plane, the worry and fear may decrease.

2. **Stop thoughts.** Again, if you worry about your plane crashing, you might visualize yourself putting those thoughts, worries and fears into a garbage bag and throwing them into the trash. You might tell yourself with some firmness, *These thoughts are ridiculous and I'm not going there anymore. I don't want these thoughts to be part of my psyche, and I refuse to give them any more time or attention.* If you are successful in stopping thoughts, you might want to fill the emptiness with something. That's when the next technique is handy.

3. **Use distraction.** Again, if you are worried about the plane going down, you might just fill up the airtime with lots of other things to do, so you don't think about it so much. You can bring reading material, watch a movie, write a letter, work on your computer or just go to sleep.

4. **Give worries and fears a distasteful interpretation.** *I believe that I'm freaking myself out in some sort of twisted effort to get attention and nurturance from someone. Maybe this was the only way that I got attention from my Mom when I was little, but it's not okay now that I'm an adult.*

5. **Be prepared for the worst.** *The kinds of things that go wrong on airplanes aren't usually that big of a deal. I can deal with some delay if it were to occur. If by some twist of fate this plane goes down and I die, then I guess I do. I have to make peace with that.*

6. **Let go of control.** *Hey, I don't have total control about everything that happens. Some things are in the hands of the universe, and I have to just learn to deal with it.*

7. **Be detached from the worries.** *I am aware of the thoughts that I have labeled as worries. I can just watch them pass through my mind like a boat going down the river. They are just thoughts, and I don't have to be attached to them.*

8. **Talk about it with a friend or loved one.** For some, just talking about a worry reduces it because it sets into motion the processing of the thoughts and feelings in a productive fashion. This also allows for the possibility that someone else might help, using one of the techniques from above. This may be felt as reassurance, particularly if the other person is also compassionate. Care needs to be taken, though, because

talking with someone else who has the same worry or fear, can make it worse.

9. **Talk about it with a trained professional.** If you are anxious about flying and have a tragic plane crash and death of a loved one as part of your developmental history, there is likely a strong association between that history and your anxiety. Speaking with a professional may help you to find ways to unlink your past to the present.

10. **Use relaxation and meditation practices.** Many people carry too much stress and are generally uptight. A whole variety of relaxation and meditation techniques are used to help people be generally calmer. Some include:

- relaxing the body by releasing muscle tension in areas that are tight
- simply *noticing* whatever passes through ones consciousness
- quietly focusing on meaningful words like *calm body* or *love*
- quietly focusing on some aspect of one's physiology like breathing
- quietly smiling to oneself
- quietly focusing on a peaceful image like waves rolling onto the seashore
- quietly focusing on the sound of a non-meaningful word like *ohm*
- quietly listening to relaxing music
- quietly focusing on the divine spirit

There are walking meditations in which sensory awareness becomes the focus. There are meditations that combine stretching and focused attention, such as in yoga. There is prayer.

11. **Use biofeedback.** A variety of physiological functions can be measured with instruments such as electrical activity in the muscles, electrical activity in the skin, electrical activity in the brain, peripheral body temperature and heart rate. By coupling the use of these instruments with relaxation techniques, we can learn to willfully change these physiological functions. By changing these functions, we may also experience changes in our feelings of tension and anxiety.

12. **Exercise.** This is one of the most important ways of reducing the anxiety that is associated with worry. Exercise brings about a change in physiology that simply decreases anxiety.

13. **Get enough sleep.** Our brains require a sufficient amount of sleep in order to operate at their best. All of the techniques mentioned above will suffer when we don't get enough sleep.

14. **Use medication.** For people who really suffer from overwhelming anxiety and panic, medication may be helpful. This would be something to review with your health professional.

See if you can be honest with yourself about the kinds of worries, fears and anxieties that you pack around, either just above or just below the level of your immediate consciousness. Anxiety is a source of great discomfort for many people, and is implicated in many mental health and physical health difficulties. Anxieties are largely a state of mind, and with some effort on your part, you can diminish them. An extraordinary number of books have been written to help you. There are also many professionals of all different persuasions to give you guidance.

Sort out what is adaptive and what is needless rumination
Methodologies:
- *Replace unwanted or irrational thoughts with new rational thoughts*
- *Stopping thoughts*
- *Use distraction*
- *Give worries and fears a distasteful interpretation*
- *Be prepared for the worst*
- *Let go of control*
- *Be detached from the worries*
- *Talk about it with a friend of loved one*
- *Talk about it with a trained professional*
- *Use relaxation and meditation practices*
- *Use biofeedback*
- *Exercise*
- *Get enough sleep*
- *Medication*

EXERCISES FOR LETTING GO OF USELESS WORRY:

1. Review the Preliminary Exercise.

2. Next to each one of the worries or fears that you have written down, assign a rating from one to ten, one being adaptive and ten being maladaptive.

3. Give each worry/fear an intensity rating, one being mildly intense and ten being extremely intense.

4. Go through the list above and select which techniques you think might be helpful for reducing each worry/fear that you listed above; write down the number of those techniques next to the individual worry/fear.

5. Select one or two of the worries/fears that you want to work on. For the next two weeks, make a concerted effort to practice the techniques that you listed on a daily basis.

6. At the end of two weeks, rate the intensity of the worry/fear that you were working on and compare it to the initial intensity rating. Make a notation of which techniques you thought were the most helpful for each problem.

7. Spend two more weeks working on the same worries/fears, or select others if you feel that the progress that you have already made is sufficient.

8. Repeat Step 6.

9. Continue this process as needed. Decreasing worries, anxieties and fears can easily take months and years.

Don't turn your shortcomings into sins.

Everyone has strengths and weaknesses, talents and shortcomings, abilities and limitations. It is part of the human condition. **Most of our strengths, weaknesses, talents, and shortcomings are a result of our genetic makeup or are a result of our upbringing. For the most part, we can neither take credit for them nor take blame for them.** They weren't a result of our efforts or self-discipline. While it is true that we acquire skills and knowledge as a result of concentrated learning and practice, even the ability to concentrate or be engaged in sustained practice has a large component of genetic makeup. Sometimes our genetic makeup is referred to as being "hardwired," meaning "wired" into the neurons of our brain prior to our birth.

It is clear that many of the characteristics that define our personalities, our problem-solving abilities, our general intelligence, our creative abilities and our temperaments are in our DNA when we take our first breath of air. Early development can also create "imprints" in our brains that are very difficult to change. For example, when you learn to talk, you develop an accent that usually lasts a lifetime in spite of efforts to change it. What we can change and what we can't change it is not always clear.

> ### *Most of our shortcomings are "hardwired."*

Our American culture creates two problems for dealing with our strengths/talents/abilities and weaknesses/shortcomings/limitations.

One problem is our competitive society **rewards certain strengths** like intellect, good looks, and athletic abilities with better grades, more attention, greater adulation or more money.

The second problem is the binary frame of reference of "good-bad" and "right-wrong" that is often used to understand and explain so much of human behavior. Thus we easily attach these positive and negative values to our strengths and weakness. This can be pretty tough to deal with, particularly if our weaknesses are in general intellect, social skills, physical abilities, attentiveness, self-management skills, appearance, etc.

> ## *Our culture values our strengths and devalues our weaknesses.*

We can all grow and improve in some area of our lives. Some of our short-comings lend themselves to change or remediation, and some don't. For example, if a child is born with dyslexia, learning to read will be more difficult. However, with sustained effort over many years, that child may be able to learn how to read just fine. On the other hand, if a child is born with a lack of coordination, she is not likely to be able to become a star athlete. In choosing what we want to try to change, we have to be discerning regarding those characteristics that are amenable to change and those that are not.

> ## *Be discerning regarding what can and cannot change.*

If you are attempting to change, good balance between accepting yourself and wanting to change yourself is important. This is *critical*. The first step in effecting personal change is being mindful of the changes that you want to make. If you are overly judgmental of yourself, it may be difficult to hold that shortcoming in your awareness long enough to do anything about it. This is one of the greatest challenges in psychotherapy and in the personal-growth movement. **If it is too painful to think about, it likely won't change.**

This entire book is filled with ideas for making personal change. If you are overly judgmental of yourself regarding any of these Rules, making progress will be more difficult. One of the main reasons for the Rule "Don't turn your shortcomings into sins" is to maximize your possibility for growth. Here are some examples of self-talk that might help you:

- I didn't create who I am. The best I can do is attempt to change this pattern of behavior.
- I'm not a bad person because of this, even though my partner doesn't like it.
- This pattern of behavior doesn't violate the Ten Commandments or the law.
- This is one part of me, but not all of me.
- I know that this behavior pattern can be annoying, and that's why I'm trying to change it. It doesn't make me evil.
- All I can do is my best to change while still remembering that I am a decent human being.

- I am still a lovable person even though I am this way.
- This is the hand I was dealt, and I'm playing the cards the best I can.

> ### *Maximize your possibility for growth by not being overly judgmental of yourself.*

To maintain good mental health, it is important to accept, "as-is," those characteristics of yourself that don't lend themselves to change. Accepting certain aspects of yourself doesn't mean you roll over and stop trying to make other improvements to your life; it means that **you don't beat yourself up for who you are.** You just make the best with whatever cards you have been dealt. **The attitudinal goal is to have an** *overall* **feeling of personal acceptance, while at the same time attempting to grow and change particular characteristics and/or skills sets that are amenable to change.** Feeling bad about who you are can overshadow the way you experience the world. It fuels depression. If it is frequently coupled with complaining and whining, it becomes a social turn-off. And if our view of ourselves is critical and self-deprecating, our view of others may also become critical and judgmental.

> ### *Don't beat yourself up for who you are.*

How do we go about accepting ourselves for who we are? It is a big job, and a lot of psychotherapy is devoted to this one task alone. Over the years I have met with many clients who have carried enormous emotional pain that has been the result of self-deprecating thoughts and feelings. Often, the therapeutic goal was to help lift the burden of those self-judgments from their shoulders. By no means am I suggesting that this book, this chapter, or this Rule can replace the work that goes on in the therapist's office. However, I am offering a few suggestions. **The first is: Don't hold yourself to blame for your hardwired shortcomings. The second is: Become less judgmental about your hardwired shortcomings.**

One way to do this is to frame those shortcomings is non-judgmental language:

- *This is the way I am.*
- *I came this way*
- *Being this way is a challenge for me.*

- *Being this way can be a challenge for some people.*
- *I don't always like this about me, either, but it is what it is.*
- *Some people like me for who I am and some people don't.*
- *If someone doesn't like this about me, there is nothing that I can do about that.*
- *This is just a small part of the overall me.*
- *I'm not going to let this one thing color all of who I am.*
- *I've worked hard to over-compensate for my limitations. I feel good about what I have accomplished.*
- *This isn't something that's bad. It doesn't make me immoral.*
- *Even if someone doesn't like this about me, it doesn't make me bad or wrong.*

> ## Don't blame yourself for your shortcomings.
> ## Don't judge yourself for your shortcomings.

Understanding and accepting your weaknesses also has other important benefits. Whether you are a contributing member of a team of two or a team of many, knowing your limitations is important so that your partner or others on the team can fill in the areas in which you are not strong. **If you act like you can do something but don't do it, you let your partner or your team down, and you may not accomplish your objectives,** be it raising children or getting a product to market. In an organizational setting, great leaders are well aware of their weaknesses and hire others to fill in where they are not so strong. Having this awareness requires being honest with yourself and not getting psychologically bogged down in thinking you are not good enough.

> ### Share your weaknesses with your partner.

Everyone has strengths and weaknesses. Look around at people in all walks of life. You will find that people with similar degrees of strengths and weaknesses have varying degrees of happiness. It's in the attitude.

Saturday Night Live made a very funny skit with Al Franken, spoofing the self-affirmation movement of the 1980s; there was value in what he said: "I'm good enough, I'm smart enough, and by gosh, people like me." Okay, I'll just practice: "This book is good enough, it's smart enough, and by gosh, I think people will like it." There, I feel better. Now it's time for you to practice.

- *Be discerning regarding what can and cannot change.*

- *Maximize your possibility for growth by not being overly judgmental of yourself.*

- *Don't beat yourself up for who you are.*

- *Don't blame yourself for your shortcomings.*

- *Don't judge yourself for your shortcomings.*

- *Share your weaknesses with your partner.*

EXERCISES FOR NOT TURNING YOUR SHORTCOMINGS INTO SINS:

1. Spend some time by yourself thinking about who you are as a person—not things you learned in school or through work experiences, or the skills that you have developed, but rather your personal characteristics. Make a written list of five to ten of these characteristics that you would consider strengths or talents and five to ten that you would consider weaknesses or shortcomings.

2. Think about each one of them and ask yourself if this is something that is "good" or "bad." Give each a rating on a scale from one to ten, one being very bad and ten being very good.

3. Go back to each characteristic you have written down, and next to each one write down whether or not you believe that this characteristic is part of your DNA or a result of your early childhood experiences (write the letters *HW* [hardwired] next to that characteristic).

4. Go back over your list again and think about whether you take credit or blame for these characteristics. See whether you take credit or blame for any of the characteristics that have the letters *HW* next to them. If so, write down how you can take blame or credit for something over which you had no control.

5. Look at your list of shortcomings. Have you assigned a value of "bad" by that characteristic? If so, write out the negative or judgmental thought that you have associated with that characteristic. Now see if you can change that thought so it is neither negative nor judgmental. Write down one or more self-statements that are incompatible with the judgmental thought about your shortcoming.

6. Write down five things about yourself that you would like to change. Think about how badly you feel about yourself for having that character- istic or behavior pattern. Give yourself a rating on a scale from one to ten; one meaning *I hate myself for having this characteristic;* ten meaning *I accept myself for having this characteristic even though I want to change it.* If you think that you are too judgmental with yourself, practice some of the kinds of thoughts above, or make some up on your own that will help you to be more accepting.

RULE #16: **Attend to priorities.**

This Rule is so easy for people to say but much more difficult to implement. It sort of begs the question: Do you *know* your priorities? This may be more difficult than it seems. For example, could you stop reading right now and write down five of your priorities for living the kind of life that you want to live? Go ahead and try it.

> **Preliminary exercise:**
> *Write down five priorities for living the kind of life that you want to live.*

What did you discover? Were you able to come up with five? Was it difficult? Do you think you are spending enough time on these priorities?

I certainly understand that much of life is consumed with the mundane tasks of daily living. That is true for all of us. How could it be otherwise? Up in the morning, attend to personal hygiene, help others who may need help in the morning, have breakfast, get transportation to work, spend time working, transport home, prepare dinner, eat dinner, help clean up after dinner, help others in the evening, get ready for bed, exercise, do chores, pay bills, fix things that break, and the list goes on and on. Perhaps you consider some of these things a priority and perhaps not. It is likely that there are things that are important to us that we just don't get around to doing. We might feel like there just isn't time, we don't have the money, we don't have the energy, or our partner isn't interested. Somehow and for seemingly good reasons, life seems to pass, one day after the next, without giving us the sense that we are doing something that has meaning or importance to us.

How do we begin to pursue the enormous ideal of **living a meaningful life, a joyous life, a purposeful life? It needs to start with mindfulness/awareness.**

> *Be mindful of what is important to you.*

If you tried to write down five priorities of living, then you have begun the process. Rather than living from one day to the next, you have stepped back for a moment and reflected on the way in which you have been living. Having categories will be helpful.

Types of tasks/activities

1. **Survival/maintenance:** These kinds of activities keep the human machine running properly: eating, sleeping, maintaining housing, exercise, relaxing/calming activities, etc.

2. **Sub-goals/dues:** These kinds of activities are necessary steps for doing something else, like going to school, developing a skill or making money.

3. **Things that are meaningful/important/joyful:** These kinds of activities are our priorities. They can be anything, including survival or sub-goal activities. Fitness can be solely for the purpose of keeping healthy, or it can be an end goal that feels both enjoyable and gives life meaning. Building a house can be solely for the purpose of having a beautiful home, or it can be an end unto itself. Going to work can be solely for the purpose of making money to do something enjoyable, or work can be an end unto itself.

4. **Unimportant obsessions/preoccupations:** These kinds of activities often arise for the purpose of decreasing anxiety, and they are often not very effective in doing that. They are sometimes repetitious. They are non-productive, not for survival or maintenance, not particularly enjoyable, and are neither important nor meaningful. They are such things as obsessive eating, drinking too much alcohol, smoking, sleeping most of the day, excessively spending time on the computer, watching too much television, arguing about things that are unimportant, doing obsessive cleaning, fighting, gossiping and demeaning others, etc.

As you reflect, you will notice that some things become priorities because they are required for your body to work well or for you to reach some other goal. All of the first three categories above have varying degrees of importance. **What becomes most important is trying to discern whether or not your activities fall somewhere into the first three categories, or into the fourth category of useless preoccupations.**

Useless preoccupations can sometimes disguise themselves as being important, when, in fact, they are not. So you have to really think about it and ask yourself questions:

- *Am I making money to fill my NWDs or is making money an end unto itself?*

- *To what degree am I trying to make money to give me social status, and is this important to me?*
- *Are my "creature comforts" comforting?*
- *How tidy do things need to be for me in order for me to be okay?*
- *Is being okay in this way important to me?*
- *Am I just drinking for fun, or am I addicted?*
- *Am I eating for enjoyment or comfort?*
- *Is sex for pleasure, closeness, or power?*
- *Are any of the things that I think I am doing for fun interfering with other important activities?*
- *Is it important to me that I be good at my sport?*
- *How good do I have to be in order to feel like I'm living the kind of life I want to live?*
- *How many dates do I have to have?*
- *How many laughs do I want to get?*
- *How many compliments do I need?*
- *How big a house do I need?*
- *How strong do my muscles need to be?*
- *How many pretty outfits do I have to have?*
- *How fast does my car have to be?*

Only you can answer these kinds of questions for yourself. But you need to begin asking and answering them to know if you are leading the kind of life that you want to lead.

> **Be specific in asking yourself if you are leading the kind of life you want to lead.**

If, after lots of inquiry, you come to the conclusion that you are not spending enough time on the pursuits that are most important to you, then it is time to begin establishing some new goals. And along with those goals, there needs to be a plan of action. It is great if you state the goal of "being in better shape"; however, if you don't have a specific plan for weight reduction, exercise and improved nutrition, you won't reach your goal, and you will be in the same place that you started. **I find that action plans that answer questions about *when* and *how* goals are going to be reached are the most helpful.** This often requires taking out a calendar and adjusting your schedule. Sometimes reaching a goal means changing your standards. While it may not require a change in your schedule, it may require some specificity, so you can know if you need to work harder at something, or stop sooner. **If you are prone to obsession, it is important that you "come up for air"** from time to time, to evaluate whether you are working at something long after you have reached a desired stopping point. See if you can put together some plans and a strategy for implementing them. It may require hard choices and self-discipline.

> ## Create goals and plans of action.

I often hear couples talk about getting stuck in arguments about things that aren't very important. By staying aware, in the moment, of what is important, you might be able to exercise some willpower, move away from what is unimportant, and attend to your priorities. It may be useful as a couple to talk about **strategies for recognizing when you are spending too much time arguing about things that are not important to you, and how to shift your focus.**

One of the exercises below is about reviewing the kinds of things that, as a couple, you get upset about and ranking them on a scale of importance. You might then develop a plan for disengaging, if you feel like you are needlessly escalating and what you are arguing about isn't very important. Both parties can silently or openly say, *Is this worth it?* And if you agree that it isn't, you might acknowledge that and say, *Isn't this just one of our differences that, for the moment, we can live with?* Perhaps it will take a bit of an effort to reverse the momentum of the moment, but you can then bring things to closure and go on to something else that is more important, like enjoying each other's company (see Rule 61, "Have a reset button").

> ## Don't waste your time and energy on arguing about things that are unimportant.

Another strategy is to keep little irritations little in the first place. I find that most couples have little irritations with one another; it's normal. I think that little irritations are part of coupling and living with someone. I also think that over time, these irritations can become less and less as we learn to adapt to each other's lifestyles and personalities. In the meantime, if you make little things into big things by emphasizing who is right and who is wrong, who's to blame or who has the biggest character flaws, the little things escalate. If little things can be contained without all of the escalations, then what is little can stay little. The irritation may continue, but it won't be such a big deal and it won't soak up your time and energy.

GRADIENT OF IRRITATIONS

Little Irritations   Significant Problems

Contain the little irritations.

- *Be mindful of what is important to you.*
- *Be specific in asking yourself if you are leading the kind of life you want to lead.*
- *Create goals and plans of action.*
- *Don't waste your time and energy on arguing about things that are unimportant.*
- *Contain the little irritations.*

EXERCISES ON ATTENDING TO PRIORITIES:

1. Spend some time by yourself, and if you haven't done so already, write down five priorities for living the kind of life you want to live.

2. Now write down ten things that you spend the most time and energy doing on a daily basis. Next to each one, write down which of the above four categories into which they fall. Your activities may fall into more than one category.

3. Go through the list of self-examination questions above regarding these ten activities to understand how important these activities are to you.

4. Next to each of these ten activities, write down whether or not they have anything to do with your five priorities of living from Exercise 1. Go through the list of self-examination questions above regarding these ten activities to understand how important these ten activities are to you.

5. Create five new written goals for yourself for living a life that is more consistent with the five priorities that you wrote down in Exercise 1.

6. Create a written plan with specifics for reaching these new goals.

7. Spend some time with your partner and discuss whether or not the two of you feel like you are spending too much time arguing about things that aren't very important.

8. Together, write down things that you often argue about. Separately, rate those things on a scale from one to ten, one being unimportant and ten being very important. Compare notes to see if you can agree on some things that are not very important and write them down. (If something is rated as important to one person but not another, it is important to the relationship.)

9. Decide on what you can say to each other when you get overly involved in arguing about something that doesn't seem worth it.

10. Discuss what you can do to keep little irritations little.

Section II
Developing Closeness

Introduction

What constitutes *closeness* with a life partner? What does it mean to have an intimate relationship? It is amazing how universal the goal of closeness is, how so many men and women alike are seeking partnership with someone with whom they can have this unique relationship. Five aspects of intimacy distinguish this relationship from all others:

1. **Friendship**
2. **Romantic attachment**
3. **Priority**
4. **Shared space**
5. **Family/partnership**

While it is possible for intimacy to develop without all of these characteristics, I believe these are the most common and most desirable characteristics.

1. **FRIENDSHIP.** All of the qualities of friendship are present in an intimate relationship:

   - companionship
   - enjoyment
   - sharing
   - interest
   - respect
   - admiration
   - lack of judgment
   - appreciation
   - care
   - concern
   - compassion
   - support
   - honesty
   - trust
   - confidence

- safety

- security

- responsibility

- connectedness

- love

2. **ROMANTIC ATTACHMENT.** An intimate relationship is different from friendship because of romantic intention and sexual desire. My use of the term *romantic intention* includes the idea of sexual desire, but it is more than just sex. Romantic intention has, at its core, a desire for connectedness in all domains: intellectual, emotional and spiritual. While we might have connectedness in other relationships, the intimate relationship has a deeper and broader connectedness and greater feelings of *attachment*. In the initial stages of romance, we feel a sense of urgency to be in the company of the other person, not for satisfying sexual desire alone but out of a compulsion to create this connection. While this sense of urgency fades, what remains is a continuing desire to be connected, to be attached, to be in each other's company, to be sexual and to share affectionate feelings towards one another. People in healthy long-term relationships have a romantic spark that never goes out.

3. **PRIORITY.** At the core of the intimate relationship is the desire to make that relationship a priority for spending time together. But it isn't time alone that is the priority. In the intimate relationship, we have a priority for attempting to achieve all the qualities of friendship at the highest level. Thus, our partner is not only our friend, our partner is our *best friend*.

4. **SHARED SPACE.** The most expedient way for couples to spend most their time together within this intimate relationship is to live together. Thus, in most intimate relationships, people share space with one another. They thus engage in all aspects of shared living, including eating together, sleeping together, creating shelter together and sharing many activities of daily living together.

5. **FAMILY/PARTNERSHIP.** While not all people choose to have children, having a sense of family with someone is another characteristic of an intimate relationship. Most couples do have children, but even when they don't, they often have pets that become family. This sense of family grows together with a desire for partnership, such that people who are intimate share resources and look out for one another. They feel as

though they are in this life together, and thus an entity begins to emerge that combines two people's way of being into one. **While separateness and differentiation remains, there is a sense of we that is profound.**

This is intimacy.

EXERCISES TO DEVELOP INTIMACY BY DEVELOPING FRIENDSHIP:

1. Find some time to be by yourself. Write down the characteristics of friendship listed above. Write down the definitions of these words, as you understand them. Ask yourself if any of these characteristics needs improvement in your relationship. Note the ones that need improvement.

2. If a characteristic needs improvement, see if you can give yourself an explanation why. Preview the Rules and write the number of a Rule that might relate to strengthening a characteristic that is too weak for you. Write down some things that you might be able to do to make this characteristic stronger.

3. As you read through the remaining sections in this book, circle back to these characteristics to see if you can add to a plan of action for making this characteristic stronger.

4. After two months, check these characteristics again.

RULE #17: **Think "we."**

Childhood is a time when most people are principally preoccupied with themselves. It can be argued that even for the child who seems to want to please his parents and others, there is an underlying preoccupation with wanting approval. As a child moves through the stages of development from childhood to teenager to young adult, this preoccupation with the self continues. There is so much to learn in order to successfully handle adulthood that young people need to spend most of their psychic energy figuring it all out. In psychology, this process of growth is called *individuation:* separating from the protection of one's home and growing into oneself. Depending on standards for success and the ability to synthesize all of the required information, this learning curve may begin to taper off in the early twenties or extend into the late twenties or beyond. During this same period of time, most people begin to enter into their most significant adult relationships. This is the time that deep intimacy with another person often begins to develop. So it becomes a challenge that during the same time frame, as young people are preoccupied with learning to be adults, they begin to develop significant relationships in which they are required to respond well to the needs and desires of another person. However, as romantic interest grows and infatuation increases, our brain chemistry creates a temporary fix for this problem and one's focus becomes much more outer directed because securing the relationship becomes the highest priority. The needs, wants and desires of one's romantic interest become keenly in focus. This very strong biochemical and behavioral response can override issues of individuation for a while. However, at some point, when the feelings of infatuation begin to subside, problems related to preoccupation with self typically rear their head. That is when the notion of "we" becomes increasingly important.

> *During the developmental years a preoccupation with oneself is normal.*

Some people develop this notion of "we" more easily than others. There may be biological differences between people, and there may be differences as a result of how they were raised. People who have had a social focus and many important relationships throughout their childhood, adolescence and early adult life, develop the notion of "we" relatively more easily. People who have had solitary interests, few relationships and who tend to be exclusively focused on their careers develop this notion of "we" with relatively greater difficulty. Some career-oriented individuals spend so much time, energy and resources developing themselves to play a significant role in society that they may have a difficult time developing their primary relationships, because they can't shift enough of their focus away from themselves and towards their partners. Unfortunately, these people sometimes lose relationships that were developed in the early parts of their lives and don't create healthy relationships until such time that they can finally shift their attention from "me" to "we."

> ## *Some people develop this notion of "we" more easily than others.*

*What is meant by **the notion of "we"**?* It is called a *notion* because it is both a thought and a feeling. It has a similar feel to a healthy parent-child relationship, but it is also very different. What is similar is the feeling that **the relationship itself satisfies our needs and protects us in some fashion.** What is different is that the adult "we" is entirely reciprocal, unlike the parent-child relationship, and **both people are active players in the development of this notion.**

- **It is the feeling that, by meeting the needs of another person, the relationship is improved.**

- **It is the feeling that when the relationship is better, I am better, and when I am better, the relationship is better.**

- **It is the feeling that when "we" are satisfied, I am satisfied.**

- **The "we" contains a unique "you" and a unique "me" with differentiation.**

- **The "we" is a constantly shifting dynamic between separateness and togetherness.**

Are you aware of this shifting dynamic? Are you conscious about when you are acting more out of self-interest or out of concern for your partner? Are you conscious about when your partner is acting more out of his own self-interest or out of concern for you? If you pay attention to this, you realize that this dynamic is usually shifting back and forth.

Thus the challenge for creating a healthy relationship is in finding a good balance between consideration of the self and consideration of someone else. The philosopher Hillel said, "If I'm not for myself, then who will be? But if I'm only for myself, then what am I? And if not now, when?" We live in a shifting dynamic on the "me-you-we" continuum, and at any given moment, our consciousness may be on "me" or "you" or "we," depending on the situation. Furthermore, the "we" might include different people at different times, like our spouse, extended family, children, friends or coworkers.

> ### The "me-you-we" continuum is constantly in flux.

Small changes in circumstance can make a big difference in how partners might feel about where they each are on the continuum. For example:

Your spouse might feel neglected at a get together with friends or with extended family if she isn't involved in good conversation. However, if she feels good about socializing with others, she may not feel neglected at all.

At the end of the day, if your spouse has expectations of being together and you had other plans, he might feel like he isn't a priority. However, if he had plans himself, the issue of "who is priority?" likely wouldn't even come up.

> ### Feelings about the "we" can change depending on the circumstances.

If either partner feels like the notion of "we" isn't strong enough in the relationship, it really needs to be brought into the open. This may be a sensitive conversation, so throwing bombs like, "You don't care about me!" or "Obviously, I'm not important to you," doesn't work well. The conversation requires kindness to create comfort in letting down the guard of both partners. Both partners' points of view need to be heard. If this doesn't happen, it is unlikely that this issue will be resolved well. If only one person's point of view is heard, the problem is likely to resurface at a later time. It is important to remember that "we" is about balance, and shifting the relative balance is going to require ongoing and good conversation and subsequent work.

Whether you have talked this over with your partner or not, take stock of yourself and ask yourself about how you operate on the "me-you-we" continuum:

- Are you concerned too much with yourself and not enough with others on this continuum?

- Are you focused too much on others and not enough on yourself on this continuum?

Getting this balance right for you and for your partner helps in developing closeness. Learning to redirect your interest, concern, attention and behavior outward or inward requires a high degree of mindfulness.

> ## *Evaluate how **you** operate on the "me-you-we" continuum.*

If you tend to be more self-centered and less considerate of others, and you want to change, you have to really make a commitment to the work. First, you have to deal with the stigma that is often attached to thinking of yourself as "inconsiderate" or "self-centered." It may be hard for you to think of yourself as "self-centered," and if your partner uses that term to describe you, you may reject it out of hand just because it feels bad. However, **everybody is "self-centered."** Even someone who may be called a "pleaser" is self-centered because she is preoccupied with her own needs and anxieties about making others happy. **Self-centeredness is on a continuum,** with some people being more self-centered than others.

There are often situational impacts on self-centeredness. For example, if someone feels threatened, he may become self-centered real fast. Or if someone is physically handicapped, he may take more time to attend to his personal needs. So it is helpful if you **don't think of yourself as a "self-centered" person or an "inconsiderate" person. Rather, think of yourself as a person who is working on being *less* self-centered or *more* considerate.** By doing this, you place yourself on the same continuum that we all are on, perhaps only at a different point on that continuum than somebody else. It's not a label or an indictment of yourself.

> ## *You can work on being less self-centered without labeling yourself as a self-centered person.*

Learning how to shift your attention away from yourself and toward others brings up a very big problem in the field of psychology and personal growth: **How does someone gain enough consciousness to think and act in a different fashion when, under normal circumstances, they don't have this consciousness?** How does someone change from being less self-centered if, while she is in her self-centered way of thinking, she is not thinking about matters of self-centeredness? Well, clearly, she has to turn off autopilot and get out of her normal way of thinking—and that requires some method for remembering to think and act differently.

Here are some methods that people use to raise the level of their consciousness:

- reading self-help books
- writing in a personal growth notebook
- going to counseling
- going to church
- meditating
- talking to a friend or partner about personal growth
- taking a class
- setting a time each day for study
- going to a retreat
- having an electronic reminder
- giving oneself daily tasks or homework
- charting one's progress anecdotally or behaviorally

> *Only after the development of consciousness and awareness can you attempt to establish new ways to think, feel and act in less self-centered ways.*

Here are some methodologies for thinking, feeling and acting in less self-centered ways:

1. **One of the first methodologies is to purposely focus your attention, thoughts and empathy on others.** What this means is when you have an awareness of being preoccupied with yourself, you purposefully ask yourself, *What is going on for (Jane)? What are her thoughts about this? How is she feeling?* You have to be not only interested in asking the questions but also interested in the answers. You have to try to develop real curiosity about others. And you have to want to know how others feel so that you can make a compassionate connection with them. You have to unleash your imagination and bring to mind the feelings that others might be having. This is *empathy.* It is fascinating that it is easy for some people to be interested and captivated by characters on the

silver screen but not towards people in real life. Is that true for you? If you can connect with characters in movies, then you can connect with people in real life. It may take some effort to remove the barriers and lower your defenses so that you can focus your attention, thoughts and empathy on others.

2. If you make yourself **be responsible for the well-being of others,** you will be less preoccupied with yourself. Feelings of responsibility are typically motivators that cause you to direct your attention outward. Ask yourself: Towards whom do you have the strongest feelings of responsibility? Many people would answer towards their children or towards their pets. What about you? Do you feel less self-centered in your relationships with your pets or your children? If you take some of the same kind of responsibility that you have toward them and direct it towards others, you will likely find it beneficial.

3. **Set up times of the day when you are purposefully going to practice more altruistic thinking** and use the suggestion above for that purpose. By doing this with some regularity, you will hopefully notice a generalization effect: that is, this new way of thinking will begin to spread to unscheduled times of day.

4. **Read material** either written by others or by you at different times throughout the day. It might be a poem, a prayer or a few paragraphs written about love, kindness or something else **that helps you to think about others.** It could be something that you have written describing your partner's qualities or things that he has done that you appreciate. If you have taken notes about something that is bothering your partner, you could read that. If your partner has written down his thoughts, you could read that.

5. People sometimes put **images of their loved ones** on their desktops at work or in their wallets to serve as a reminder that they shouldn't be totally preoccupied with their jobs. If it isn't too much of a distraction, you can look at the picture and remind yourself that that is someone who is important in your life and you are hopeful that his day is going well. At some other time of day, use the picture as a reminder that you are trying to shift attention away from yourself and onto him.

6. **Sounds and music can also be a cue** for thinking about others. Perhaps you have a particular song or songs that help generate warm feelings

about your partner. You can sing it to yourself, or play it, thus shifting your attention onto a loved one.

7. In a more general sense, you might be able to help yourself to be more outer-directed by doing **volunteer work.** Particularly if you do volunteer work that evokes your feelings, you will be drawn out of yourself and towards others.

Some couples have the problem of one partner being too much of a *pleaser.* Being a *"pleaser"* just doesn't carry the same stigma as being "self-centered." Having an attitude of wanting to please one's partner is wonderful, but it can be taken too far. Ask yourself if you are this kind of a person. **If you are, try to recognize that, by not stating your own needs and wishes, you are limiting closeness that will only be achieved when your needs are met as well as your partner's.** You might also begin to develop low-level resentments. And, even worse, you might begin to try to get your needs met by someone else, threatening the integrity of your spousal relationship. **If you have this *pleaser* way of being with your partner, you will likely be anxious when stating your needs, particularly if they conflict with your partner's.** It will require courage to let your needs be known, but it will be easier if you learn some of the Tools from this book about dealing with differences and conflict.

> *Being overly pleasing can also create limitations on closeness.*

Consideration of your partner's thoughts, feelings, desires, needs, preferences, and idiosyncrasies are all part of establishing deeper intimacy. For most couples that are having difficulty, developing *consideration* is one area of work that will make a big difference. Consideration often gets derailed when there is conflict; during conflict, it is far too easy for it to be all about the "me" and not about the "we." This can have a snow-ball effect that creates even further alienation. It may take a conscious effort to turn things around by reengaging in acts of consideration. Again, this is not to forget about what is important to you, but rather to help rebalance the relationship with acts of consideration that go in both directions.

> *Try to have consideration of the "we" even when you are in conflict with your partner.*

- *Evaluate how you operate on the "me-you-we" continuum.*
- *You can work on being less self-centered without labeling yourself as a **self-centered person**.*
- *Only after the development of consciousness and awareness can you attempt to establish new ways to think, feel and act in less self-centered ways.*
  - *Focus your attention, thoughts and empathy on others.*
  - *Make yourself be responsible for the well-being of others.*
  - *Set up times of the day when you are purposefully going to practice more altruistic thinking.*
  - *Read written material that helps you to think about others.*
  - *Look at images of your loved ones.*
  - *Listen to music that helps you to think about a loved one.*
  - *Do volunteer work.*
- *Being overly pleasing can also create limitations on closeness.*
- *Try to have consideration of the "we," even when you are in conflict with your partner.*

EXERCISES FOR DEVELOPING THE "WE":

1. Spend some time with your partner talking about the notion of "we." Talk about whether you experience this notion of "we" with one another, and if you do, how you experience it. Read the definition that I have written above out loud to one another and discuss whether this is anything that you have experienced in your relationship together.

2. In this same conversation, discuss whether there are circumstances in which you experience the "we" stronger or weaker. Write down ones that come to mind.

3. If you and your partner come to the conclusion that you could do a better job in developing this notion of "we," either in specific circumstances or in general, give some thought to courses of action that you both could take to develop the "we" better. Consider this after this first conversation and a second conversation. Think mainly about what you can do to make the "we" stronger.

4. In a subsequent conversation, talk about what each of you might do to make the "we" stronger. Use your best listening skills and try to avoid saying things that will hurt your partner's feelings. Listen to your partner's suggestions for herself and try to give support. If you think her idea can be improved upon, carefully make those suggestions.

5. Spend some time by yourself, if you haven't already, thinking about where you are on the "for myself/for other" continuum. If you are not where you would like to be on that continuum, identify it to yourself. Draw a line with *for myself* on one end and *for other* on the other end, and indicate where you currently are on the line and where you would like to be. This will represent your goal.

6. Create an action plan for developing greater consciousness of where you are on this continuum. Look at the list of suggestions above and select from that list or create some ones of your own and write them down.

7. Create an action plan for how you will adjust where you are on the continuum of "for myself/for other."

8. After two weeks and after four weeks, return to your line graph and date and mark any progress you have made.

RULE #18: **Enjoy each other's company.**

After all, isn't this the point? **Isn't this just an extension of one of the most important aspects of our reason to live—to enjoy life?** In our fast-paced, make-money, be-successful and cope-with-the-stress-of-it-all way of living, we can easily lose sight of the importance of joy. It seems like so many couples start out with such great joy in having found one another and doing things together that bring happiness. And for so many couples, this joy dissipates over time with money issues, children, arguing and having unresolved conflicts. Enjoyment with one another gets put on the back burner. The difficulties get worse, and feelings of closeness drift away.

One of the most important elements for enjoying another person's company is being present with that person. (Rule 1, "Be present with a joyful spirit.") It is almost universal in Western cultures that in the courtship phase of a relationship, two people find great enjoyment together. The enjoyment is *here and now*, whether it is an experience in nature, being entertained, being involved in a sporting event, enjoying a cultural experience together or making love. The "here and now" property of enjoyment is important, but unfortunately for many couples, it dissipates over time. When couples are trying to re-infuse their relationship with enjoyment, it is helpful to look for experiences that they can do together that give them this feeling of presence.

> ## *Find enjoyment together in the "here and now."*

To this day, I still think that my clients are going to turn to me and say, *Are you stupid or just dumb? We know that.* But that never (okay, *rarely*) happens. They say, *You know honey, we aren't spending enough time with each other.*

And that's it. That is usually the biggest problem, *time* together. If you want to more fully enjoy your partner's company, you will need to spend **more time together doing something that you both enjoy.** And this has to be done with regularity and with some frequency...and not once or twice a year, either; at least a couple of times a month. No kids. If you can spend time with each other and at the end be able to say, *That was fun!* or *I sure enjoyed that,* or *I'm glad we did that,* then you are on the right track. There is no "right" amount of time to spend with your partner. Everyone has slightly different time-together/time-apart ratios, and compromise may be required.

> ## *Make spending more quality time together a priority.*

While spontaneity is wonderful, as life becomes more complicated, scheduling becomes more important. Couples often have good intentions for spending time together but with a crowded schedule and competing demands, if it doesn't get on the calendar or if something doesn't occur at a standard time weekly, it might not happen. Make structure your ally, not your enemy. In fact, I think that it is a very good practice to *have a regular time each week just to review the calendar with your partner.* If you have something important to talk over and you aren't finding the time, schedule a time to talk. If you don't think that you are spending enough time together having fun, schedule an activity-planning session with your partner. If you create structure, it is more likely to happen.

> ## *Make structure your ally.*

When relationships begin, it often doesn't matter what partners do because it is just so great to be in each other's company:

> *Hey, want to go down to the dump and watch the pigeons?*
> *Yea, that would be great, let's go!*

When smitten with infatuation, it's easy to have a great time at the dump. But infatuation wears off. Then the selection of mutually agreeable activities of interest becomes more important.

I think that **there are several misconceptions about spending time together.**

1. If we love each other it will just happen.

2. Fun things are mostly spontaneous.

3. Our partner's interests don't change.

Since all of these things are not necessarily true, spending time with each other might require conversation and planning. Talk it over with one another and **generate some ideas of things to do together that you can both enjoy.** Try to make a robust list for various times of the day or evening, different days of the week, and different seasons and weather conditions. Make it fit your budget. Don't let life pass you by. There are too many things to do that can be enjoyable. If you let yourself become a couch potato, you might be slipping into a withdrawn state with your partner, and, frankly, with your own living. Try to be active and enjoying life with one another.

> ## *Make a list and plan activities to do together.*

While not taking time to be with your partner is a huge barrier to enjoying his company, another barrier is remaining stuck in negative feelings. To enjoy your partner's company, you have to have **an attitude of *wanting* to enjoy each other's company.** Too often, couples allow themselves to just go through the motions of being together while clinging to old feelings of hurt or anger. This requires, at the very least, a suspension of those feelings and a willingness to focus on the present moment. Better yet would be the desire and effort made to reduce the feelings of hurt and anger so that you might enjoy the moment. Sometimes by focusing on the moments of enjoyment, our motivation to decrease feelings of anger and hurt increases, and we make a bigger effort to resolve those feelings. Sometimes by focusing on the moments of enjoyment, we realizes that our anger and hurt was way out of proportion to all the goodness in the relationship, and it dissipates on its own accord.

> ## *Enjoying each other's company helps reduce angry and hurt feelings.*

One principle characteristic of intimacy is sex, and one principle sexual activity is lovemaking. This is an incredibly important activity to be enjoyed by people who are involved in romantic relationships. Just like other activities, it is important to maintain an active and regular sex life. In the early development of a romantic relationship, lovemaking is one of the most spontaneous activities for creating intimacy. However, over time, the spontaneous aspect of lovemaking can become more difficult. Because of the variety of demands and constraints that couple's experience, the frequency of lovemaking can decrease even when couples would like it to be more frequent. Couples may feel awkward talking about the logistics of lovemaking when neither was previously required. **Unfortunately, without talking and planning, lovemaking can become so infrequent that the relationship suffers.** (Rule 32, "Keep feeding the fires of romance.")

> ## *Have a willingness to talk and plan regarding lovemaking.*

Mutual understanding about frequency should apply to all activities that help couples enjoy each other's company. Now, of course, don't try to fix something that isn't broken. If you and your partner are currently into a great pattern of enjoying each other's company, fabulous—keep it up! But if you are not, then you need to find a way to turn this around. **This Rule is extremely important, and if you don't find ways to enjoy each other's company, other attempts to attain closeness will likely fail.**

- *Find enjoyment together in the "here and now."*
- *Make spending more quality time together a priority.*
- *Make structure your ally.*
- *Make a list and plan activities to do together.*
- *Enjoying each other's company helps reduce angry and hurt feelings.*
- *Have a willingness to talk and plan regarding lovemaking.*

EXERCISES FOR ENJOYING EACH OTHER'S COMPANY:

1. Write down five activities that you would like to do with your partner that you think would give you a feeling of greater closeness. These activities should not take more than a few hours to complete. Fantasize about having fun with your partner doing these activities.

2. Spend time with your partner discussing these activities. Arrange to do a least one activity per week from each person's list, for the next four weeks.

3. Arrange a time each week to talk with each other about how these activities are going. Discuss whether there are any big interpersonal barriers, like anger and hurt, standing in the way of being with each other. If so, try to identify the problem without solving the problem, and set up a time to talk about it further.

4. Spend some time alone and write down logistical barriers that you think exist for lovemaking.

5. Talk to your partner about those barriers. See if you can work through logistical constraints with good problem-solving skills. Talk to your partner about an ideal frequency for lovemaking. If the two of you have differences about that frequency, see if you can compromise. See if you can create a plan or some guidelines for lovemaking that would create an improvement. This is a sensitive subject, and consequently, problem-solving may be more difficult. Problems may arise that are discussed in other sections in this book, and you may have to put off this discussion until your skills improve.

RULE #19: Engage by sharing.

Perhaps this is another "no-brainer," but it is a lot easier said than done. What is there to share?

- your experiences of the day
- your future plans
- your thoughts and feelings about matters of importance to you
- your thoughts and feelings about people in your life
- your thoughts and feelings about each other

We have public and private types of thoughts and feelings. Awareness of our thoughts and feelings may come easily, may come with difficulty or may not come at all. Generally, we reserve our most private thoughts and feelings for people with whom we are closest and most trusting. The personal sharing of private thoughts and feelings is one of the elements of intimacy.

> ### Sharing private thoughts and feelings helps to create intimacy.

Language is the primary vehicle for sharing thoughts and feelings, so it is important to **develop a language of self-disclosure.** If you have nothing to say, it can be difficult for your partner to know how you are doing and what you are experiencing. Consequently, it may be tough for her to make a connection with you. It may take an effort to formulate your thoughts and your feelings. You need to put your thoughts and feelings into words.

> ### Put your thoughts and feelings into words.

- "We didn't talk about feelings when I was growing up."
- "I don't think that I ever heard my parents say that they loved one another. And they never said they loved me."
- "The only feeling that was ever expressed in my family was anger."
- "If I talked about my feelings, my mom told me that I was just getting too full of myself."
- "It just didn't take much for me to get a beating, so I just kept my mouth shut."

Maybe that wasn't your experience growing up, and maybe it was. The point is, for some people, knowing and expressing feelings was not encouraged, and for some, expressing feelings was punished. Because of those developmental experiences, some people need a high degree of confidence that sharing feelings is not going to go badly. Some of that confidence is achieved through the slow testing of the waters, and some of it is comes from faith.

Our feeling life is one of the most personal aspects of who we are. Our feelings might give us the highest high in one moment, and in another moment give us the lowest low. The potential for this kind of change causes many of us to want to have a high degree of control over our sensitive feelings for fear our strong feelings will be overwhelming. **The higher our uncertainty is about becoming overwhelmed, the greater is our need for trust.** When trust is developed and feelings are shared, it can be very satisfying. This is one of the most important elements of intimacy.

> *Develop trust that if you share your feelings with your partner, there will be a positive outcome.*

When your feelings are shared in real time and out loud, they can be processed more effectively. This is because the processing stays linear and active. Sometimes all it takes is talking and good listening; no suggestions, no advice. Ten to fifteen minutes later, you might feel light as a bird. *Voila!* And how do you feel about your partner? Well, pretty darn good. And she feels closer to you because of the sharing. This is the experience that is repeated hundreds of thousands of times every day in relationships all over the world. It is special, and it is intimate.

> *Sharing your troubles with someone you love usually helps you to feel better.*

You can share more than just negative feelings. **It is equally as important to share your good feelings:**
- things you felt good about in the course of your day
- your accomplishments
- something that moved you
- an insight
- a pleasant exchange with someone

- something funny
- a song you enjoyed
- a visual delight

Share your good feelings, too.

Sharing your feelings of joy the very moment **you experience them is a wonderful way to create a sense of closeness and connection.**

You know, I really liked _____.
You know, I did too."

It just feels good when that happens. But you have to remember to be present and talk about the pleasantries, not just keep them inside.

Share your feelings in the moment.

It is important to share your feelings about one another, positive and negative. Sharing negative feelings will be discussed in subsequent rules (like Rule 43, "Give and receive feedback without condemnation"), since it can be more difficult. This discussion is about sharing the positive feelings that you have for one another. It starts with getting in touch with those feelings. Positive feelings about your partner don't have to just happen spontaneously. You can actively bring positive thoughts into your consciousness, if you choose to do that. You can pause right now for a minute and begin to think about ways you love your partner, and immediately you will start to have warm feelings. And believe me, if you walked into the next room and started sharing those feelings with your partner, he would likely start to have some of those warm feelings, too. When you happen to be feeling positive about your partner, share your feelings. Don't wait for inspiration to hit you. **Love isn't inspiration alone. It is also about using your mind to direct your consciousness towards the feelings of love and then disclosing those feelings.** We do it all the time when it is a special day, like someone's birthday. We don't love our spouses more on their birthdays; it is just that we have directed our minds towards those feelings of love and, lo and behold, we begin to feel those feelings.

Bring your feelings of love to the surface.

And finally, sharing isn't all about you. Make sure that when sharing happens, it is a two way street. That will be the next Rule.

- *Sharing private thoughts and feelings helps to create intimacy.*

- *Put your thoughts and feelings into words.*

- *Develop trust that if you share your feelings with your partner, there will be a positive outcome.*

- *Sharing your troubles with someone you love usually helps you to feel better.*

- *Share your good feelings, too.*

- *Share your feelings in the moment.*

- *Bring your feelings of love to the surface.*

EXERCISES FOR SHARING THOUGHTS AND FEELINGS:

1. Spend ten to fifteen minutes by yourself and think about several things that you would like to share with your partner. Think in terms of both thoughts and feelings.

2. Every other day for the next two weeks, do the following exercise: Spend no less than ten minutes with each other—hopefully in person, but if not, on the phone. Take turns sharing something about yourself or your day for approximately five minutes. This sharing is not to be about the other person. The listener is to practice good listening skills asking for further clarification if needed. The emphasis in this exercise is more on the sharing and not on listening, acknowledging or showing compassion. For this exercise there will be *no reacting or problem-solving* (or even showing gratitude). After approximately five minutes, switch roles with your partner.

3. For a few minutes each day, write about how well you did in:

   a. sharing your thoughts.

   b. sharing your feelings.

   c. how you might improve.

4. Every other day for the next two weeks, spend a few minutes by yourself and think about ways you love your partner. Find a moment on that same day to tell your partner at least one positive thought that you have about her. Make sure that she is paying attention when you tell her. Make note of how you feel when you say this positive thing. Make note of how she feels.

RULE #20: **It's not all about you.**

This Rule addresses the quality of mutuality in your relationship with your partner and with others in general. Some people enter into a dialogue with others asking questions and showing interest in what they have to say. They are sufficiently curious that they will draw out the other person through inquiry.

Others only want to tell stories—their story. They will talk about their life experiences or what interests them without regard for the interests, experiences or points of view of the other person. They treat other people like an audience, and they are the performer. They may think that everyone is having a good time listening to them; that they are quite the entertainer and a lot of fun. But this is self-deception. Most people don't find this attractive. **Most people don't like it when somebody dominates the conversation without giving anyone else a chance to be heard. Most people want a give-and-take experience** in which both parties are talking and listening, each party is interested in the other person, and both are sharing. This is the richest of all interpersonal interactions. When all of the elements discussed in the Rules on developing closeness are combined together in this give and take fashion, intimacy really emerges.

> *Most people want a give-and-take experience.*

Ask yourself what your dialogue is like when you are engaged in casual or serious conversation with others, particularly your partner. Is it all about you, is it all about him; or is there a nice balance? **One of the simplest measures of this is airtime. Another is whether or not you ask any questions and listen to the answers.** If you are dominating most of the airtime and rarely asking your partner questions, perhaps it is time to converse in a different way.

> *Don't hog the microphone. Draw-out your partner by asking questions.*

> - *Don't hog the microphone.*
> - *Draw-out your partner by asking questions.*

EXERCISES FOR NOT HAVING THE CONVERSATION BE ALL ABOUT YOU:

Please refer Rule 22, "Be interested in your partner," as there are many suggestions in that section on how to draw out another person.

1. For the next week or so, try to be conscious about the way you converse with your partner and your friends. Be extra attentive if you are in a social setting. Try to pay attention to two elements: airtime and questions.

2. At the end of the day, write down your observations regarding the way you conversed. Also write down whether or not your conversation was more like two people just telling stories to each other, or whether there was real dialogue.

3. If you concluded that you were dominating airtime and not asking many questions, see if you can correct that in future conversations with awareness and effort; withhold another story and ask for details about the other person.

4. Write about your progress.

5. After spending a couple of weeks with this, have a conversation with your partner and share with them what you have observed. If one of your observations is that your partner tells a lot of stories, too, see if you can gently encourage him to have more dialogue with you. Talk about whether or not you both engage in give-and-take and in drawing each other out.

6. If you have concluded that you can do a better job together, spend time focusing on this aspect of your relationship making the behavioral corrections as needed. Allow each other to point out when the dialogue slips back to too much storytelling and not enough engagement. Try your best to not be defensive when you get this feedback. Continue trying to make corrections so that there is more give-and-take engagement.

RULE #21: **Acknowledge feelings and be compassionate.**

You may be getting the idea that I believe feelings are important. How we feel about our experiences may well determine our sense of satisfaction with life itself. Certainly the way we feel about someone is a highly important factor in determining the closeness of that relationship. Nonetheless, feelings can be elusive (see Rule 6, "Know thyself"). If you ask someone the question, "How was your day?" what do you expect to hear? Do you expect to hear about what he accomplished or didn't accomplish; what he saw or heard; how he was treated by others; what happened in the news; what his children are up to, or how he is doing physically? Do you expect to hear about any of the associated feelings? It is common that people converse about all of these things, never being mindful of any of their feelings, even when strong feelings exist. It is ironic that even when feelings are unknown, they may be the most important factor in determining whether or not we have a good or not-so-good day.

> ### *Be aware of feelings.*

In the introduction to "Developing closeness," friendship, caring and having a sense of responsibility were mentioned. Over the years I have talked to couples who have very strong feelings of responsibility and caring for their children and weak feelings of caring and responsibility for one another. While it is important at any age, I believe that as we get older, our need for our partners to look out for us increases.

Ask yourself now if you have a sense of caring and responsibility toward your partner and, if not, see if you can develop it. It will provide some motivation for acknowledging feelings and being compassionate.

> ### *Have a sense of caring and responsibility for your partner.*

Acknowledging feelings means that through verbal and non-verbal cues and phrases, we let our partners know that we are aware of their feelings. Here are some examples:

- "I can see that you are feeling pretty sad."
- "I can hear how angry you are."
- "I know that you are scared."
- "I can tell that you are in a lot of pain."

Acknowledge your partner's feelings.

Compassion is all about these feelings. **It is about noticing someone else's feelings, finding similar feelings within ourselves (empathy), and sharing that relatedness with a sense of caring.** It may verbally sound something like this:

- "I really understand and care about how you are feeling."
- "Boy, I'd find that situation really upsetting, too."
- "I'm so sorry to hear that your friend died."
- "What you are telling me is really scary and I'm concerned for you."

These are all compassionate comments, and if you are on the receiving end of hearing them, they may help you feel better. Such comments may also help you feel closer to the person who says them. If you are feeling compassionate, you will experience a greater readiness for making a connection.

Be compassionate.

Making a connection. What does this phrase mean? It means **creating a state of being in which the way one person experiences circumstances and the way another person experiences the same circumstances begin to blend with each other.** For most people, this process of blending with another is comforting and satisfying. It is more than simply feeling the presence of another person. It is feeling that in a specific moment, your psychological presence and that of another person occupy the same space in a satisfying way. When this happens, negative feelings often melt away, replaced by a sense of wellbeing. Acknowledging feelings and being compassionate are pathways for making a connection.

Make a connection.

Becoming a compassionate person is easy for some and harder for others. **It requires that we not be so consumed by our own feelings, needs, wants and desires that we can't engage in the experiences another person is having.** The more preoccupied we are with our own needs, be they physical or psychological, the harder it is for us to be compassionate. It takes intentionality and a concerted effort to be compassionate, if it doesn't come naturally. Many people find that an unexpected result of being compassionate is that some of their own needs vanish. They may have thought that the only way they could feel better is by *getting*, when *giving* works just as well.

- *Being compassionate requires a person to suspend a preoccupation with oneself.*

- *Be aware of feelings.*

- *Have a sense of caring and responsibility for your partner.*

- *Acknowledge your partner's feelings.*

- *Be compassionate.*

- *Make a connection.*

- *Being compassionate requires a person to suspend a preoccupation with oneself.*

EXERCISES FOR ACKNOWLEDGING FEELINGS AND BEING COMPASSIONATE:

Some of the exercises in Rule 17, "Think 'we,'" may be very helpful, particularly relating to becoming preoccupied with oneself. Raising one's consciousness is the first step. Driving one's attention outward is the next. Not being preoccupied with oneself is important for intimacy, and it is a necessary prerequisite for both this Rule about compassion and for the next Rule about showing interest.

1. Spend some time alone. What are some of the most significant feelings you believe your partner is having today? Write them down.

2. How might you express an understanding of those feelings with your partner? Write down some examples of those expressions.

3. Spend some time contemplating your partner's experience. Close your eyes and review her circumstances. Try to put yourself in her shoes. Can you draw forth that same feeling in yourself that you think she might be having? Are you having any other feelings? Can you find a place inside yourself that cares about the feelings that your partner might be having? Hold on to that feeling of caring just a little longer than you might usually hold on to it.

4. If you were to share those feelings of care, what might it sound like verbally? Write it down.

5. Spend time with your partner every other day for the next two weeks. Spend at least ten minutes with each other, hopefully in person, but if not, on the phone. Take turns sharing something about yourselves or your day for approximately five minutes. This sharing is not to be about the other person. The other person is to practice good listening skills, acknowledge feelings, and show compassion. For this exercise there will be *no reacting or problem-solving* (or showing gratitude). After approximately ten minutes, switch roles with your partner.

   During this exercise it is important that the person who is sharing feel heard, noticed, acknowledged, important to the listener, understood and cared about. If the person who is sharing doesn't feel understood, he can gently restate his feelings to help the listener better understand him.

6. Spend time alone for no more than ten minutes each day and write about Exercise 5. How well did you do in:
   a. using good listening skills?
   b. acknowledging feelings?
   c. showing compassion?
   d. not reacting or problem-solving?
   e. helping your partner feel noticed, acknowledged, important and understood?
   f. managing your negative emotions?

7. Also in this same ten minutes, make a note of any aspect of this exercise on which you particularly need to concentrate so that you might do it better. Write it down.

RULE #22: **Be interested in your partner's thoughts, ideas and priorities.**

Interest is the counterpart to compassion. It is closely related, since thoughts and feelings merge with one another. It is a separate Rule because many people describe what is important to them with thoughts and ideas more than with feelings. **If you want to create a connection, show interest in what your partner finds important.**

Have an attitude of interest.

If your partner does not readily share his thoughts, it may require that you ask some questions to show that you are interested. Not everybody likes to be asked questions, but most people who are seeking closeness like questions. There are *open-ended questions,* like:

- "How was your day?"
- "Did you hear anything on the news that was interesting to you?"
- "How was your get-together with the Johnson's?"

And there are *closed-ended questions* like:

- "Did you have bacon for breakfast;"
- "Who won the game;" or,
- "Did you know that the Johnson's got a new car? "

If you start by asking open-ended questions, your partner has greater opportunity to choose what is most important to him. Sometimes, to get the ball rolling, you might have to start with a specific question and then move to open-ended questions.

Be able to use both open-ended and closed-ended questions.

At times, your partner may not be in a mood to talk. You can say, "You know, I really would like to hear about how you are doing. Maybe we could talk later. What do you think?" Hopefully you and your partner will be able to make a time to talk later. However, if your partner doesn't ever seem to want to talk, you may have to arrange a meeting to talk about talking. At that meeting, you could talk to your partner about the importance of sharing. Perhaps your partner would be willing to listen to you read out loud Rule 19, "Engage by sharing," or even the Introduction, "Developing closeness."

Many people start with good intentions of finding out about someone else, but something derails the effort. These are some of the things that are said or done to create *pitfalls*.

1. **You know, something like that happened to me.** And before you know it, you are *talking about your own experience* rather than listening to his experience.

2. **Your Aunt Margaret didn't pass away in April, she passed away in March.** You might find yourself *correcting a detail* of what your partner is saying and totally be missing the forest for the trees.

3. **Well, here is what I would do about that.** Trying to *solve the problem* before it is fully aired cuts your partner off from talking about it. Your partner may just want to talk without seeking a solution.

4. **Well, I don't agree. I think all our political problems really rest with the congress not with the president.** Or, **That really makes me mad.** If you *react too quickly* to what your partner is saying, you will never know what she is thinking.

5. **Well, I appreciate what you did.** Even though you think you may be doing something nice by showing appreciation, if you *cut off your partner's expression* before she is finished or before you have acknowledged what she said, she may not appreciate your appreciation.

6. **What are we having for dinner?** If you *ask an unrelated question* while your wife is talking about the difficulty she had with one of the children that afternoon, she might just think you aren't paying attention, and you probably aren't.

7. **I know where you're going with this, and frankly I don't agree.** If you *interrupt* your partner, he won't be able to finish his thought, and that can be very frustrating. In my office, this is one of the biggest pitfalls of all and it often totally derails a conversation.

Be aware of common pitfalls.

If you want to draw your partner out you might **ask yourself:**

- *What makes what she is saying important to her?*
- *Are there some feelings attached to her thoughts or ideas?*
- *Is this a subject matter in which he has shown previous interest?*
- *Is this a subject matter in which he is trying to acquire a body of knowledge?*
- *Is this an area of particular intellectual curiosity?*
- *Can I find something about this subject matter for me to learn?*
- *Can I find an interest in this subject matter independent from my partner?*

You might ask if you are just being a phony if you try to show interest in something that is not inherently interesting to you. An analogy can be made to a music appreciation course that helps you develop an interest and appreciation in a subject matter in which you have previously not been interested. It is fascinating that these courses often work. The point is this, interests can be developed if you try to pay attention and find new things about which you used to know nothing. This is not being phony. It is about changing yourself to become more interested. In Rule 1, "Be present with a joyful spirit," I discussed developing your sense of curiosity. Curiosity is an important ingredient of interest, and I encourage you to develop curiosity and interest both for your own joy of living and for a richer relationship with your partner.

> **Be curious about your partner's interests and show it.**

Another step in showing interest is **remembering what your partner has told you.** If your partner shares something of importance with you and a few days later you show interest with a further inquiry, how do you think he will feel? Usually people feel pretty good about that. And if you are in an intimate relationship, your partner might feel cared about because you remembered and inquired about his interest.

> **Ask a follow-up question the next day.**

- *Have an attitude of interest.*

- *Be able to use both open-ended and closed-ended questions.*

- *Be aware of common pitfalls.*

- *Be curious about your partner's interests and show it.*

- *Ask a follow-up question the next day.*

EXERCISES FOR SHOWING INTEREST IN YOUR PARTNER:

1. Every day for a week, spend about ten minutes with your partner. Take turns sharing something about yourselves or your day for approximately five minutes. This sharing is not to be about the relationship or the other person. After about five minutes, switch roles. The listener is to practice showing interest by:

    a. having an interested frame of mind.

    b. paying attention and being present.

    c. acknowledging some of what has been said.

    d. using opened-ended and closed-ended questions.

    e. trying to determine the level of importance to the speaker.

    f. not interrupting.

    g. not talking about oneself.

    h. not correcting a detail.

    i. not trying to find solutions.

    j. not reacting too quickly with thoughts or feelings.

Remember that the emphasis in this exercise is on the listener showing interest. During this exercise it is important that the person who is sharing feel heard, noticed, acknowledged, important to the listener and understood.

2. For no more than five minutes each day, write about how well you did in showing interest. Rate yourself on a scale from one to ten on how well you did in the ten areas listed above. Write down any pitfalls that need special attention and concentration on your part. Write down any other ways you need to work on becoming a better listener.

3. During moments of meditation or contemplation, think about something in which your partner is interested. Review in your mind what makes it important for your partner. See if you can develop some curiosity about her interest. Write down five questions that you could ask her to follow up things she already told you.

RULE #23: **Give support to your partner.**

Many people are confused about what it means to be supportive. They have a true desire to be helpful, and it can often feel like being helpful means doing something active to take away a person's pain. So they may give advice or make an effort to solve their partner's problem, yet their partner still may feel unsupported. In fact, making a suggestion may actually trigger a response like, *I've tried that already,* or *That will never work,* or *You just don't understand.* Both parties can feel frustrated, when the intentions of the helper were so good. The helper may ask herself or say out loud, *What went wrong here? I was just trying to be helpful!* And she *was* trying to help. Unless someone asks for advice, typically it is best to assume that he wants understanding, not a teacher, and not a quick fix.

> ### *Advice and problem-solving may not feel supportive.*

Giving emotional support doesn't start with solving the problem; it starts with recognizing and understanding the problem (see Rule 21, "Be compassionate"). It is almost universal that people want to feel understood and cared about when they are having a problem. This type of support is often called *TLC* or *tender loving care* because it resembles the kind of care children may receive from their parents.

When a little boy falls down and skins his knee, his parent might say, "Oh, honey, you scraped your knee." And if the child says, "Uh huh, and it hurts," the parent might say, "I'm so sorry that it hurts you." And then the parent might give it a kiss and say, "There; that will make it better." And it often does make it better. It works because the parent is soothing the anxiety of the child, which may be a bigger problem than the pain of the scraped knee. It really wasn't the kiss that made it better; it was the caring, the compassion and the TLC.

When one adult gives TLC to another adult, it really isn't that much different than what happens with a child. If an adult gets hurt, his partner might say, "Oh, honey, you hurt yourself. Are you in pain?" And if his partner says, "Yes, it really hurts," he might say, "Oh, honey, I'm sorry that you are in so much pain. Is there anything that I can do to help?" Often the answer will be no, so he adds, "Can I just give you a hug?" That might be followed by a hug, an arm on the shoulder or a gentle kiss. This type of support is helpful because **anxiety is**

soothed and there is a sense of connectedness. The feelings of aloneness that can arise when one is in pain decrease because of caring and compassion.

> ## One of the best ways to give support is with TLC.

In a partnership there will be times in which one person needs support and times in which the other person needs support. One partner may need more overall support than the other. All of this may be fine if it is acceptable to both parties. However, two related problems can emerge:

- One partner wants more support than he is receiving and is upset with his partner for not providing it.

- One partner feels guilty or defensive that she isn't giving more support.

Concerns about the *amount* of support that is needed and given tend to be more difficult to resolve than concerns about *how* to give support. For acute difficulties, the issue of the amount of support is usually resolved with greater ease than if the difficulties are chronic. Consequently, people with chronic difficulties more easily feel insufficiently supported. Resolution of the need for support typically requires direct conversation. *If that conversation contains excessive blame, guilt, shaming, humiliation, put-downs and anger, it probably won't go well.* Productive conversations about support need to be calm and respectful, recognizing both the needs of one party and the limitations of the other. As previously stated, having a need creates vulnerability (Rule 8, "You can't always get what you want"). Thus, if a satisfactory resolution is not reached for the person in need, she may have to get the remainder of support elsewhere or manage on her own. This is a tough reality in facing chronic difficulties. If both parties can be in touch with their feelings and express how they experience the difficulty of lack of support, understanding can occur, even if one person's needs are not totally filled by the other.

> ## Imbalances in giving and receiving support may require non-judgmental conversation.

Giving and receiving support in a relationship can be very helpful in bringing about a sense of closeness. No one feels on top of her game all the time. Try to notice when your partner is not on the top of her game and find a way to be supportive.

> - *Advice and problem-solving may not feel supportive.*
> - *One of the best ways to give support is with TLC.*
> - *Imbalances in giving and receiving support may require non-judgmental conversation.*

EXERCISES FOR GIVING SUPPORT:

1. Spend time alone and think about the way in which you give support to your partner. Ask yourself if you tend towards showing care and compassion or if you tend towards trying to solve your partner's problems. Think about ways in which you could show support better.

2. Spend some time talking to your partner about the way in which you show support. Ask him if you could make improvements in the way you show support. See if your partner can give you specific examples. Also talk to your partner about the way in which he gives you support. Try to make suggestions regarding how he gives support to you.

3. Talk to your partner about any disparities you feel between his giving and receiving support. Ask him to express his feelings about this, and you do the same. See if you can come to some mutual understanding about difficulties that arise concerning disparities.

4. When the occasions arise, try to be mindful of what you have learned to see if you can give support to your partner in a better way.

5. Talk to your partner about difficulties that have arisen concerning the *amount* of support that is being given. Using your best conversational skills, see if you can both show understanding of the other person's feelings and perspective. Pay attention to reducing blame and guilt.

RULE #24: **Show appreciation.**

By the time couples get to my office, they are often feeling pretty unappreciated. It's typically not because they don't appreciate one another. Usually it is because: they don't think about it.

- they don't take the time to express it.
- there are other things on their minds.
- they are feeling distant and unconnected.

Most of us like to know that we are appreciated by our partners. And if we don't feel appreciated, we often feel sad and resentful. This is an unfortunate, particularly when there *are* feelings of appreciation but they just aren't expressed.

> ### Feelings of appreciation need to be expressed.

The last Rule was about giving support. Typically, if you are giving support to your partner, she is giving support to you, too. And she is doing a lot more than that:

- Every day your partner is sharing in your joint responsibilities of living. No matter the division of labor, she is making contributions to the household.
- She is trying to be a good friend to you.
- He is committed to the family, however that is defined.
- He gets up in the morning with interest in you and in your relationship with one another.
- She may be thinking about you at various times throughout the day even if she never says so.
- She loves you and cares for you.
- He is trying to fill your needs even if he isn't always successful.
- **Your partner is on your side.**

While the things I just said above may not all be true for you, many of them, or at least some of them, are. Having an attitude of gratitude (Rule 2) is important within the context of your relationship as well. But don't just feel it—show it! It is so nice to feel appreciated, particularly when you are wrestling with a difficult issue. It can cut through tense feelings and soften one toward another. **When you get in touch with your feelings of appreciation for your partner and express them, it will help you move closer to your loving spirit, towards acts of loving-kindness, and towards gentleness and tenderness.**

> • *Feelings of appreciation need to be expressed.*

EXERCISES FOR SHOWING APPRECIATION TO SOMEONE YOU LOVE:

1. Every day for the next week, spend about ten minutes in the morning thinking about ways you appreciate your partner. Write those things down.

2. Each evening for the next week, spend about ten minutes with your partner expressing some of the things that you thought about. Take turns. Take no more than five minutes and talk about one to two things for which you are appreciative. The listener needs to *really* pay attention. If the listener doesn't understand, she should ask for further clarification. The listener needs to let her understanding of what has been said sink in. She then needs to express thanks for whatever has been said.

3. This is not a time for sarcasm or left-handed compliments. This is a time to be on good behavior, particularly if you are upset about something else or one another. Do whatever you need to do to get yourself into the proper frame of mind for exercise 2 of this Rule, particularly if you are upset. Make note of what happens to your mood when you attempt to do this.

4. Spend some time with yourself writing about your experience expressing and receiving appreciation, particularly when you are not in the mood for either. You can break it down by thinking about what happens inside of yourself before the sharing, during the sharing, and after the sharing.

RULE #25: **Be kind and caring.**

Boy, do people want to be cared about. I would say that it is on most people's top-ten list. When you can find a way to do the little things that help your partner feel cared for, he will likely love it. If you don't already know, ask your partner what some of those little things are. Then put them on your to-do list. They are some of your most important to-dos of the day.

Most of you will have an immediate intuitive feeling as to what it means to be kind. You will likely have a sense of what "Be kind to animals," or "Be kind to the elderly," or "Be kind to the sick," means. Apply the same kindness to your partner, frequently, daily, in as many of your interactions that are possible. Make kindness and caring be the predominant feeling and behavior in all your interactions with your partner. **If you are struggling in your relationship and you practice kindness every day, you will see a remarkable and rapid change in the quality of your relationship.**

> *Make kindness the predominant feeling and behavior in interactions with your partner.*

Showing kindness and caring starts by having an attitude of kindness and caring. If you have this attitude, your acts of loving-kindness will be reflected in the way you talk, how you look at your partner, and the small, tender expressions you show throughout the day.

> *Have an attitude of kindness for your partner and it will be reflected in your behavior.*

Small acts of loving-kindness are very personal for each of us, but for the purposes of illustration, here are some examples:

- Ask how your partner slept.
- Make him a cup of coffee or a cup of tea.
- Help her look up something on the computer.
- Make your partner breakfast.
- Start your partner's car and warm it up or cool it down before she leaves.

- Remind your partner of any special appointments he has that day.
- Kiss your partner goodbye with a five- to ten-second kiss and hug.
- Phone your partner during the day just to say you love her.
- Ask your partner how his day went and really listen to the answer.
- Have dinner already prepared.
- Arrange a special event that you can do together.
- Do chores that aren't on your list.
- Take time to express appreciation.
- Tell your partner something nice about himself.
- Write your partner a personal note.

Perform small acts of kindness daily.

As stated in the Introduction, the length of the explanation does not necessarily connote the importance of the Rule. This Rule requires very little explanation because it is so easily understood. Nonetheless, it is extremely important.

- ***Make kindness the predominant feeling and behavior in interactions with your partner.***

- ***Have an attitude of kindness for your partner and it will be reflected in your behavior.***

- ***Perform small acts of kindness daily.***

EXERCISES FOR BEING KIND:

1. Spend about ten minutes by yourself and write down no less than ten kind things that your partner could do for you that would give you the feeling of being cared about. Ask your partner ten things you could do for her that would give her the feeling of being cared about.

2. Spend about ten minutes with your partner reviewing each other's list.

3. Read each other's list at least twice a day for the next two weeks.

4. Try to do at least two of the things on your partner's list daily.

5. Spend time by yourself contemplating or meditating on the attitude of kindness. Use any readings, poetry, songs or images that might assist you. Perhaps you could write something yourself.

The following is a meditation that may help. If you like, use the bones of this meditation and modify it to suit your own personal tastes.

I Can Be Kind

Now I bring into my awareness
My ability to have an attitude
Of kindness.

I know kindness.

Kindness is when my mother
Picked me up from school
On a rainy day.
Or when my Dad
Stayed up late,
To help me
With my homework.
When my brother
Helped me carry the load of wood
To the back of the shed.
Or when my sister
Sat with me,
When my dog died.

I've observed kindness.

When the young man in the grocery store
Helped the older woman
Pick up the fruit
That she knocked over.
When the woman behind the register
Patiently waited
For the disabled man
To give her the correct change.
When the mail carrier
Stopped for a few minutes
To talk to my neighbor.
When that random stranger
Gave aide
To the wounded
In Tucson.

I have felt my partner's kindness.

She smiles at me
In the morning.
He makes me laugh
When I'm down in the dumps.
She makes the bed
So warm and cozy.
He looks out for me
When I'm not
Looking out for myself.

I know I can be kind.

I can start with a smile.
I can notice what is needed.
I can give with warmth and caring.
And I can do it again.

I know kindness.
I've observed kindness.
I have felt my partner's kindness.
I know I can be kind.

And I can do it again.

RULE #26: **Be honest.**

One characteristic of an intimate relationship is that two people can share some of the most sensitive and vulnerable sides of who they are. When people expose their bellies, they don't want to be punched in the gut. So, they have to have confidence and trust that they are going to be safe if they are going to be vulnerable. Without trust, they can easily be afraid to be vulnerable. It is difficult for a healthy intimacy to grow in a climate of mistrust. While the word trust has multiple definitions, **this kind of trust, confidence in one's emotional safety,** is a central ingredient of intimacy. A second kind of trust is **confidence that what one is told, is the truth.** We use the same word, *trust,* to describe both states of mind. **Dishonesty erodes trust that what we are told is the truth and that, in turn, erodes trust in our emotional safety.** In the thirty years that I have been doing this work as a psychologist, I can't remember a time in which the party that has been lied to didn't tell their partner that it was a breach of trust and that it might take some time for the trust to be rebuilt. I also can't remember a time in which the person who was lied to didn't feel less safe.

> *Trust is having confidence in one's emotional safety.*
> *Trust is also having confidence that what one is told is the truth.*

Not all acts of dishonesty feel the same. Dishonesty about an act of infidelity is likely to feel different than dishonesty about being told that a chore was finished when it wasn't really finished. There is the **type of dishonesty** and the **content of dishonesty.** Both are important in determining how we feel if we are not told the truth. (See the graphic below.)

TWO TYPES OF DISHONESTY ARE LIES AND BROKEN PROMISES
LIES
There are two kinds of lies, lies of commission and lies of omission. *Lies of commission* are active lies, out-and-out lies, lying–to-your-face type lies, misrepresentations and cover-ups. *Lies of omission* are passive lies, non-disclosures, lack of transparency and "Oh, I didn't think you wanted to know" type lies.

    Cover-ups are lies of commission because they are active even though they might not be right in your face. Over time, cover-ups can sometimes become so extensive, with one lie being told to protect other lies, that the truth begins to get lost for the person who is now living a life of lies.

Misrepresentations of feelings or intentions to get something are lies of commission. There are common examples of misrepresentations that occur during the dating process. One person says that she loves the other person for sexual favors, or one person says that he has helpful intentions when he really has intentions of taking advantage of the other person. That type of dishonesty can really hurt. Another example might be one person denying being angry at her partner and then gossiping about him behind his back. The reasons for the misrepresentation, the content of the misrepresentation and the resulting damage all contribute to an understanding of the severity of the misrepresentation.

Multiple lies of commission and omission all strung together are perhaps the worst. While single lies of omission may not seem quite as egregious as multiple lies of commission, most acts of dishonesty begin to erode trust.

BROKEN PROMISES

Some people argue that once a promise is made, it should be kept, and if we doubt our ability to keep a promise, we shouldn't make it in the first place. They say that "our word is our bond." **Nonetheless, most people consider broken promises to be on a scale of least egregious to most egregious with *intent* and *circumstances* being factors.** If a person makes a promise knowing full well that he is not going to do what he said, it may seem like he was lying when he made the promise. It seems intentional. However, if a promise is broken due to unavoidable circumstances, that may be different. For example:

If you were told that you would make a 25 percent sales commission, and after multiple sales, you were only given a 10 percent commission, you would likely think it was an intentional lie and feel betrayed.

If your partner told you that she was going to be home to get the house ready for a dinner party and you later found out that she already had something else scheduled, you may also feel like she lied, if you thought it was intentional. However, if it was an oversight, you might feel like it was unintentional and feel differently. On the other hand, if she arrived home late as a result of becoming over committed at work, you might be confused about your feelings, particularly if it happened repeatedly. And if she got home late because she had a flat tire and the spare tire also turned out to be flat, you might feel like it was just an accident and it might never cross your mind that dishonesty was involved. Of course, if you later found out that there was no flat tire, you would definitely think that it was a lie, and you would probably be very upset.

CONTENT

The content of a promise may also bear upon the feelings that we have if a promise is broken. For example, a broken promise about doing the laundry is different than a broken promise about using protection during intercourse. The content of something that isn't disclosed may be critical in determining the offense. There are many types of non-disclosed activities that couples wouldn't think are acts of dishonesty at all. For example, what you had for lunch or what you were doing on the computer may not be of any concern to your partner. On the other hand, if you went to lunch repeatedly with the same person, or you started making expensive purchases on the computer and didn't disclose either, *that* may be a big concern. Each couple has to determine for themselves what constitutes egregious activity. **Usually this is on a continuum of least egregious to most egregious.**

One of the biggest acts of dishonesty for most couples is infidelity. This is because couples typically have agreements of exclusivity with one another that they have established very early in their relationship. Also, our culture supports monogamy as the standard of behavior in marriage such that infidelity would violate that standard. Secret violations of the law are also typically thought of as breaches of trust for most people. While these major violations are usually recognized as breaches of trust, there may be more minor activities that are not recognized as breaches of trust to both members of a partnership. In the exercises below, you will be asked to discuss with your partner what types of non-disclosed activities you both would consider to be dishonest.

> *You and your partner need to know what types of non-disclosed activities are considered dishonest.*

SUMMARY OF DISHONEST ACTS

DISHONEST ACTS
Content highly important
Content mildly important

LYING
Lies of commission
Out-and-out lies
Cover-ups
Misrepresentations
Lies of omission
Non-disclosures

BROKEN PROMISES
Intentional
Unintentional

Many people feel like honesty is a matter of black and white, a person is either honest or dishonest. When trust is impacted and fear is activated, black and white thinking is reinforced as a protective mechanism. Many people believe that where there is one act of dishonesty there are others. Perhaps more important, where there is one act of dishonesty, there is *suspicion* that there are others. Even when there are feelings of mistrust, the overall damage that results from different types of dishonesty may vary, and it may not always seem so black and white after all.

Trying to repair the mistrust that arises from perceived acts of dishonesty may be different depending on what has occurred, and how often it has occurred. If you believe that your partner has lied to you or has been dishonest with you, it is important that you give him an opportunity to explain himself. **This is tricky, because your trust in his explanation may be low, and you may be so upset you don't even want to talk to him.** Nonetheless, you need to try, because when there is a perception of dishonesty, more information is better than less information. It is important to understand that your partner's explanation is not the same thing as a justification; but in order to give your relationship a chance to heal, you have to talk about why the dishonesty has occurred. If you discover that the dishonesty continues even while you are trying to heal the situation, you may find the problem simply can't be fixed. On the other hand, couples that have been able to work through issues of dishonesty, sometimes supported by counseling, are often rewarded by greater closeness.

Here are some of the reasons why people are dishonest in relationships:

1. One reason is simply for someone **to be able to get what she wants without negative consequences from her partner.** An example of this would be spending money that, if known, would receive disapproval and thus it isn't mentioned. Another example would be engaging in substance abuse and lying about it.

2. Another reason is **to cover up something that occurred for which he *might* get in trouble from his partner.** This would be something like having an exceptionally long lunch with a coworker with whom his partner might think there is a sexual attraction, and not mentioning it.

3. There is **dishonesty about a forbidden act that was planned.** This is like having an affair.

4. There is **dishonesty about a forbidden act that was unplanned.** This is like going out after work, having too much to drink, gambling away a large sum of money, and covering it up.

5. People are sometimes **dishonest in an attempt to avoid conflict** even if he is unsure his partner will be upset. He just doesn't want to take the chance. This is like going somewhere with a friend that his partner might consider to be a little too edgy and not mentioning it.

6. People may be **dishonest to just avoid criticism or embarrassment.** This is like having a clothing malfunction, or forgetting to take one's medicine, and not mentioning it.

7. People are **dishonest about reporting that they haven't done something that they were supposed to do.** This could be something like not doing the income taxes when there was an agreement to do it, and not mentioning it.

8. There may be **dishonesty as a means of protecting someone else's secret or protecting a secret of her own.** This could be not talking about a mutual friend who committed a crime, or having committed a crime herself.

9. People also **cover up secrets from their own past** like sexual activities, encounters with the police, hurtful things that happened to them, or things that they did that they are ashamed to admit.

10. People are **dishonest about their feelings by using them as a means to an end.** That would be like proclaiming love for sex when a partner knows she doesn't feel that way.

11. **People break promises that they never intended to keep.**

12. **People break promises that they thought they were able to keep but found too difficult to keep at a later time.**

These are just a few of the reasons for dishonesty. You may have experienced other reasons for dishonesty as well. The feelings each of you have about various acts of dishonesty and the reasons for that dishonesty are very personal. Part of intimacy is sharing those feelings with your partner and attempting to be on the same page with him. Some of the exercises below will help you do that.

- *Dishonesty erodes trust that what we are told is the truth and that, in turn, erodes trust in our emotional safety.*

- *Once a promise is made, it should be kept, and if we doubt our ability to keep a promise, we shouldn't make it in the first place.*

- *You and your partner need to know what types of non-disclosed activities are considered dishonest.*

EXERCISES IN CREATING HONESTY:

1. Spend some time with your partner reviewing this section together. Talk about honesty and the impact it has on trust.

   a. Do you think that there are different kinds of trust?

   b. What are they?

   c. Do different kinds of trust all impact one another?

   d. What do you think about lies of omission vs. lies of commission?

   f. Do you think that they are equally as egregious?

   g. Do you think that people always know when they are lying?

   h. What do you think about cover-ups?

   i. Do you think that all broken promises are the same?

j. Do you think that misrepresentations of feelings are always acts of dishonesty?

k. Under what circumstances are they and are they not?

2. See if the two of you can come up with a couple of examples of dishonesty that have occurred with friends, family or in the public. Talk about what type of dishonesty this was. Talk about why you believe this dishonesty occurred. See if you agree on how egregious an act of dishonesty this was, on a scale from one to ten.

3. Have a discussion with your partner about non-disclosed activities. See if you can generate a list of non-disclosed activities, starting with activities that you would not consider egregious at all to activities you would consider highly egregious. Rate the activities on a scale from one to ten.

4. Have a discussion with your partner about broken promises. Do you think that broken promises can be on a gradient of less egregious to more egregious? If so, what does that gradient look like for you?

RULE #27: **Have a lightness of being and a sense of humor with your partner.**

Can you name one person who doesn't feel good when laughing? And when two people are laughing together, they are also usually feeling pretty good about each other. **Laughter restores balance in a relationship** so that problems aren't out of proportion to enjoyment.

Humor can help to restore balance.

All of us have concerns about serious matters. We have to-do lists and lists of grievances. But "all work and no play..." (Rule 4, "Have a sense of humor") is important for individual health. It is equally as important in relationships. Find a way to laugh and be silly with your partner. See if you can laugh at the ridiculous parts of yourself and the clumsiness that we can all have. Don't take yourself too seriously. Humor is not only a healing balm for stress and illness but also a healing balm for developing closeness. Put a smile on your face. Notice how much better you feel when you are smiling!

Let your light-hearted self have presence in your relationship.

Some things are useful to do even when you don't feel like it. Lighthearted fun is one of those things, and it usually has a good payoff. If you or your partner are feeling in the dumps, watching a funny movie can be very uplifting, even if you don't feel like doing it at first. If your partner wants to tell you something funny that happened to him that day, make time to listen and try to get yourself into a lighthearted frame of mind while he is talking. Try to find something in your day that you can laugh about with your partner. Make the effort.

Push yourself towards a lightness of being.

There *will* be times that you or your partner have a serious problem and just not be in the mood for laughter, and you may not want to be pushed. Under those circumstances, it is important not to push. If there have been serious breaches of trust, if a climate of fear has developed in the relationship, or if there are strong resentments, it may be difficult to get to a lighthearted feeling. The difficulty that couples have in being lighthearted can be a barometer for how serious the relational difficulties are. If you are noticing that you rarely laugh with one another or rarely have lighthearted feelings, it is time to have a conversation to see if something else might be going on that is causing problems.

> *A lack of light-heartedness in a relationship may be a barometer for other difficulties.*

With the exception of serious difficulties—and even sometimes when there are serious difficulties—laughing helps people feel better about and with one another. In Rule 4, I suggested that you have a list of various movies, television shows, YouTube videos, or comedic writers that cheer you up. The suggestion is the same for you and your partner. It can be a safety net for turning an unpleasant or neutral moment into a pleasant moment and a good time.

- *Humor can help to restore balance.*
- *Let your light-hearted self have presence in your relationship.*
- *Push yourself towards a lightness of being.*
- *A lack of light-heartedness in a relationship may be a barometer for other difficulties.*

EXERCISES FOR HAVING A SENSE OF HUMOR:

1. Spend time with your partner to see if you can come up with several stories about your relationship that put a smile on your face. Give each story a title and write the titles down. Tell the stories to each other out loud, making sure each of you have a chance to tell part of the story.

2. Discuss with your partner whether or not it is okay to be pushed towards light-heartedness and humor. Discuss when it is and when it isn't okay.

3. Discuss with your partner whether or not there are problems in your relationship that are making it difficult for you to be light-hearted. If such problems exist, make a list of what they are and write them down. This list of problems will require more serious conversation at a later time.

4. With your partner, generate a list of movies, television shows, YouTube videos and comedic writers that you both enjoy. See if you can acquire some of these items and put them in a mutually acceptable place. They should be available for your use at any time.

RULE #28: Share fond memories and future fantasies.

Long-term relationships have a past, present and will likely have a future. We don't know the extent to which other creatures have this sense of past and future, but it does appear to be distinctly human. We have a choice. We can remember the past with fondness and we can think about the future with wonderful anticipation, or we can think about the past with regret and guilt and we can think about the future with worry and dread. The former leads to joyfulness and the later leads to despair. Intimacy grows with the former.

> *Remember the past with fondness.*
> *Think about the future with positive anticipation.*

It might take a little self-discipline between you and your partner to remain positive when discussing the past and the future. When you are looking at old photos together or just reminiscing about past experiences or adventures, try to remember what you enjoyed about those experiences. Stay open for lightness, laughter and warmth. Shared memories give depth, fullness and a sense of time to a relationship.

There will always be a need to avoid pitfalls in any plans that you make for the future, however, try to share in those parts of the vision that excite you. If your partner has an idea that doesn't suit you, don't be a downer; just see if you can come up with an idea that does excite you. And when you land on an idea that excites both of you, enjoy it together to see if you can expand the fantasy. You may not realize all of your future fantasies, but you sure can enjoy thinking about them together. This is sometimes called *window-shopping*. There are many different kinds of window-shopping, and when partners "shop" together, it can be a lot of fun.

> • *Remember the past with fondness.*
> • *Think about the future with positive anticipation.*

EXERCISES FOR SHARING MEMORIES AND PLANS:

1. Sometime in the next two weeks, have a "sharing fond memories" date. You don't have to leave the house for this date if you don't want to. For at least twenty minutes, discuss happy memories from times together with your partner in the past. No one person should dominate the time, and only positive thoughts and feelings should be expressed. A give-and-take walk down memory lane works very well for this exercise.

2. Sometime in the next two weeks, have a "sharing future fantasies" date. You don't have to leave the house for this date if you don't want to. For at least twenty minutes, discuss ideas about things you and your partner could do together in the future. This is to be a "brainstorming" session with the primary emphasis on the production of ideas, not on editing those ideas. If you don't find that your partner is particularly interested in discussing one idea, move to another. Try to not get caught up with ideas that come only from you. Start with big ideas, and narrow them down as you discover mutual interest. Discuss details only after you both agree on an idea. No one person should dominate the time. Try to make it a positive atmosphere, even when an idea comes up that doesn't particularly interest the other partner. Write down ideas with mutual interest for future planning.

3. Discuss with your partner whether or not you would like to repeat Exercise 1 or 2 sometime in the future. If so, when and how often?

RULE #29: **Your home is not your castle.**

Most of you have heard the expression, "Your home is your castle." For some people, this means that they can relax and let down their hair a bit more at home than in the workplace. If this was the way in which most people interpreted this expression, we would be fine. Unfortunately, for others, it is a declaration of freedom that the social rules of the community do not apply in one's home—that anything goes. Far too often, the consequence of this kind of thinking lead to domestic violence. Rules of conduct need to be followed in all of our human interactions, even when we are at home...no, *especially* when we are at home. It is ironic that people are willing to put on the brakes and be constrained in the workplace so they don't lose their jobs, but they are not willing to permit constraints so they don't lose their partners.

Part of living in civilized society is exercising restraint on our behavior. It is also having codes of conduct, such as manners, so that the natural intrusions that occur by living in close proximity with other humans can be smoothed over without offense. This Rule requires you to **treat your partner as well as you might treat your guests, colleagues and friends—if not better.**

> ### *Exercise restraint over your hurtful behavior in your home.*

Sociologists cannot readily explain why certain rules of conduct in our society seem to be eroding away. There seems to be an increasing lack of courtesy by students toward their teachers, children toward their parents and spouses toward one another. One of the points in writing this book was to emphasize the importance of adhering to a set of rules by which to live, not only for better individual and relationship health but also for improved civility in general. As an abandonment of civility, "your home is your castle" begs for outside restraints because restraints aren't enforced by oneself.

In some small measure, this book is being written to say, if we can gain that balance between freedom and responsibility within ourselves, we will not have to turn to others to create that balance for us.

> ### *Don't stop following the rules inside your home.*

It is likely obvious to most of you that one of the most destructive, unbridled forces in one's home is anger. Anger can be destructive when acted out in many different ways: through hitting, insult, humiliation, shame, rage, destruction, contempt, etc. These destructive expressions are one of the principal reasons that people living under the same roof have difficulty with each other. We all have angry feelings from time to time, and most of us express angry feelings from time to time. **Anger should not be expressed in any way you want just because you are angry: not in the workplace, not on the streets, not in business establishments and *not in your home*.** It can be so helpful if you and your partner can have several honest discussions about how you both express your anger and what causes difficulty for the other person. If your partner tells you that your use of certain swear words, expressions or voice tones is very upsetting to her, try to understand exactly what she is talking about and put it at the top of your list of things to try to change. It is difficult to develop closeness when you are trying to stop the bleeding from your partner's assault, physical or psychological. Following rules regarding the expression of anger in your home is very important. **Your home is *not* your castle.**

- *Exercise restraint over your hurtful behavior in your home.*
- *Don't stop following the rules inside your home.*

EXERCISES FOR CREATING GREATER CIVILITY IN YOUR HOME:

1. After you and your partner both read this section, have a discussion about whether you think you need to increase codes of conduct in your home. If you do, write down these codes of conduct as they might be applied to your own behavior. Rule 53, "Develop rules of engagement," might help. Pay particular attention to how you express anger. Write down changes that you would like to make in a way that makes them measurable and observable, so you can be accountable for the changes that you make.

2. Review these written suggestions every morning for two weeks and rate yourself on how you are doing.

3. At the end of two weeks, have another discussion with your partner to see how you both think you are doing. Continue your efforts.

RULE #30: **Don't kick the cat.**

It is human nature to have days that don't go smoothly, and to be anxious or frustrated. When this happens to you, what do you do? Do you acknowledge your feelings to yourself? Do you practice self-soothing? Do you share your feelings with your partner? Or do you externalize your frustration and anxiety in the form of anger at your partner, who has nothing to do with it? I'm sure that you have all heard the expression, **"kicking the cat." It essentially means taking out your frustrations on a totally innocent party.** If your partner literally kicked the cat when she came home from work because she had a rough day, you probably would find it horrifying. And if it wasn't a cat and it was one of your kids, you might find it even more horrifying. Perhaps people don't literally kick their partners when they come home from work, but they might take out their frustrations on their partners in some other way, like picking fights, stone-walling, being cold and snappy, or in a multitude of other ways.

> *Don't take out your frustrations and axieties on an innocent party.*

If you are the one doing this, see if you can do a better job. **Don't externalize.** Try to remember that your partner is perhaps the most special person to you in the whole world and that he is there to support you. Tell your partner that you have had a hard day, you're frustrated, anxious, or in a bad mood. But don't rag all over him. It's not his fault. He didn't do anything to deserve that. If you feel like it, ask for his support and tell him what is bothering you. Otherwise, **try to find other ways to settle down that doesn't include barking at your partner or blaming him for something he hasn't done:** lying down for fifteen minutes, reading something, turning on some music, exercising or meditating. I know that a lot of people use alcohol as a way to relax, but drinking alcohol when frustrated can create other problems. Because alcohol disinhibits, it can raise the risk for "kicking the cat" and decreases the potential for containing frustrations while working them out in a healthy fashion.

> *Find other ways to decrease your frustrations.*

Sharing feelings, being compassionate, listening well and giving support are all ways to develop greater closeness. Frustration creates an opportunity for these things to happen…if the process isn't derailed by "kicking the cat." When you start off feeling frustrated, you may actually end up feeling much better when you can experience the care and compassion from someone you love.

> • *Don't take out your frustrations and anxieties on an innocent party.*
>
> • *Find other ways to decrease your frustrations.*

EXERCISES FOR NOT KICKING THE CAT:

1. Have a sit-down conversation with your partner and discuss each other's thoughts about whether the "cat gets kicked" by either of you, how often, and under what circumstances it occurs. With your partner's help, see if you can set up a plan of action for dealing with your frustrations differently.

2. Set up a second meeting two weeks later and discuss this again to see if there was any progress. Set up another meeting two weeks after that for the same purpose.

RULE #31: **Make eye contact and touch one another.**

This Rule is about making a connection in two very basic ways. It is not about having sex. Having a connection with one another is a critical ingredient of intimacy. Quietly looking in each other's eyes is a one of the most fundamental ways for quieting the mind and joining together with your partner. When the fast pace of life begins to slow, when you can experience your breath, and when your focus can be on your partner's eyes looking back at you, a very special feeling of intimacy begins to emerge. It can help to strip away defenses and create a gentle, delicate, and open vulnerability. It is truly one of those experiences that can never be adequately described in words and can only be felt.

> *Remind yourself to make eye contact with your partner.*

Gently touching one another is also a fundamental way of making a connection. While there are individual differences when it comes to our desire to touch and be touched, being touched in an affectionate fashion activates the chemistry of feeling close. During the early stages of a developing relationship, touching often activates sexual feelings. As a relationship matures, touching in non-sexual ways can be very helpful in promoting feelings of a deep and secure intimacy. This might include giving each other a hug and a kiss during ritualistic moments such as getting up in the morning, saying goodbye when leaving for work, saying hello when coming home from work and saying goodnight. Finding random moments for a simple touch at non-ritualistic times also gives a strong message of caring that fuels passion for one another. One of the differences between ritualistic and non-ritualistic touching is the length of time of the touching. It is not surprising that a brief kiss hello or goodbye gives us one kind of feeling, and a more lengthy kiss gives us another kind of a feeling.

> *Touch one another in both ritualistic and non-ritualistic ways.*

It may be difficult to make eye contact or touch one another when couples are feeling angry. This is particularly true if the anger isn't just on the surface but feels very deep. Before being able to make eye contact or touch one another, efforts may need to be made to resolve this deeper anger. On the other hand, when the anger is just on the surface, and sometimes even when it is deep, making eye contact and touching one another can restore the balance between two people and remind them of their love for one another. Sometimes it is difficult to know, when having an argument, whether or not to yield and turn towards one another in these ways or whether it is important to wait to gain a greater degree of resolution. Sometimes people just get stuck in their negative feelings and stubbornly resist reconnecting. Ask yourself if you are just being stubborn, and if so, see if you can push yourself a little bit to reconnect. You can start with gentle eye contact and a gentle touch.

> ## *Push yourself to reconnect if you are just being stubborn.*

Over time, couples often became complacent about doing the things required to maintain feelings of closeness. Two of those things are making eye contact and touching one another. Our lives often become preoccupied with children, work and other activities, and our partnerships can easily be taken for granted. Often, if partners are asked during the early part of this complacency if they still feel "in love," they will respond that they *do* still feel in love. However, as the years go by, inattention to the relationship can deteriorate its foundation and couples can fall out of love. **Being mindful about doing little things that send messages of caring and love is as basic as brushing your teeth, and these need to be done daily.**

> ## *Acts that send a message of caring need to be done daily.*

> - ### *Remind yourself to make eye contact with your partner.*
> - ### *Touch one another in both ritualistic and non-ritualistic ways.*
> - ### *Push yourself to reconnect, if you are just being stubborn.*
> - ### *Acts that send a message of caring need to be done daily.*

EXERCISES FOR TOUCHING ONE ANOTHER:

1. Spend about twenty minutes with your partner and have a conversation about eye contact and touching. Talk about what you like and what you don't like. Each person is to take about ten minutes. The other person should use good listening skills only seeking clarification; no judgments and no admonitions about the past.

2. Over the next week, try to do the kinds of things that your partner likes daily.

3. After a week have another conversation discussing what happened. Discuss how it felt. Discuss improvements that can be made. Discuss what pleased or displeased you, and not what was right or wrong.

4. Over the next month practices mindfulness and try to do some of these things daily.

5. After a month, have another conversation as you did in Exercise 3.

6. Continue being mindful about eye contact and touching—make eye contact and touch one another.

RULE #32: **Keep feeding the fires of romance.**

In Rule 3, I wrote, "romantic love is deserving of a thousand songs and a thousand more." It could be argued that no other positive feeling has the power and the passion of romantic love. It is the theme of some of the greatest novels, movies and works of art. A sizable portion of our economy revolves around all aspects of romantic love. A cycle of romantic love can create some of the highest highs and some of the lowest lows. Yet after the passions of infatuation wear off, after a home together is established, and after a first child is born, romance often begins to dwindle. In part it is physiological, and in part it is the stresses of blending a life together in a new relationship, stress and strains of life in general, shifting attentions, and new preoccupations. **No matter the cause for diminishing romance, the results can be corrosive to a relationship.**

Romantic expressions usually begin with romantic feelings. Romantic feelings were discussed in the Introduction as deep feelings or connection and attachment that coincide with feelings of romantic desire and wanting to be close physically. Romantic desire has a strong sense of presence: something is desired right now. While sexual desire is part of romantic feelings, romantic feelings are far more than sexual desire alone.

Many people think that romantic feelings arise automatically, since that's how they typically get started at the beginning of a new relationship. That may be part of the problem. After a relationship matures, we may continue to believe that if romantic feelings aren't automatic, they don't exist. **That is why romantic thoughts and images may need to be brought into our mind actively and intentionally.** Some possible ways for stimulating romantic feelings are listeded below. As you are looking at this list of suggestions, it is important to keep in mind that your partner is in a completely unique role in your life. She is your one and only, your most special person and if you stay together, she will follow you to the end of life. Many of your major life experiences will be with her. You will likely own property together, have your dinners together, spend your weekends together, spend your holidays together, travel together, plan together, socialize together and sleep together. You may have children together. This is the person that will support you if you are ill or hurt. Your partner cares for you unlike anyone else. Your partner is sharing your life and her life with you in the most profound ways. You want to be able to have special thoughts and feelings towards this person who is so important.

- Think about the qualities of your partner that you like.
- Think about what attracts you to your partner.
- Recall past loving moments.
- Bring to mind the image of your partner's face smiling.
- Think about the many things that your partner does that you appreciate.
- Think about things that you have done in the past that your partner appreciates.
- Listen to a romantic song or poem, and in your imagination, make your partner the subject of that song.
- Think about ways in which you are physically attracted to your partner. Create visual images for yourself.
- Look at pictures of your partner that give you feelings of attraction.
- Look at pictures of you and your partner together that bring up fond memories.
- Remind yourself of feelings of longing that you had for your partner after you first met.
- See if you can hold on to those feelings and strengthen them. Remind yourself of those feelings during times of separation.
- Think about embracing your partner and the good feelings that are associated with being in your partner's arms.
- Remind yourself of particularly romantic moments with your partner.
- Try to have a light heart and a loving attitude as you think of all of the above.
- Put a smile on your face as you think about these thoughts and images.

Actively and intentionally bring romantic thoughts and images into your mind.

There are many ways you can express your romantic feelings. However, it is important to keep in mind that your expression isn't romantic if it doesn't feel romantic to your partner. There is a great scene in the movie *Taxi Driver* in which the taxi driver takes a young woman to a pornographic movie on their first date. He doesn't understand why she is upset; he thought that it was a romantic thing to do. Some years, ago I saw a couple in which the man continually bought his wife roses in a romantic gesture. Not until they were in therapy was she able to tell him that she appreciated the gesture but hated roses. In the exercise below, you will be asked to share romantic expressions that you like or would like with your partner. Once you are sure that you know what to do, see if you can increase the frequency of those expressions.

> ***If it doesn't feel romantic to your partner, it isn't romantic for the relationship.***

There is one special type of romantic act that is called *courtship*. Courtship is the way relationships begin. It may begin with a little dance in which two people start to show interest and attraction towards one another. Romantic behavior may be overt or covert and involves all kinds of flirtatiousness, seduction and pursuit. Courtship usually involves putting your best foot forward and trying to make a positive impression on the other person. At the beginning of a relationship, courtship provokes interest and heightens one's passions. One of the major intentions behind courtship is to create exclusivity and ultimately marriage. But courtship behavior doesn't have to end after marriage. **In fact, courtship-type behavior can last the life of the marriage, and it tends to be cherished by both parties.**

> ***Courtship doesn't have to end after marriage.***

Part of a romantic relationship is a sexual relationship, and romantic feelings, romantic acts, and courtship are all important in creating a healthy sexual relationship. Romantic feelings between couples are rarely generated by sexual acts alone. **The pathway for a healthy sexual relationship within the context of a long-term committed relationship typically starts with loving and romantic feelings.** That is the foundation. Romantic acts and courtship-type behavior further increases a couple's sexual passion for one another. When touching comes from a place of presence and sensuality, arousal can be further activated. An attitude of "Come on, let's get on with it" can be a real mood killer for romantic sexual passion.

> **Romance needs to be part of a healthy sexual relationship, in a long-term committed relationship.**

Couples can be sexual in many different ways. **You and your partner get to create your own guidelines for how to have a good sexual relationship.** As a young person, your sexual relationship may have started quietly and in the dark. It probably didn't take much to satisfy you because you were so highly aroused. But as the years progress, that level of arousal diminishes and satisfaction in a sexual relationship likely requires more than whatever occurred in the first six months after marriage. **If you try to continue having a sexual relationship without talking about it, you may not keep pace with the changing nature of your relationship.** This is particularly true if you have children. You likely need to talk. Your sexual relationship can be a very sensitive topic, so **when talking about it, don't be angry, judgmental, shaming or condescending in any way.** It is a time to use your very best listening skills. **And it is not the kind of conversation that can happen just one time and it's over.** Talk about logistics, circumstances, frequency, likes and dislikes. What constitutes a good sexual relationship for one couple may be completely different from what constitutes a good sexual relationship for another couple. One couple may like marathons, and another couple may like strolls in the woods. For some couples, a sexual climax is important; for others, it doesn't matter, and cuddling is what is most important. It is personal to your relationship. Good conversations about sexuality can release a lot of tension in a relationship. Creating mutual understandings about sexuality and having a good sexual relationship is an important part of having an overall healthy romantic relationship.

> **Conversation is important for a good sexual relationship.**

The same feelings of hurt and anger that might interfere with enjoying each other's company in general can interfere with lovemaking. So, again, if healthy lovemaking is going to occur **there needs to be a desire to enjoy lovemaking with one another.** Without this desire, lovemaking will likely turn into a chore for at least one of the partners...if it occurs at all. Willingness to work through feelings of hurt and anger becomes even more important when it comes to lovemaking, since this is such an intimate activity. **One pattern that I have seen many times is the couple that stopped having sex because the individuals were hurt and angry, and then they became more hurt and angry because they weren't having sex.** Working through negative feelings is very important; there are other chapters in this book that will help you to do that.

Work through hurt and angry feelings so they don't stop your sexual relationship.

It has been said that humor is one of the greatest aphrodisiacs. Seriousness tends to not stoke the fires of romance all that well. A loving, light-hearted attitude will likely serve you much better. A playful mood just makes romance so much more fun (Rule 27, "Have a lightness of being").

Try to be lovingly light-hearted.

One common sexual problem for couples is frequency. Often there are three major issues:

- differences in sexual desire that are physiologically based
- lackadaisical attitudes from both partners about having sex
- a decrease in sexual desire because of other problems in the relationship

Discussion is helpful in dealing with all of these issues, and having a heightened sensitivity to your partner's feelings is important because of the subject matter. There are many issues that might be useful to talk over:

- how to get in the mood
- when is a good time
- spontaneity vs. planning
- children
- windows of opportunity
- changing libidos
- pregnancy
- birth control
- physical concerns

- health related issues

- circumstances that arise

- worries

- feelings of rejection

- feelings of insecurity

- attitudes about having sex when one partner isn't as interested

- assumptions about what constitutes enjoyable sex

When couples appear to have lackadaisical attitudes, it is often because one or more of the topics just mentioned needs to be discussed. It is also possible that other issues of dissatisfaction with the relationship in general are bubbling beneath the surface, and neither person wants to bring it up. There is a collusion of silence that suppresses sexuality. **It is important when talking about sexuality to be able to acknowledge underlying issues.**

> *Have an open attitude in taking about issues that impact your sexual relationship.*

The Introduction stated that romantic intentions contain a basic desire for connectedness. A romantic connection combines romantic thoughts, images and feelings; a merging of self with another; and the experience of occupying the same space, mind, body and spirit. This is the passion, the heat, the fire of romance.

- *Actively and intentionally bring romantic thoughts and images into your mind.*

- *If it doesn't feel romantic to your partner, it isn't romantic for the relationship.*

- *Courtship doesn't have to end after marriage.*

- *Romance needs to be part of a healthy sexual relationship, in a long-term committed relationship.*

- *Conversation is important for a good sexual relationship.*

- *Work through hurt and angry feelings, so they don't stop your sexual relationship.*

- *Try to be lovingly light-hearted.*

- *Have an open attitude in talking about issues that impact your sexual relationship.*

EXERCISES FOR FEEDING THE FIRES OF ROMANCE:

1. Having spontaneous romantic feelings isn't the only way to have romantic feelings. You may have to actively and intentionally bring thoughts, images, and feelings into your awareness. Spend some time alone and write down things that you could do or thoughts that you could have that would bring up romantic feelings. Over the next few weeks, make a concerted effort to spend time alone reviewing what you have written. Some of the things that you have written will require you to meditate on a thought. See if you can hold a single romantic thought in your mind for at least ten seconds. See what happens if you try holding the thought in your mind for longer than ten seconds, or if you replace it with a new romantic thought. The goal of this exercise is to see if you can generate romantic feelings towards your partner when they aren't present. Use the list of suggestions above to help you.

2. You and your partner are each to spend time alone creating a list of things that each other could do or say that you would consider to be romantic acts. Make sure that there are at least five things on your list.

3. Spend time with your partner sharing your lists with one another. Each person is to read out loud the other person's list and ask any questions for clarification. Talk about ideas that you have for showing your romantic feelings, and ask him if that idea could be added to his list. Keep the list that your partner made for you and add things to the list as they occur to you. This list should be kept somewhere you can refer to it easily. This list is to be a work in progress and as you think of new romantic ideas, you can share them with your partner and write them down.

4. Try to do at least one or more of the things on the list every day, or every few days, at the very least.

5. Talk to your partner about courtship. Is courtship part of what you do? Would you like it if courtship were more a part of your relationship? If it were, what would it look like? What would actually happen? Add any of those suggestions to the lists of things that you can do or say to be romantic.

6. Talk to your partner about establishing other guidelines for a good sexual relationship with one another. Write down any mutually agreed upon guidelines. Review the guidelines on your own. Try to implement those guidelines.

7. Spend some time with your partner talking about the barriers to love-making that the two of you think exist. Use your very best listening skills in talking about these barriers, always acknowledging feelings when you become aware of them. Try to be as non-defensive as possible.

Section III
Bridging Differences

Introduction

Differences between people have been a source of conflict for civilization through-out the ages, whether at the personal level, the tribal level or the national level. What is it about differences between people that are so bothersome? It probably boils down to fear. Fear that, as a result of differences, we will be harmed or hurt; we will lose something that we already have, or we won't be able to get something that we want. There might be fear of not being able to control our situation, or being required to do something undesirable in the face of this difference. Or there might be fear of embarrassment. Some people think that differences activate fear of the unknown.

Successfully navigating the waters of difference requires, first, the desire to do so. To many of you, this might seem silly to say; however, this problem is so difficult, so widespread, and the fear runs so deep, that many of us would rather maintain the status quo than venture into these unknown waters. We have to be *committed* to learning how to get along with our neighbors, learning how to share the planet with others who are different from ourselves, before any progress can be made in solving the problem. And it can't be lip service. It has to be a real commitment.

Once we are committed, the work begins. Chapters III and IV are devoted to teaching human relationship skills for bridging differences and solving problems. Many of these skills can be applied in many relationships, but I am mainly going to address long-term partnerships. Developing these skills will take practice, both on your own and with your partner.

Most of the skills in this chapter, "Bridging differences" are achieved by making changes in yourself. However, no matter how hard you work within yourself to bridge differences, you will ultimately get to a point where you will want to ask for change in the other person. Rule 43, "Giving and receiving feedback," begins to lay out an approach for asking someone to change, or someone asking you to change. This will then lead into the final chapter, "Conflict resolution, problem-solving, and negotiation."

RULE #33: **Love doesn't conquer all.**

Most people in healthy, long-term committed relationships will tell you that it takes work. Problems have to be worked out; if they are just swept under the carpet, over time, they can make things worse. **Important differences of opinion don't get resolved simply by having fun.** At the beginning of most relationships, it often seems like there are few problems and those that pop up are easily solved. Dark days are gone. Weeks and weeks may pass by with never a harsh word or a difference of opinion that doesn't get resolved in two minutes. It may really feel like "love does conquer all." However, in time, the euphoria typically lifts, and couples are faced with difficulties that take more than two minutes to resolve. **If either person believes that "love [is supposed to] conquer all," then the relationship is in trouble.**

Love and feelings of closeness are essential, but not sufficient for a healthy relationship. Loving feelings are essential because:

- love creates a very strong desire to bridge differences, and that desire will help both people in the relationship have the willingness to stay in the tension of a disagreement long enough for a resolution to be reached.

- love motivates people to seek compromise.

- loving feelings can help people to be on good behavior when there are difficulties.

- love helps to create goodwill, caring and compassion between people.

Yet, even with strong motivation and caring, love doesn't give us *methods* for resolving conflict. There are so many wedding vows spoken with real commitment, hope and love. Unfortunately, partners might develop antagonistic feelings towards one another because they don't know what to do when problems emerge, even when caring remains strong. Parental models may be inadequate or may not even exist as divorce rates increase. Relationship skills are not taught in school nor are they a prerequisite for marriage. It can be difficult to learn these skills by the seat of your pants. That is one of the reasons for this book. I recognize that love *doesn't* conquer all, and learning relationship skills helps couples make their wedding vows a reality.

Embrace your partner's differences.

The first step in bridging differences between yourself and others is establishing a strong desire to do so. Most couples begin getting to know one another based on their commonalities, not their differences. Often the attraction is profound and intense. In fact, feelings of infatuation can be so strong that the awareness of differences is muted or pushed to the sidelines. However, in time, feelings of infatuation become less intense and differences begin to be noticed. Differences include:

- ways of thinking
- feelings
- beliefs
- temperaments
- aptitudes and skill sets
- ways to communicate
- ways of doing things
- priorities
- interests
- patterns of spending and saving money
- views on work and play
- ways to raise children
- attractions in friends
- upbringings
- cultures

The desire to bridge differences can be very strong at this point. Unfortunately, methodologies for dealing with these differences may be underdeveloped; consequently, differences may be pushed under the carpet. One or the other partner may establish the attitude of "go along to get along." If that is the pattern, inevitably frustrations build, along with hurt, blame and anger, and together they make bridging differences more difficult. Many couples allow this to go on for years. This decreases their desire to bridge their differences, because the bridge seems so big and the ground on which it needs to be built seems so unstable. It is far better to deal with differences right away, before it gets to this point. However, to do this means that both partners need to have the willingness to face all of the associated anxieties and fears. More often than not, **the fears are more about the process of facing and confronting the differences than about the differences themselves.**

> ## 1. *Bridging differences starts with the desire to do so.*

The second step is developing awareness of your worries or fears associated with facing the differences that you perceive. What are the worries or fears, and are they adaptive?

- *Will my partner be mad at me if I bring this up?*
- *Will it just lead to a fight?*
- *Is there anything we can do about it anyway?*
- *If we can't do anything about it, won't it just become a source of tension between us?*
- *What if I find out that my partner can't or won't change, and it drives me nuts?*
- *If I bring up the difference will it obscure all the commonalities?*
- *Could this just be the tip of the iceberg?*
- *Shouldn't I just let sleeping bears lie?*
- *If I bring it up will I end up having to do all the changing?*
- *What if it means we don't want to be with each other anymore?*

> ## 2. *Develop awareness of your worries or fears.*

The third step is acknowledging those worries and fears as possibilities. Bringing up differences with your partner can be unsettling. Some of the things you might be worried about could, in fact, happen.

- Your partner might be upset with you.
- You may not be able to find a resolution.
- It could remain the elephant in the room and continue to be a source of tension.
- Other problems could come out as a result.
- You might have to change to create a resolution.
- It could end the relationship.

3. Acknowledge the possible reality of your worries and fears.

The fourth step is confronting those worries and fears with rational thinking and new attitudes. Many sections in this book are devoted to helping you face those fears.

- *If my partner is upset, we'll just talk it over. I don't need to be a victim.*

- *While I may not be able to find a resolution, I probably will. And just talking about it will likely help me to feel better.*

- *It could continue to be a source of tension, but it probably won't, because I'm going to do something about it. And if I keep talking about it, it won't remain an elephant in the room. Not talking about it is what makes it an elephant in the room. If I am able to find something in the difference to appreciate, what initially gave rise to tension will give rise to enjoyment.*

- *Other problems could come out as a result of bringing up a difference, and that is a good thing. In the end, it will only make my relationship with my partner stronger.*

- *I might have to change in order to create a resolution. The good news is that unless I'm dealing with my own boundary, I can change. While I might have to change, my partner is in the same boat. The change doesn't all have to come from me.*

- *Yes, it could end the relationship. There is always that chance if I confront my differences with my partner. However, if I don't wait until we are at the end of our ropes, neither of us is going to want the relationship to end. I'm sure that we are both going to do everything in our power to bridge our differences so we can stay together. If one of us truly has a boundary, the other one is likely able to be accommodating. If my partner really doesn't want to work on bridging our differences, then I have to ask myself if this is a healthy relationship after all. While ending our relationship would be very sad for me, living in an unhealthy relationship is likely worse.*

4. Confront your worries and fears by developing new attitudes.

The fifth step is trying to understand, appreciate, and even enjoy the differences between yourself and your partner. To ultimately have good feelings about your partner's differences, have an open attitude about them. Don't be judgmental. Be interested and curious. Suspend concluding too quickly whether or not you agree with your partner or whether you like or dislike what he has to say. Part of being curious is trying to understand how your partner came to have his position, and why it has value for him.

There are such riches in difference if we can come to appreciate it. One of the great beauties of this planet is its diversity—geological, biological and cultural. And one of the great beauties in us humans is our individual differences. Each person is unique, even when one person's story sounds similar to someone else's story. There is always something to be learned about everyone, always something fresh and interesting. Closeness with another human is accomplished not only when we can delight in our sameness but also when we can delight in our differences. That is the best bridge of all.

> *5. Try to understand, appreciate and even enjoy your partner's differences.*

> *1. Bridging differences starts with the desire to do so.*
>
> *2. Develop awareness of your worries and/or fears.*
>
> *3. Acknowledge the possible reality of your worries and fears.*
>
> *4. Confront your worries and fears by developing new attitudes.*
>
> *5. Try to understand, appreciate and even enjoy your partner's differences.*

EXERCISES FOR EMBRACING YOUR PARTNER'S DIFFERENCES:

1. Spend some time by yourself thinking about differences that you have with your partner. Write down five of those differences. They can be differences in personality, patterns of behavior, beliefs, interests, aptitudes or skill sets, etc. Since you are going to be asked to share your perception of these differences with your partner, make sure that your selections don't include a subtle (or not-so-subtle) putdown or condescending attitude. Think about whether you have ever talked to your partner about these differences.

2. See if you can identify any worries or fears that might make it difficult for you to talk to your partner about your differences. Look at the questions above for guidance. Write down your worries or fears.

3. What sort of rational thinking or different attitudes can you have for confronting your fears and worries? Write them down.

4. Think about what you can appreciate, value or like about the differences and write them down.

5. Spend some time with your partner over a period of two weeks and do the following:

   a. Find a twenty-minute period of time in which you can share. Each person is to take no more than ten minutes apiece.

   b. Select one of the items on your list and share it with your partner.

   c. Your partner is to reflect back her understanding of the difference that you mention. Your partner is not going to state whether or not she agrees that this is a difference.

   d. Once your partner reflects back an understanding of this difference, tell her how you have come to appreciate this difference.

   e. Your partner is then going to reflect back an understanding of this appreciation.

   f. Switch roles.

RULE #35: **Be open to accepting your partner's influence.**

If you are open to the influence of another, you allow that person to change the way you think or feel. Usually this is known by the person's verbal behavior. It can be in the form of book, lectures, speeches, discussion, debate or one-on-one conversations. Right now, you might be open to the influence of this book. Being open to others' influence is essential for learning, growing and improving adaptation to the environment. Like other psychological characteristics, being open to others' influence is on a gradient. **Openness requires an attitude that recognizes that someone else might have more information on a subject than you, or a useful new perspective. It also requires that you trust you won't be worse off by listening with an open mind.**

> *Being open to others influence is recognizing that there is always something to learn.*

Accepting the influence of others is particularly important for personal and interpersonal growth, because:

- you may not be aware of how your behavior impacts others.
- you not be aware of what to do to improve a relationship.
- you may not know how to get unstuck from a pattern of behavior or thinking that is causing you difficulty.
- you may have difficulty figuring out exactly how you feel and think.

Other people's observations and feedback can be very important for your improved performance, functioning, resolution of differences, creation of mutual satisfaction and increased overall adaptation.

> *Being open to influence can help you with awareness and getting unstuck.*

Being open to your partner's influence means that what your partner thinks and feels has the potential to change your thinking, attitudes and behavior. **Several attitudinal prerequisites are needed to have if this is going to happen:**

- having an open mind
- not being a "know-it-all"
- not having to be right
- not being stuck on doing things only one way
- not being stuck on getting exactly what is wanted
- believing that your partner has good ideas and a legitimate perspective
- understanding and respecting his feelings
- trusting that she isn't "out to get you"
- trusting that your partner isn't just out for himself
- trusting that she is being honest
- trusting that you won't be worse off by listening to what he has to say
- trusting that this Rule is likewise being practiced by your partner

---

In order to be open to your partner, you need to value and trust him.

Being open to your partner's influence doesn't mean abandoning your own point of view and accepting her point of view, lock, stock, and barrel. It is about modification. It may be a subtle change, or it may be a substantial change. Being open to your partner's influence means that when you are at an impasse, it is *not* because you are just too stubborn to listen to her and consider what she has to say. It is for some other reason. If you are at an impasse, you can be confident that you and your partner *aren't* thinking or saying, *You are too closed minded to even listen, What good does it do for me to talk? You don't care what I think anyway. You think you are just too perfect the way you are. You'll never change!* **What is important about accepting your partner's influence is that you have allowed yourself to be in a dynamic process of give and take that brings about a result with which both you and your partner can be happy.** In fact, when you can come to enjoy this process rather than see it as burdensome, your relationship with your partner (and everyone else) will be at a different level.

> ### *Being open doesn't mean totally abandoning your own point of view.*

Having a close relationship or living with someone creates opportunities for becoming more self-aware. There are so many little things that we do, little nuances in behavior, verbal expressions, or repeated habits, of which we are unaware.

- We may say or do things repeatedly that don't produce the results that we would like.

- We may have difficulties at work for which we just don't see a solution.

- We may be upset about a conflict with someone else and can't see our part of it.

- Our partner may become upset with us, but we don't see another way to act.

All of these are examples of things that we might improve, if we had someone else to give us insight or suggestions. Our partners are often in the best position of anyone to help us. These are circumstance in which being open to their influence can be very helpful.

> ### *Our partners may be able to help us to act better and feel better.*

Partners are not always aware of the changes the other is making to improve the relationship. It can be useful for this information to be shared. It helps develop trust in feedback that is given. This can give a great sense of satisfaction that conversations are constructive, helping partners to feel good about themselves and about their relationship.

> ### *Tell your partner what you are doing for self-improvement.*

- *Being open to others' influence is recognizing that there is always something to learn.*

- *Being open to influence can help you with awareness and getting unstuck.*

- *To be open to your partner, you need to value and trust him.*

- *Being open doesn't mean totally abandoning your own point of view.*

- *Our partners may be able to help us to act better and feel better.*

- *Tell your partner what you are doing for self-improvement.*

EXERCISES FOR ACCEPTING YOUR PARTNER'S INFLUENCE:

1. Spend some time by yourself reviewing the attitudinal prerequisites above. Rewrite all of them using the word "I" and using your partner's name. If you think a statement it isn't true for you, write it down as a topic of conversation to have with your partner at a later time. Think about what concrete steps could be taken so that it *would* be true, and write that down as well.

2. Spend some time talking to your partner about the changes that you are both trying to make to improve yourselves and the relationship. Use good listening skills and do not be judgmental.

3. Spend some time talking to your partner about this topic, whether influence already exists in your relationship, and how it could be improved upon.

RULE #36: **Develop the construct of relative right and wrong. Your opinions are not absolute.**

Preliminary exercise:

Write down several things about your partner that distress you and several things that please you. Write down the first things that come to your mind in whatever way the ideas form.

Many people simply think that they are right. And it is entirely understandable. We were raised to think that way. **From the time that we are little, our parents instructed us in the ways of the world by telling us the right and wrong way to act.** We were disciplined for doing things that were wrong and praised for doing things that were right. Girls and boys were told that they were good when they helped out around the house and they were bad if they hit their sibling. In school, this way of thinking was reinforced even more. It was all about giving the right and the wrong answer. Our political system also reinforces this way of thinking by convincing the electorate that voting for one candidate is on the side of *right* while the other is on the side of *wrong*. The institutions of home, school and government often appear to have little grey area. So it makes sense that tensions and difficulties between people are approached within this same framework: *I'm right and you're wrong, and I'm sure of it.*

There is a developmental and cultural basis for thinking in terms of right and wrong.

This developmental basis for settling tensions in childhood easily becomes the basis for settling tensions in adulthood. Consequently, when tense moments arise between couples, both parties can quickly begin to think about who is right and who is wrong. It seems pretty straightforward: figuring out who's right and who's wrong determines who is supposed to change. Unfortunately, it rarely works out very well when couples take this approach, for several reasons.

First, two people often have different views of what is right and wrong, particularly when it comes to domestic and social issues. And second, people often have a hard time being told that they are "wrong."

The kinds of issues that couples have don't lend themselves to this absolutist way of thinking that we may have learned in childhood. **Consequently, it is useful to develop the construct of *relative* right and wrong.** This is not to say that right and wrong don't exist or we should abandon morality, generally agreed upon standards or the laws of the land. If there are violations at that level, it is important to call a spade a spade and to be accountable for our behavior.

> ### Develop the construct of **relative** right and wrong.

This construct of relative right and wrong works for a multitude of differences that have nothing to do with morality or legalities. In practical terms, when a behavior is bothersome, it might be expressed as not being **"right *for me"* or as being "wrong *for you."*** This becomes a useful construct in discussing differences, because we don't then need to defend our behavior in terms of what is right or wrong for the community, the universe or on some other order of morality. **Differences can be expressed as discomforts, comforts, pleasures, displeasures or benefits.** When both partners' points of view are presented from this perspective, defensiveness is minimized. Rather than discussing who is right or wrong, couples can discuss **the relative importance and strength of feeling that each person has about the problem, thus creating a more negotiable basis for resolution.**

> *"This is not **right for me**."*
>
> *"It is **wrong for you**."*
>
> *"I don't **feel right** about this."*
>
> *"It just **feels wrong** to me."*

Most of the things that couple argue about have no right and wrong: who takes out the garbage; whether to spend $500 on a new piece of furniture, put it into savings or give it to charity; whether the kids should be in bed by 8:00 or 8:30; whether to drive the speed limit or five miles per hour below the speed limit; whether the grass is cut once a week or every other week. **As soon as the conversations turn into *I'm right and you are wrong,* good listening diminishes, as each of us becomes preoccupied with proving our point.** The conversation isn't about the importance of the problem or the feelings associated with it. It's about trying to win a debate—which is quite different than a constructive conversation. **Also, when people think they are right, there may be a lot of passion, the passion of self-righteousness.** Ask yourself about your own arguments with your partner. Have the elements of who is right and who is wrong become part of the argument? Has it added to the heat between you and your partner? Did it help bring about resolution? **When you have a difference with your partner, the goal is to gain mutual understanding; arguing from the perspective of who is right and who is wrong creates a roadblock for that understanding.**

Thinking in relativistic terms means developing a mental framework for thinking about others' behavior outside of the concept of good or bad, right or wrong, correct or incorrect, appropriate or inappropriate. Some additional alternatives are:

- what works/doesn't work for me
- what fits/doesn't fit for me
- what I like/don't like
- what is comfortable/uncomfortable for me

An important premise for this type of thinking is the idea that it is okay to have positive or negative feelings about another person's behavior based on your own individual needs, wants and desires, and not on the quality of his behavior. Absolutist verses relativistic thinking can also be called judgmental and non-judgmental thinking.

NON-JUDGMENTAL THINKING

*"This **doesn't work** for me."*

*"This is **not a good fit** for me."*

*"I'm **uncomfortable** with this approach."*

*"I **don't like** the way you're doing that."*

*"I **want** to do it another way."*

*"It just **feels better** this way."*

*"When it is done that way, I **feel anxious**."*

Having a perspective of uncertainty can be very helpful when trying to resolve differences. This uncertainty opens up the possibility that there may be something new to learn from your partner, allowing you to consider a problem from another perspective. Rule 9, "Accept uncertainty," discusses uncertainty from the individual perspective. This Rule discusses it from the relationship perspective. Obviously I think this concept is very important for our overall mental health.

Sorting through differences of opinion with your partner is not school. You are not going to be graded on having the correct answer. Opinions are only opinions. **Considering another person's point of view and agreeing with her may require you to adapt, change or be accepting. If you want to have intimacy, you have to be prepared to do all of these. Part of being in a relationship is having the willingness to shift your thinking and behavior.** The *willingness* is the important variable here. It doesn't mean that you will agree, but it does mean that you are willing to listen with an open mind. When you have this willingness, conversations will be much calmer and caring, and differences more easily resolved.

Have the willingness to shift your thinking and behavior.

- *Develop the construct of "relative" right and wrong.*
  - *"This is **not right** for me."*
  - *"It is **wrong for you**."*
  - *"I **don't feel right** about this."*
  - *"It just **feels wrong** to me."*
- *Develop non-judgmental thinking.*
- *Have the willingness to shift your thinking and behavior.*

EXERCISES FOR DEVELOPING THE CONSTRUCT OF RELATIVE RIGHT AND WRONG:

See also review the exercises in Rule 9, "Accepting uncertainty"

1. Review the Preliminary Exercise. Rewrite what you wrote in language that describes your feelings *(non-judgmental)* more than the quality *(judgmental)* of your partner's behavior.

   Example (Absolute, judgmental thinking):

   - *It was really good that Mary was able to get the laundry done right.*
   - *Mary shouldn't be yelling at little Billy for not doing his homework. It's just wrong.*
   - *John doesn't care about the kids; he only cares about himself.*
   - *I'm glad that John finally learned how to do the dishes properly.*

   Example: (Relative, non-judgmental thinking):

   - *I appreciated Mary getting the laundry done.*
   - *I have trouble with Mary yelling at Billy.*
   - *I would like it if John would spend more time with the kids and I think they would like it too.*
   - *I felt good that John did the dishes the way I like to have them done. I felt like he heard me.*

2. Spend some time with your partner talking about the concept of relative right and wrong and judgmental and non-judgmental thinking. Discuss whether or not you feel like the two of you talk in absolute terms and use the language of right and wrong, good or bad behavior.

3. Talk about whether you feel judged by your partner in conversations with one another. Talk about this exercise that you have completed and also the exercise in Rule 9 on "Uncertainty," and consider whether using a different frame of reference might help.

RULE #37: Your partner knows his or her thoughts, feelings and intentions better than you.

"I know you are mad at me." "You don't like my mother."

"You don't like spending time with my friends."

"You just don't care about having the house look nice."

"You're not interested in sex."

"Your more interested in your job than you are in me."

"You're more interested in the kids than you are in me."

First of all, no one is a mind-reader, and no one knows for sure how his partner feels, unless, of course, she tells you. Second, when feelings are expressed this way, your partner will often end up in a defensive posture. The couple will fight about the veracity of the statement and never get around to talking about the real issues: discomforts and difficulties with what is going on in the relationship. **It is far more productive for you to talk about what you want, need and feel than it is to make assumptions about what someone else feels.**

> ### Talk about your own feelings not your partner's feelings.

"I'm nervous that you might be mad at me."

"I'm upset because it doesn't seem that you like my mother."

"I want us to spend more time with my friends, and I don't think you do."

"I would like us to be on the same page about keeping the house looking nice."

"I'm wanting to make love more frequently. What about you?"

"I wish we could spend more time together, but it doesn't seem like you feel the same way."

"I would like to spend more time with you that doesn't include the kids."

204

It may seem subtle, but there is a difference between saying:

- "I feel like you are mad at me," "it seems like you are mad at me," or "I think you are mad at me," and

- "You're mad at me."

It may seem like semantics, but the connotations are different.

The first statements acknowledge a qualifier, filter or perceptual quality that can be attributed to the person who is making the statement.

The second statement doesn't make this attribution and makes an absolute statement that the observer is correct about how the other person feels.

It is the absolutist nature of this second statement that can cause trouble. **It particularly causes trouble because it is not a statement about a *behavior* that has been observed; it is about a feeling in the other person that is *interpreted* from her behavior.** While we might have a pretty good idea what our partner is feeling based on her behavior, the final word on what she feels rests with her.

> ## *The final word on what someone else feels rests with him.*

If this Rule is not accepted by both parties, endless arguing will ensue with increasing agitation from the person who's feelings are assumed: "You don't know how I feel! Stop trying to tell me what I feel or what I think. You aren't a mind reader!" It is best to assume that the thoughts and feelings in one's mind are known best by that very same person.

> ## *Both parties in a partnership need to accept this rule.*

If you want to know how your partner feels about something or someone, you can always ask. However, if you ask without saying why, he may not want to answer, because he may feel exposed or unsafe. It is usually better to state your own feelings first as in the examples above. That makes it much easier for your partner to respond to your request.

> ## *If you are having feelings about a topic, state your feelings first before asking your partner how she feels.*

- *Talk about your own feelings, not your partner's feelings.*
- *The final word on what someone else feels rests with him.*
- *Both parties in a partnership need to accept this rule.*
- *If you are having feelings about a topic, state your feelings first before asking your partner how she feels.*

EXERCISES IN NOT MAKING ASSUMPTIONS ABOUT HOW YOUR PARTNER FEELS:

1. Spend some time reflecting on whether you make assumptions about how your partner feels. See if you can come up with five to ten examples and write them down.

2. Using the examples from Exercise 1, state your own feelings about what your partner did; for example:

   - *I feel upset that you...*
   - *I'm sad that...*
   - *I'm very confused about...*
   - *I'm concerned that...*
   - *I'm mad that...*
   - *I wish that...*
   - *I would like it if...*

3. Have a conversation with your partner about this Rule. Share whether or not you think you make assumptions about how the other person feels. Give her some feedback, if you think that she does this to you. Use examples if you have them.

4. On the basis of your partner's feedback and on the basis of your own thinking, decide if this is an area you need to practice. If so, practice the kinds of statements from above or come up with similar expressions of your own and write them down. Try to review your written words every other day for the next couple of weeks.

RULE #38: **Expectations do not necessarily lead to obligations; agreements do.**

This rule is essential for having healthy relationships! This Rule is so important because it answers the question, *What is required of me just by being in this relationship? Is there anything that I have to do that doesn't require my agreement?*

> *What are you obliged to do by virtue of being in a relationship?*

This Rule basically says that the people in a relationship, *together*, determine how that relationship is supposed to work. No single person gets to call the shots. **By virtue of being in that relationship, one person is not obliged to meet the needs, wants, desires (NWDs), and expectations of the other person.** Conversation needs to take place if there are unmet NWDs. If mutual understandings, agreements or contracts are the result of that conversation, each partner is required to follow through with that agreement. **Thus, a requirement or obligation to fill the other's NWDs is not inherent to the relationship; it is the result of the agreements that the parties reach with one another.**

> *An obligation to fill someone's needs is not inherent to a partnership.*

Examples:

"I can't believe that you didn't bring me home something for lunch when you were out. You knew that I was hungry."

"I didn't know that you wanted me to."

"Well, you should have known."

"Why didn't you do the laundry? I don't have any socks."

"I didn't know that you didn't have any socks."

"Well, if you looked in the drawer, you could have seen that they were all gone."

"Hey, there's no toilet paper in the bathroom!"

"Well, then, get some from the closet."

"Didn't you use the last of it?"

"Yes."

"So why didn't you replace it?"

"Because I wasn't using the bathroom next. You were."

"It's the person that uses up the toilet paper that is supposed to replace it."

"Not according to me."

"Turn off the light. I'm trying to go to sleep."

"How about just closing your eyes. The light doesn't bother me, so it shouldn't bother you."

"I can't believe how rude you are!"

Each of these examples is filled with assumptions regarding how one partner thinks the other partner should behave, based on his own needs and expectations. In each case, a conversation, along with some understanding or agreements, will help to solve the problem. Without such understandings, the problem will likely continue.

There are exceptions to this Rule in certain types of relationships. **The most important exception is in the parent-child relationship.** As a result of their age and lack of development, children are not able to meet their own needs. If a parent doesn't feed the baby, the baby will die. Thus, the parent is obliged to meet certain needs of the child. This requirement goes one way, particularly when the child is an infant.

An exception is the parent-child relationship.

As the child gets older, the requirements of the parents to meet the child's needs change. If the parents don't change and continue to give the child everything she wants, the child may end up feeling entitled to have her needs met by her parents or someone else. As an adult, that person may have difficulty when her partner is unable or unwilling to fill her NWDs. She may rage like a spoiled child. She may have never learned that "You can't always get what you want" (Rule 8).

There are other relationships in which there is an exception to this Rule; there are differences from one person to the next and from one family to the next regarding obligations inherent to relationships. Those obligations are not the same for every family. **Some kinds of relationships that may be exceptions are: children's obligations to parents as they age, siblings' obligations to one another, grandparents' obligations to their grandchildren, and obligations to extended family members.** Notice that marriages, friendships and relationships with neighbors aren't included on that list. While we might like it if people had the desire to help their neighbors or friends, they aren't required to help. Business relationships also aren't on the list, and that is why business partnership agreements are so important.

On the surface, this Rule may seem very straightforward and easy to understand, but with friends, neighbors and marriages, it might create a moral dilemma, particularly if one of those people is hurt or sick. That's when this Rule can be very troubling.

While it is true that relationships get started because many desires get met automatically, at some point, a need or desire will go unnoticed or will conflict with what the other person wants to do. **If the partner with the unmet need feels that the other person is "obliged," and if the need continues to go unmet, he is likely to be upset. Conflict and fighting can often occur based on this premise alone. Unless there is mutual understanding concerning obligations, the conflict will probably not be resolved.**

> *If there is no agreement concerning what constitutes obligations to one another, there will likely be conflict.*

Of course, there are unspoken mutual understandings and agreements that are based on the laws of the land and commonly held cultural beliefs. Most people accept "Ten-commandment" type laws. In our grandparents' generations, there were more cultural beliefs and roles that were accepted without negotiation or discussion. For them, many expectations and mutual understanding were assumed. However, during the last half of the twentieth century, a great deal of cultural change has occurred as women have joined the work force in huge numbers. Thus commonly held beliefs have shifted and roles have become less well defined. What was once thought to be inherent to the relationship is no longer so. Therefore couples have to affirm or reaffirm what each accepts of cultural expectations. What may seem to be a requirement for one person may not be a requirement for another. **Good communication and negotiation aimed at reaching mutual understanding has therefore become much more necessary.**

> *What seems to be an obligation for one person, may not be an obligation for the other.*

Once parties arrive at a mutual understanding, make an agreement, or reach a commitment, they have an obligation to follow through with that understanding. The obligation grows out of that mutual understanding, and not out of the original expectations. **Expectations based on agreements and mutual understanding are different than expectations that are *not* based on agreements and mutual understanding.** Since mutual understanding and agreements are the bridge for unmet NWDs and expectations, it is very important that they be taken seriously. It is also important that understandings be stated explicitly and out loud so that both partners are clear about their agreements at the end of a conversation. If it is your NWD that is being addressed by this agreement, you will want there to be follow-through. **So it is important that the agreements with your partner be very clear.** It is far better to not agree to do something than to agree and not follow through.

> *You are obliged to follow through with the agreements you reach with your partner.*

It is true that not every agreement has the same degree of importance, because the importance of different needs may vary. Thus an agreement to do the dishes may not be as important as an agreement to pick up the kids after school. But **not keeping agreements, at any level of importance, can become a slippery slope, particularly if it turns into a pattern of behavior. When agreements are broken, trust and confidence begins to deteriorate, and this is caustic to relationships.** Not following through with agreements is one of those "end-of-my-rope" kinds of problems. It can totally erode confidence, respect, feelings of dependency, and love, ultimately destroying the relationship. **Mutual understanding and follow-through is one of the most important ways of bridging unmet needs and expectations.** Doing it well is extremely important for the success of the relationship.

> *Confidence in one's partner grows when agreements are kept.*

- *An obligation to fill someone's needs is not inherent to a partnership.*
- *An exception is the parent-child relationship.*
- *If there is no agreement concerning what constitutes obligations to one another, there will likely be conflict.*
- *What seems to be an obligation for one person may not be an obligation for the other.*
- *You are obliged to follow through with the agreements you reach with your partner.*
- *Confidence in your partner grows when agreements are kept.*

EXERCISES ON EXPECTATIONS, OBLIGATIONS, AGREEMENTS:

1. Review this Rule along with all its exceptions. Do you agree or disagree with this Rule? Talk it over with your partner. Do you and your partner agree with this Rule? If you don't agree, continue talking with your partner about the issue of unmet needs and the requirements of each of you to fill the needs of the other person.

2. Are there cultural norms that you both mutually agree upon? Write some of them down.

3. Spend a little time by yourself and write down at least five expectations that you have of your partner. Next to each one, write down whether or not you believe that you and your partner have a mutual understanding regarding that expectation. Write either *yes we do, no we don't,* or *I don't know.* Try to write down at least one expectation for each of the three ratings.

4. Spend about twenty minutes with your partner reviewing what you wrote. See if she agrees with you on your ratings and write down her answers.

5. If your ratings don't agree, see if through conversation you can figure out why one of you thought that there was a mutual understanding and your partner didn't. Talk to each other about what you have learned from this conversation.

6. In another conversation each of you is to pick one unmet expectation from your list to see if you can arrive at a mutual understanding. If you do, use language that is clear and explicit. If you don't arrive at a mutual understanding, set this issue aside to be discussed again at a later time.

RULE #39: Use "I" language.

Preliminary exercise:
Write down 5-10 things that you regularly get upset about with your partner. Write then down however you normally think about these things.

Paying attention to the language used when discussing difficulties can make a big difference in how the conversation goes. I often find myself coaching my clients by helping them to restate their feelings in a less accusatory and judgmental language. This is difficult for many people, because one partner's upset feels like it is caused by the other partner. First, it is their partner's fault, second, whatever their partner is doing is wrong, and third, they are sure of themselves. It is so difficult for people to get away from this type of thinking. The basic formula for this type of thinking is simple: "I'm upset, so therefore you (not me) must have messed up."

Complaints often start with blame and judgment.

This Rule about "I" language will probably not work without a new attitude.

The new attitude is: **This problem may not be totally a result of my partner's Behavior. My behavior and my sensitivities are also in the mix. My partner didn't necessarily do anything wrong, and her point of view is also important.**

Talking in non-accusatory and non-judgmental language begins by introducing your concern using "I" language. This means entering into a discussion first by describing your frustration or difficulty as your personal experience of the problem. If you get hit in the leg with a baseball, you might start by saying, "I'm in pain," or, "My leg hurts!" rather than, "What did you do that for, you jerk?" or, "Can't you do something?"

Start by describing your personal experience in feeling language.

I like to think of "I" language as language that expresses our "comfort" level.
This can be done by following the word "I" with a true feeling. Here are
some examples:

- "I sure was worried that I didn't get a call from you to let me know
  that you were coming home late."
- "I'm angry that I have to do the dishes after you said you were going
  to do them."
- "I feel so alone in the evenings when you are drinking."
- "I feel out of control in my own kitchen when your mom comes over."
- "I feel pretty unimportant when you don't make time to talk to me."
- "I'm frustrated with how much we argue."
- "I can't stand how messy the house is."
- "I'm upset about the way we are disciplining the children."

> ## Use "I" language that expresses your comfort level.

**If you use the expressions *I feel that you*…or *I feel like you*…, they may sound
just as accusatory and judgmental as if you didn't use the word "I."** *I feel like*
or *I feel that* are not true expressions of a feeling. This is particularly true if the
words *I feel that you*…are followed by a characterization: *I feel that you are a
son-of-a-gun.* I'll give you some examples by rewriting the statements above
using I *feel like you*…or I *feel that you*…This is *not* the way to use "I" language:

- "I feel like you are incredibly irresponsible for not calling to tell me you
  were coming home late." (vs. "I was really worried…")
- "I feel like your agreement to do the dishes doesn't mean a thing to you."
  (vs. "I'm angry that you agreed to do the dishes, and…")
- "I feel that you are an alcoholic." (vs. "I'm very frustrated with your drinking.")
- "I feel like your mother wants to control everything including my kitchen.
  (vs. "I get so angry when I'm in the kitchen with your mother. I feel like
  I'm unable to do things the way I want to do them.")
- "I feel that you're selfish and that you are more interested in your
  computer than you are in me." (vs. "I feel so unimportant . . .")
- "I feel like you are a slob and that it is perfectly fine with you if I do
  all the cleaning." (vs. "I really get upset about the house.")
- "I feel like you're tyrannical in the way you discipline the kids."
  (vs. "I'm worried that…")

> ### Don't use the words "I feel like you," in accusatory and judgmental ways.

The same words can be used in a softer, less-accusatory fashion if there aren't characterizations, particularly when compared to the alternative of starting the sentence with the word *you*. Here are some examples:

- "I feel like you're not interested in my work." (vs. "You're not interested in my work.")
- "I think that your sister doesn't like me." (vs. "Your sister doesn't like me.")
- "I feel like you aren't interested in sex." (vs. "You're not interested in sex.")
- "I feel that you don't want to help with the chores." (vs. "You don't want to help with the chores.")

> ### Use the words, "I feel like you," in softer and less absolute ways.

If "I" language is used in the examples above and the tonal emphasis is on the word *you* rather than the word *I*, it may make no difference at all that you started the sentence with the word *I*—it is still going to sound accusatory. Say the sentences above to yourself and emphasize the word I and then emphasize the word *you* to see how it changes the meaning of the sentence. If you have an accusatory attitude, you can find a way to use "I" language in an accusatory fashion.

Using "I" language isn't necessarily a *panacea*. The "I" word can also be used in other ways to cause trouble. For example the "I" word followed by words like ... *know that you* or ... *am sure that you* can make a statement absolute and cause difficulty for your partner. I'll use some of the same examples as above:

- "I know you're not interested in my work." (vs. "I feel like you're not interested in my work.")
- "I'm sure that your sister doesn't like me." (vs. "I think that your sister doesn't like me.")
- "I know you're not interested in sex." (vs. "I feel like you aren't interested in sex.")

> ### "I know that you" statements can also sound absolutist.

Learning to speak by using "I" language requires attention and practice. While using the word "I" can be a big help, be careful to not use the word "I" and still be accusatory, judgmental and absolutist. Using language in a new way may feel contrived and awkward at first. However, one of the most important parts of bridging differences is understanding each other's point of view. Conversations that are filled with *What's wrong with you?* typically end in frustration. Conversations that are filled with *This is what's going on for me* have a much better chance of ending on a positive note and with a positive outcome.

- *Complaints often start with blame and judgment.*
- *The new attitude is:*
  - *This problem may not be totally a result of my partner's behavior*
  - *My behavior and my sensitivities are also in the mix*
  - *My partner didn't necessarily do anything wrong*
  - *His point of view is also important*
- *Start by describing your personal experience in feeling language.*
- *Use "I" language that expresses your comfort level.*
- *Don't use the words "I feel like you," in accusatory and judgmental ways.*
- *Use the words "I feel like you" in softer and less absolute ways.*
- *"I know that you" statements can also sound absolutist.*

EXERCISES FOR USING THE "I" LANGUAGE:

1. Review the Preliminary Exercise.

2. Go back and reread each of those statements to see if you can get in touch with a feeling that you are having about whatever you wrote down. See if you can rewrite each of the statements using "I" language and lead with your feelings. Try to be open to any feelings that you are having other than anger. You can model your language after the examples given above or come up with your own way of saying it.

3. Spend about twenty minutes with your partner talking about this exercise. Without discussing the particular things with which you are upset, talk about anything you learned by doing this exercise on your own. Also discuss with your partner the various ways in which "I" language may be used that can still cause difficulty.

4. In the same conversation, talk about what you might do when you are having a conversation and one of you would like the other to use "I" language more. What can you say to one another that will be well received? Can you have some agreement about this? Also talk about what you can do if "I" language is being used but still causing difficulty. What can you say about that, in the middle of a conversation, that will be helpful?

5. In future conversations in which you are talking about things that are troublesome between you and your partner, practice using "I" language.

6. Using "I" language is not a panacea for all communication with your partner. It is one of many tools to use. It won't always work. If you find that you are having trouble framing your expression with "I" language, just tell your partner that you are doing your best but you just don't know how to express it any other way. Be understanding that using "I" language doesn't always apply.

RULE #40: **Don't blame "lack of love" for not getting what you want.**

Preliminary exercise:

Do you have any needs, wants or desires that aren't met by your partner because you think he/she doesn't care enough about you or what you want. Write them down plus any other examples of unmet needs to create 5 examples.

When people have incompatible differences with one another, a developing relationship usually doesn't get out of the starting gate. When relationships take off, it is usually because there is commonality that is automatic and easy to achieve. As people find mutual satisfaction in one another, love can develop, and it often does. **Once two people are in an established loving relationship, they will inevitably run into differences, bump into each other, and fail to meet some of their partners' expectations. Rarely does this result from a lack of love.** If feelings of love are truly diminishing, there will likely be many more indicators other than simply not getting what is wanted on occasion. Nonetheless, a person can feel unloved when her needs aren't being met by her partner, even when her partner feels in love with her.

Feeling unloved and being unloved are two different things.

Over the years, I have often heard people talking about being unloved and relating it to their unmet needs. This is how it is often stated:

- *If you really loved me, you wouldn't argue with me so much.*
- *How can you say you love me and still treat me like that?*
- *I think if you loved me, you would be more caring.*
- *You say you love me, but you forgot my birthday.*
- *How many times have I asked you to _____? Maybe you just don't love me anymore.*
- *You know, you are spending so much time working/talking on the phone with your friends, I just don't believe you love me anymore.*

The failure to have needs met cannot be assumed to be from a lack of love. Typically it has nothing to do with love. By the way: that's not only true in marriage, but it is also true for the parent-child relationship. Most parents love their children. There may be many reasons why they aren't very good parents, but lack of love is typically low on the list. Likewise, when needs aren't met in marriage, there may be many other explanations:

- not noticing a partner's NWDs
- not remembering to pay attention to them
- not having the same standards as the other person
- not really knowing how to fill the needs
- not having the ability
- having poor organizational skills
- having poor self-management skills
- not being able to set priorities very well
- being stressed out or over whelmed
- being depressed
- being self-centered
- having difficulty controlling one's feelings
- generally having personality differences

> *When needs are unmet there are usually good explanations that aren't about love.*

You may be very much in love with your partner but still be unable to fill his expectations. While there are many different points of view regarding what constitutes *loving behavior,* and while it may seem to you that your partner is acting in an unloving fashion, **your partner and only your partner knows** if he loves you. Again, you may feel unloved, but that doesn't mean that he doesn't love you.

> *Only your partner knows for sure if he loves you.*

"The love in your heart isn't put there to stay; love isn't love till you give it away." This is a statement that encourages us to put our loving feelings into action. And it is important to find many ways to be loving toward your partner. However, love is in the eyes of the beholder. If it isn't "given away" according to the expectations of another person, that doesn't mean that "love isn't love." No matter how you act, no one can speak for you regarding whether or not you have loving feelings in your heart. **Nonetheless, those feelings need to be translated into loving behavior that is felt by your partner.** While that loving behavior may not bridge all of the differences, it creates a wonderful climate in which to try to build the bridges for those differences.

> ## Translate your loving feelings into loving behavior.

Making the assumption that your partner doesn't love you will only make you and your partner feel worse. On the other hand, if you are feeling neglected, it is important to let your partner know how you feel and why. By talking about this without the accusation that she doesn't love you, together you will be more able to work on your difficulty and seek a solution.

Sometimes, when we don't feel like our partner loves us, it is because our own feelings of love are fading and we just don't want to admit it to ourselves. This is sometimes called *projection;* that is, the feelings that one person is having are being projected onto the other person. If you are thinking that your partner doesn't love you, ask yourself if your own feelings of love for your partner are beginning to fade. If that is the case, this is a serious problem— one that you want to discuss with your partner right away. Sometimes by going through the exercise below and having some understanding and compassion for why your partner doesn't meet some of your needs, your loving feelings towards your partner can be restored.

In addition to not assuming that your partner doesn't love you, you also don't want to turn your partner's shortcomings into sins. That will be the next section.

- *Feeling* unloved and *being* unloved are two different things.
- *When needs are unmet, there are usually good explanations that aren't about love.*
- *Only your partner knows for sure if he loves you.*
- *Translate your loving feelings into loving behavior.*

RULE

#40   Don't blame "lack of love" for not getting what you want.

EXERCISES ON NOT GETTING YOUR NEEDS MET— DON'T BLAME LOVE:

1. Review the Preliminary Exercise.

2. Spend at least twenty minutes with your partner sharing your Preliminary Exercise. Make sure that your partner really understands what you are talking about.

3. Ask for your partner's perspective on why she doesn't fill your need. Your partner needs to frame her explanation in terms of her own limitations or difficulties (look at the list above for examples) and *not* in terms of the quality of your need. (Examples of things *not* to say: "You're just too demanding;" "Your standards are too high;" "You're a bottomless pit when it comes to that.") Write it down.

4. After you meet with your partner, spend some time by yourself and compare his explanation about why he has been unable to meet your need to the ones you wrote down originally. See what you can learn from that.

5. Spend a little time by yourself and think again about your partner's unmet needs that were presented to you, and how you explained your inability to meet those needs to him. Write down these explanations that you gave to see if you can think of any other reasons why you have been unable to meet his needs.

6. After a couple of days, spend at least another twenty minutes with your partner reviewing the same lists of unmet needs. Discuss any that you didn't have time to discuss in the previous session. Add further explanations that you thought about in the time you spent by yourself. Write down new information.

7. Spend a little more time by yourself and review again all of your notes from this exercise. See if you clearly understand that the reasons why your partner has been unable to meet your need. Does it seem to you that her explanation has anything to do with whether or not she loves you? Do you feel like you have clearly communicated your reasons for not being able to meet her needs?

RULE #41: **Don't turn your partner's shortcomings into sins.**

Rule 15 is "Don't turn *your* shortcomings into sins." This Rule is about *your partner's* shortcomings. *Shortcoming* is defined in a relative sense here; that is, the inability of your partner to satisfy your need. For example:

- Jason and Louise have below average intelligence and are married. *They do not* have a "shortcoming" relative to each other, even though *they do* relative to the world at large.

- Margaret has excellent executive functions, or self-management skills, and Steve's skills are average. Relative to the world, Steve does fine. Relative to each other, they have a problem. Steve's standards for domestic tasks are lower than Margaret's. On occasion, Steve abandons a task partway through, fully intending to return to it later. Margaret feels neglected or uncared for as a result. She characterizes Steve as lazy, incompetent and a slob.

> *Try to develop some understanding and compassion about your partner's shortcomings.*

While there are ways to resolve these problems and other differences, **acknowledge your partner's shortcomings as just that and try to not characterize him as "bad" for having the shortcomings that he does.** If you get historical data on a bothersome behavior pattern of your partner, you may find that this has been a pattern for his whole life. The fact is, most people want to do their best, and they don't want others to be upset with them. People with shortcomings have to work hard, given the level of the difficulty, particularly when there is a developmental history. Some behavior patterns are in the nature of the individual and some behavior patterns have been habituated over time and may be very difficult to change.

What about being a hard worker? If someone is not a very hard worker relative to her partner, can that be considered a shortcoming? **We are not all born with the same ability to be industrious.** It is not only a matter of willpower. Some people can work an eight-hour day and have a lot of energy left over for more work. On the other hand, some people work eight hours and have nothing left. Sure, there are other factors, like having enough sleep and eating properly, but it isn't just a matter of "trying harder." Some people just have more trouble finding the energy. Some people are good sleepers and feel refreshed in the morning, while others can be in bed the same number of hours and awake feeling sluggish. This is not to say that we shouldn't try to "push ourselves" to do better. Most of this book is about pushing yourself in one way or another for self-improvement. This is simply to say that some people have an easier time than others at working hard.

> ### *Don't assume that everyone has the same ability to work hard and complete tasks.*

Even "pushing oneself" comes easier to some and is more difficult for others. We don't all have the same amount of willpower. We certainly don't all have the same ability to be self-disciplined. Some people can set out with goals in mind, and before you know it, they are accomplishing their goals—while others get distracted more easily or have difficulty even getting started. Some people can delay gratification more easily or persevere longer, while others have difficulty with both. If you are the one that has the easier time, it might seem like it is just a matter of your partner trying a little harder, but it just isn't that simple.

> ### *Don't assume that everyone has the same amount of willpower.*

How about addictive tendencies or depression? Again, if you don't have a tendency toward addiction, you may not know what it feels like to have cravings or how hard it is to turn off an obsession. And if you have never been depressed, you may not understand how someone's brain can tell her that she has a good life yet she still feels like she doesn't.

> ### *Acknowledge innate aspects of depression and addiction.*

These are many types of human frailties, and your partner may have some of them. Some of these frailties may contribute to your relational difficulties. **If you find yourself becoming impatient with your partner because of his limitations, try to remember that we are all human and we all have flaws and foibles.** It is understandable that you may be frustrated at times. Nonetheless, **try to take a non-condemning approach to your partner's shortcomings, and**

work together with him to create the best compensatory solutions for the two of you. Boundaries and structures may have to be set in place for things to work out. You may have solutions available that you have not thought of because you have been so frustrated. Try to do whatever you can to be in touch with your loving feelings towards your partner in spite of his shortcomings. At times this may seem like a very tall order, but it is one that is worth the effort.

- *Try to develop some understanding and compassion about your partner's shortcomings.*
- *Don't assume that everyone has the same ability to work hard and complete tasks.*
- *Don't assume that everyone has the same amount of willpower.*
- *Acknowledge innate aspects of depression and addiction.*

EXERCISES FOR NOT TURNING YOUR PARTNER'S SHORTCOMINGS INTO SINS:

1. Spend some time by yourself and review the explanations that you wrote for not meeting your partner's needs in the previous section. Think about your explanations and do some further introspection about these explanations. Think in developmental/historical terms about your explanation. Think about how your past may be tied to a personality characteristic. Think about how your past might be tied to changes in the circumstances of your life. Think about how your past might be tied to changes in your body. Write down your thinking, so you can it share it with your partner. Try to not be judgmental of yourself as you think about your explanations.

2. Spend at least twenty minutes with your partner sharing your notes on his unmet needs. Your partner will select a need that he has that is not being met from his list of five unmet needs. Offer your explanation in greater detail than you did previously. Your partner can ask you questions to further understand your explanation. These questions will *not* carry a hidden message of disapproval. They will only be for the purpose of understanding your explanation better. Good listening skills will be used. Your partner will take notes.

3. Spend time by yourself reviewing the notes from the previous session with your partner. Think further about what your partner has explained to you. Use your skills of compassion and caring to try to understand your partner's explanations. Use empathy and put yourself in her shoes. Try to understand what it would be like to be unable to meet the need you presented and the explanation she gave you. Next to the notes that you have taken on your partner's explanations, write these words, *Concerning this explanation, I believe that my partner feels* _____, and fill in the blank. Spend some time reflecting on the feelings that you think your partner has regarding this.

4. If the two of you have not had enough time to complete all five of the needs that you have listed, spend additional sessions with each other repeating the steps above.

RULE #42: What's good for the goose may not be what's good for the gander.

We are all different and we all have different needs, wants and desires. Because of these differences, couples may have division of labor differences, different responsibilities, different leisure activities, different ways in which they show caring, different sleep habits, etc. Often couples have no conflicts about these differences even though, technically speaking, they are double standards. In fact, rigid equality rarely exists in partnerships. Unequal distributions (double standards) may evolve or may be negotiated. Couples figure out what works for their relationship. Some things lend themselves more readily to unequal distribution.

Equality may make sense for things such as discretionary spending, time spent walking the dog, or time spent on leisure activities. But it is a matter of negotiation based on feelings and individual needs, wants and desires. Generalities like "What's good for the goose is good for the gander" or, "You have double standards" tend to cloud the issue and lead to dead-end conversations.

> *Equality is not a given in relationships. There are many more inequalities than equalities.*

Often we argue for what we want by pushing the *fairness* button.

- "It isn't *fair* that I have to get up with the baby."
- "It isn't *fair* that I have to work all day and you get to stay home with the kids."

It is not likely that the person listening to those statements is going to say:

- "Oh, not fair. Sure, I'll get up with the baby."
- "I'll go get a job myself."

"It's not fair" is the cry of the victim saying, "You're taking advantage of me." At best, it says, "This feels like an unequal distribution and I don't like it." Using the words *not fair* implies that somebody did something wrong. Arguing about whether or not something is "fair" in relationships is usually a ridiculous, go-nowhere argument. "It's not fair" typically doesn't explain feelings behind wanting redistribution. It may take more effort to think about how to express feelings, but the resulting understanding is well worth that effort. If it feels unfair, explain why it feels that way. It will make a big difference in resolving problems. For example, perhaps parents can say:

- "You know, I am really exhausted with getting up with the baby every night. I'm really struggling, and I'd like to see if there is some way I can get some relief. I know you have to get up for work in the morning, but I'd like to just go over our schedule to see if there is any way we could do things differently."

- "You know, being the sole provider for this family is really hard on me. I feel so responsible and guilty. I feel like I don't have any time to do anything but work, eat and go to bed. I really would like to talk about the possibility of doing this differently than we do now."

Slow down on pushing the "It's not fair" button.
Instead, explain how you feel.

In both of these cases, using the expression "What's good for the goose is good for the gander" or some facsimile is not likely to resolve the issue.

- **Equality is not a given in relationships. There are many more inequalities than equalities.**

- **Slow down on pushing the "It's not fair" button. Instead, explain how you feel.**

EXERCISES FOR NOT USING THE "GOOSE OR THE GANDER" EXPRESSIONS:

1. Spend some time with your partner talking about this Rule. Talk about whether the two of you use "goose or gander" type arguments with each other. Talk about whether you use expressions like *double standards or fairness* when you are upset about something. Talk about the kinds of situations in which this expression has been used.

2. Write a list that designates areas of concern where you can agree that equality is required and a list that designates areas of concern where you can agree that equality is not required.

3. If you determine that either of you use expressions about fairness when you both agree that it is not appropriate, discuss other ways you can express your feelings without using terms like *fairness* or *What's good for the goose is good for the gander.*

RULE #43: **Give and receive feedback without condemnation.**

This Rule has been left for last in Chapter III because by mastering previous Rules, giving and receiving feedback will be easier. **Giving and receiving negative feedback and complaints is essential for growth in relationships.** In primary relationships, our behavior is rarely (perhaps never) *completely* acceptable to our partner. Consequently, from time to time, we are going to ask our partner to change her behavior. This is typically done by giving feedback, complaining or making a request for change. This can be difficult both on the giving and receiving end. In fact, **this is one of the greatest sources of conflict in all relationships, personal or work-related.**

DIFFICULTIES ASSOCIATED WITH GIVING AND RECEIVING NEGATIVE FEEDBACK

We are exposed to negative feedback starting at a very early age and continuing throughout the developmental period. This feedback is critical to our survival and our ability to adapt to a complex social world. It is on the basis of these early childhood experiences that we develop our patterns of responsiveness to feedback. **Several elements can contribute to making feedback difficult to give and receive:**

1. *Arousal.* When children behave in ways that parents considers unacceptable, the parents often get upset or angry. When parents get upset, children usually also get aroused by becoming alert, cautious and maybe fearful. It is physiological and it has consistency throughout the world. Typically, the more arousal there is from parents, the more arousal there is in children.

2. *Judgment.* Parents often tell children how to behave by emphasizing what they consider to be proper behavior, what is good and bad, right and wrong.

The combination of parental arousal and judgment is powerful for children and the internal response that a child develops to this combination of behavior can last a lifetime.

When children are parented well, arousal in a parent may signal a need for greater attentiveness, not fear. Being scolded alerts the child to modify a specific behavior, rather than indicating that, as a person, he is wholly unacceptable. **Unfortunately, many children grow into adulthood fearing the arousal associated with feedback, and they think that they are, in fact, wholly unacceptable when they hear a complaint. Their typical response at both the physiological and psychological levels is thus defensiveness.** His body gets tight and becomes consumed with issues of safety, and his mind wants to shut out what feels like condemning thoughts or statements. It may be difficult to distinguish between his partner's statements and the self-deprecating thoughts that her statements provoke.

> *The internal and external response to perceived arousal and judgment is often defensiveness.*

3. *The assumption of blame* is a third element that can make feedback difficult. That is, if Jane is bothered by something that John did, then John is to blame for bothering Jane. This is a very common assumption, perhaps one of the most common assumptions when negative feedback is given. Both partners often buy into this assumption, thus setting into motion frequent and active defensive patterns, particularly denial. **When judgment gets into the mix, it can feel like condemnation, and John feels blamed for having done something bad.** And if Jane is particularly upset, John might react with yelling or withdraw because he's upset, too.

> *Three elements of negative feedback that can make it difficult:*
> 1. *Arousal*
> 2. *Judgment*
> 3. *Blame*

THE ASSUMPTION OF BLAME, CAUSALITY, AND RESPONSIBILITY

The attribution of causality or blame is central to many disruptions in human relations. Defensiveness can easily escalate in a climate of blame and incrimination that puts couples into a tailspin. When sorting out blame and "responsibility," the person who initiates the feedback needs to take responsibility for his sensitivities. The person on the receiving side of the feedback needs to take responsibility for her behavior that was the trigger. **When one partner is bothered by the other's behavior, sometime one is to blame because of his behavior and sometime the other is to blame because of her sensitivities — and most of the time it is a combination of both behavior and sensitivity.** If it is generally assumed that the person receiving the feedback is in the wrong, that partner is going to be reluctant to hear it. On the other hand, if there isn't a preconceived idea about who's to blame, it will go much better.

- If Jane is upset with John because he said he was going to pick up dinner for the family on the way home and he is late and forgets, Jane's upset is mostly his fault.

- However, if Jane is so upset with John that she starts breaking dishes, she needs to be responsible for her overreaction, even though John has to be responsible for not bringing home the dinner.

- If John brings home dinner with the wrong salad dressing and Jane is so mad that she doesn't speak to him for two days, Jane has to take the lion's share of the responsibility for her overreaction. While it is true that the John's behavior served as a stimulus for Jane's response, it is not the same thing as causing her response.

The objective in human relations work is to promote change on *both* sides of the stimulus response chain, so that the interaction improves (Related Rules: 10, "Don't be a victim- Appendix," 9, "Accept uncertainty," and 36, "Relative right and wrong").

> *When one person is upset by another person's behavior, usuallyboth parties need to be responsible for their contribution to the difficulty.*

GIVING NEGATIVE FEEDBACK

Negative feedback can be difficult to hear for all of the reasons stated above: arousal, judgment and blame. So when you give negative feedback, it is important to do it in ways that make it easier on the your partner. (See adjunct discussions of this topic in Chapter IV "Conflict resolution.") When giving negative feedback:

1. **Talk about the impact of your partner's behavior without being judgmental.**

2. **Be non-accusatory and use "I" language.**

3. **Have a calm voice.**

1. **Having a non-accusatory attitude for giving negative feedback begins with trying to understand your own sensitivities to the other person's behavior.** This is a tall order and it takes a lot of practice. It means driving your understanding deeper than "what they did makes me mad." Other possible helpful thoughts are:

- *I know that I'm sensitive about things like this.*

- *I'm sure that she didn't know that would upset me.*

- *I've had trouble getting used to that behavior in my partner.*

- *This isn't something we have ever discussed.*

- *We don't have a mutual understanding about this.*

- *I know that I am more upset than I want to be about this.*

- *Maybe I'm just in a bad mood.*

- *I know that I won't feel so upset in the morning.*

- *This kind of thing has bothered me ever since I was little.*

- *I think I feel this way mostly because of how I was treated by someone else.*

- *I think that I'm mostly upset because I don't feel very good about myself.*

All of these thoughts make the assumption that there is a relationship between what bothers you about someone else's behavior and your *own* set of needs, desires, sensitivities and patterns of reactivity. It may be helpful to think, *If I didn't have my particular sensitivities, I probably wouldn't be bothered by what the other person is doing.* It is also helpful to understand that your particular sensitivities are not necessarily universal or correct, but that they are important to you. You may or may not be able to change them. It helps to recognize that when you are in a relationship and you are upset, part of the problem rests with you and part of the problem rests with what your partner is doing; **by lodging a complaint, you are just opening a dialogue in an effort to create some resolution.**

> ## *Develop a non-blaming attitude before giving negative feedback.*

2. **Use non-judgmental language when giving negative feedback.** Try to think about your partner's behavior in terms of the impact it has had on you, and not in terms of what is right and wrong or good and bad (see Rule 36, "Relative right and wrong). If you use "I" language when you give negative feedback it is much more likely to go well (see Rule 39, "I language").

> ## *Use non-judgmental language.*

3. **Using a non-accusatory and non-judgmental attitude makes it much easier to start giving negative feedback in a calm voice.** Starting in a calm voice can make a big difference in how well your feedback will be received. He will likely be less defensive, which will make it easier for him to understand your feelings and take responsibility for his own behavior. (Refer to Rule 50, "Start by calmly stating the problem.")

> ## *Calmly introduce your concern.*

THE SMALLEST UNIT OF BEHAVIOR

When you want to talk to your partner about something she did that is bothering you, it helps to keep your focus on **the smallest unit of their behavior** while still giving pertinent feedback. This is called ***containment.***

1. **Situation-specific behavior** is typically the smallest unit of behavior. Some negative aspect of your partner's character or a pattern of behavior is not the smallest unit of behavior. For example:

- "I'm upset that you didn't do the dishes tonight."

    vs.

- "You never do the dishes," or

- "You never pick up after yourself," or

- "You don't care about helping me, do you?"

2. Behavior that has occurred several times in similar situations is the next smallest unit of behavior. Even if it is something that your partner has done before, it is helpful to talk about the most recent occurrence of that behavior. Later you can mention that it isn't the first time.

- "I'm upset that you didn't do the dishes. I'm more upset tonight because it seems like you haven't been doing the dishes hardly at all lately."

3. A pattern of behavior is the next smallest unit of behavior. This is behavior that has occurred repeatedly and in a variety of situations. This is the most difficult to discuss because patterns of behavior *do* begin to define character. So when giving negative feedback about patterns of behavior stay away from negative judgments and be mindful of how the feedback may be received.

- "I'm upset that you didn't do the dishes tonight like you agreed to. I'm particularly having a hard time with this because you have repeatedly agreed to help clean up the kitchen, and I have ended up doing all the work."

  vs.

- "You are incredibly irresponsible and a liar. You have repeatedly told me you were going to help in the kitchen, and I'm left holding the bag. The only person you care about is yourself."

More often than not you will have the best success in giving feedback if you can contain the feedback by keeping it situation-specific. Even if it has occurred more than once or it is a pattern of behavior, start by talking about the event that is most recent. It will be less difficult for your partner. If you can come to some understanding regarding the most recent event, it will be easier to then talk about other past occurrences of that behavior.

> *Use the smallest unit of behavior possible when giving*
> *negative feedback.*

When you give negative feedback, it is useful to begin with an **optimistic attitude:**

- Giving feedback is important to the wellbeing of your relationship, and this begins a process that is necessary for achieving resolutions of difficulties.

- You understand that while this may be difficult, it is important.

- You understand that while there are times when you might be unable to reach an early resolution of some difficulty, you have to start trying at some point. Resolutions often take a little time.

- You know that even if you don't reach an easy resolution, adaptation and acceptance are more easily achieved when you talk things over.

- Not resolving something important may bring up a number of hard feelings; however, it is important to not put the cart before the horse and assume the problem can't be solved until adequate effort is made.

Guard against having a defeatist attitude, otherwise the anticipated negative feelings may become so intense that you can't even get into the topic with your partner without a huge degree of agitation.

RECEIVING NEGATIVE FEEDBACK

When you are on the **receiving** end of negative feedback, attend to the same three elements: arousal, judgment and blame.

1. **Take responsibility for your behavior, but not your partner's sensitivities.**

2. **Listen for the impact of your behavior on your partner and don't judge yourself.**

3. **Listen calmly and non-defensively.**

1. **It is helpful to have the same assumption that you have in giving negative feedback; i.e., there is a relationship between your behavior and your partner's set of needs, desires, sensitivities and patterns of reactivity.** The problem your partner has presented to you is a two-way street that depends both on her needs and sensitivities and how you triggered her sensitivities or didn't meet her needs. Some thoughts that might help establish a positive attitude are:

- *This isn't all about me.*

- *I really have to think about both sides here; what I did and how she feels.*

- *If there is something here for me to learn, then that is what I want to do.*

- *I need to take responsibility for what I do.*

- *This is just a conversation not an indictment.*

- *I know that it is important that we talk about our problems.*

- *I'm confident our problems are solvable by one or both of us engaging in some sort of behavioral or attitudinal change.*

- *I'm not going to let myself get all jacked out of shape until we really talk things over.*

- *I know that sometimes we will have to talk over the same problem several times.*

> ### Your partner's negative feedback is a two-way street when it comes to blame.

2. **It is important that you recognize most of the time neither party has some moral high ground regarding what your partner is upset about.** Your job isn't about defending the rightness or wrongness of what you did. It is first about understanding all of your partner's feelings that are associated with his complaint. You can understand your partner's feelings even when you are uncertain about your contribution as a trigger for those feelings. Even if he slips and begins to talk about the problem in moral terms, it is possible to reframe the problem in your own mind.

- *I don't have to feel like a bad person because of this complaint.*

- *My partner is not my parent telling me that I have done something wrong.*

- *I am a grownup now and I get to decide for myself what is right and what is wrong.*

- *I can hear that what I did upset my partner and that is what is most important.*

- *While it may not bother everyone, it did bother my partner.*

> ### Your behavior can be wrong for your partner without being wrong.

3. Listening to negative feedback calmly and non-defensively might be hard to do but you must learn how to do it if you are ever going to be successful in your relationships. Having a good attitude will help, as you won't get overly hooked by your partner's judgments of you or your own judgments of yourself. Recognize the two-way street when it comes to blame and responsibility. It might be harder to keep yourself calm if your partner is not relatively calm, try nonetheless. You might be physiologically activated particularly if your partner

is highly aroused. Thus, previous practice with meditation or other relaxation or calming techniques may be helpful. If you get too agitated, you will have a hard time listening and an even harder time responding calmly.

Even if your partner is calm when she is giving you feedback, you might become agitated. It will help you to remain calm if you make a very concerted effort to first understand the impact of your behavior on your partner. **If you direct yourself towards that level of understanding and have an attitude of curiosity, it will be easier to listen without reacting.** At the first awareness of your own reactions, calm yourself by asking your partner a question to further understand what she is talking about. This practice of active listening will help you to remain calm by reducing the possibility of being triggered into an old pattern of reactivity. It will help you to stay present, stay in the cognitive domain by engaging your intellect, and hopefully activate empathy as you engage with your partner's feelings. You can think:

- *I want to know what my partner thinks and feels.*
- *I feel bad that she is upset.*
- *I'm not going to let myself get all jacked out of shape before I even know what my partner is upset about.*
- *This doesn't have to be the last word on the subject. We can talk about it again later.*

> *Have an attitude of interest and concern regarding your partner's feedback.*

There is one more attitude that will help you in both giving and receiving negative feedback. That is an attitude of *caring*—remembering and acting throughout the conversation that you love your partner and he loves you.

- You don't want him to feel awful, so do your best to speak kindly.
- You want to be constructive, not destructive.
- You want to solve problems, not create new ones.
- You want to show caring for what is important to him.
- You want him to know that you understand his concern, even though it might be a difficult situation for you as well.
- You want him to know that his position matters to you.

- You want him to feel your care, even though you may be finding it difficult to immediately apologize or find a solution.

- Caring can be in the room even when there is conflict. When you are caring you:

- Don't try to dominate the conversation by spending time just stating and restating your position;

- Spend time showing understanding of your partner's position;

- Use controlled voices that aren't too loud;

- Use "I" language;

- Don't make demeaning accusations;

- Don't go "nuclear" on either the giving or receiving end;

- You aren't in "battle mode;"

- You are in "owning-up mode;" "negotiation mode" or "let's-make-a-deal mode."

This caring is not just directed outwardly but it is also inward. That is important for reducing defensiveness. This overall attitude of caring tends to make the giving and receiving of negative feedback much easier and can eliminate the experience of being in a fight. Moving through the process successfully helps create intimacy, and doing it well one time makes it easier to do it well the next time.

> *Have an attitude of caring when giving and receiving negative feedback.*

1. *Several elements can contribute to making feedback difficult to give and receive: **arousal, judgment,** and **blame**.*

2. *The internal and external response to perceived arousal and judgments is often defensiveness.*

3. *When one person is upset by another person's behavior, both parties need to be responsible for their contribution to the difficulty.*

4. *When giving negative feedback:*
    - *Have a calm voice (arousal).*
    - *Calmly introduce your concern.*
    - *Talk about how the other person's behavior has impacted you without being judgmental of them (judgment).*
    - *Use non-judgmental language.*
    - *Be non-accusatory and use "I" language (blame).*
    - *Develop a non-blaming attitude before giving negative feedback.*

5. *Try using the smallest unit of behavior possible when giving negative feedback.*

6. *When receiving negative feedback:*
    - *Listen calmly and non-defensively.*
    - *Have an attitude of interest and concern regarding your partner's feedback.*
    - *Listen for the impact of your behavior on your partner and don't judge yourself.*
    - *Your behavior can be wrong for your partner without being wrong.*
    - *Take responsibility for your behavior but not your partner's sensitivities.*
    - *Your partner's negative feedback is a two-way street when it comes to blame.*

7. *Have an attitude of caring when giving and receiving negative feedback.*

EXERCISES FOR GIVING AND RECEIVING NEGATIVE FEEDBACK:

1. Write down the three elements that can make giving and receiving feedback difficult.

2. Write down five things that your partner has done in the past few weeks that upset you. For each one give a rating:

    a. How upset am I about it? (ten being very upset; one not upset.)

    b. Do I think what she did was wrong? (ten being very wrong; one not wrong.)

    c. Do I blame her for how I feel? (ten being all her fault; one all my fault.)

3. Review the concept of responsibility and how our sensitivities can be as important as our behavior. See if by making attribution to your own sensitivities you can modify your answer to 2c. If so, write down the thinking that helped.

4. Review Rule 9, "Accept uncertainty," and Rule 36, "Relative right and wrong." Review the self-statements in this section that pertain to judgment. See if any of that modifies your answer to 2b. If so, write down the thinking that helped.

5. Did Exercise 3 or 4 help modify your answer to 2a? If so, write down the new rating.

6. Review the concept of *containment* and *smallest unit of behavior.* Review the five things that your partner did and, if necessary, rewrite them in terms of the smallest unit of behavior.

7. Write down your positive and negative thoughts about giving and receiving negative feedback with your partner. Do you think that you have an optimistic attitude?

8. Rate yourself on a scale from one to ten on how well you receive negative feedback, (one being poorly and ten being excellent). Write down what you can do better.

9. Rate yourself on a scale of one to ten regarding how well you give negative feedback, (one being poorly and ten being excellent). Write down what you can do better.

10. Review these exercises with your partner.

Section IV
Conflict Resolution, Problem-solving, and Negotiation

Introduction

Many people hear the term *conflict* and they become concerned. To them, conflict means a fight, raised voices, high tension, lots of intensity and winners and losers. In the context of this book, the term *conflict* does not mean a fight, something violent or something volatile that requires a winner or loser to resolve. *Conflict* is a strong disagreement and *conflict resolution* is similar to *problem-solving* or *negotiation,* but with more passion and stronger feelings. The more important the topics of disagreement and the greater the differences of opinion, the more difficult the conflict is to resolve. Like so many other psychological and human relations topics, conflict and problem-solving are on a continuum from neutral to passion-filled, and from easy to difficult.

This section is written to discuss how to negotiate, problem-solve and have healthy conflicts. It is a difficult subject, and it is one of the most common problems that people say they have when they come to see me with relationship difficulties. What they often say is, "We are having communication difficulties." The problem they describe is about communication, but not communication problems alone. Typically the problem is about not knowing how to deal with conflict in general. Because this is a pervasive problem that causes such disruption in relationships, it is important to give it substantial attention. Most of the previous Rules are important either directly or indirectly for creating a good climate for solving problems. Hopefully, by practicing these remaining Rules, you can improve your ability to negotiate, solve problems and deal with conflict in a healthy fashion, while avoiding some of the most common pitfalls.

This section of the book will primarily address "process" issues; that is the "how-to" of problem-solving, negotiation and conflict resolution. However, at the end of this section, I will introduce two topics that are primarily about *content* and not *process* that commonly create conflict—finances and division of labor issues. By practicing all of the previous Rules in this section, resolution of differences regarding these two topics will be easier.

RULE #44: **Don't avoid healthy conflict.**

Far too many couples end up leading separate lives because they are so conflict-avoidant. When they think that they are going to disagree with their partners, they are filled with dread. They fear activating their partners' disapproval, starting a fight, provoking anger or just creating tension. So they find ways to "do their own thing" without making waves. They learn that to "go along" is to "get along." And it often works, at first. Couples who practice this avoidant method often report with some sense of pride that they "never fight." **However, over time, conflict-avoidant people may discover that they don't feel very close to each other and that they have developed deep pockets of resentment over festering problems.** What once was pride turns into disdain.

Perhaps during an era when roles were more clearly defined, it may have been easier for couples to operate successfully by avoiding conflict. But as our society has evolved, with over 50 percent of the workforce being woman and with dads spending increasingly more time with their children, these roles are not so clearly defined. Couples find that they have to talk over things like division of labor, how money is spent, and what methods of discipline will be used with the children. Ours is also a much more mobile society, with couples moving frequently from house to house and town to town. Relocation is a stressful process for families, requiring more communication. The stability associated with being born and staying put in one place is no longer common for many people. And the days of job stability and the twenty-five-year gold watch are long since gone as well. The economy adds further stressors. Unemployment unleashes social psychological unrest of gigantic proportions. The increasing climatic volatility also creates less stability, more challenges, and catastrophic events that weigh on our psyches. All of these changes in our society, our culture and our earthly presence create greater emotional unrest that demand increased conversation and problem-solving. "I don't want to talk about it" only leads to increased stress. Learning how to be a good communicator has never been more important for couples. Learning the skills of problem-solving has become essential. Avoiding discussions around common domestic and partnership issues is no longer an option.

EXERCISE FOR NOT AVOIDING HEALTHY CONFLICT:

Spend some time with your partner. Talk about whether either one of you or both of you avoid conflict. If you do, see if you can come up with some of the reasons why. Write them down.

RULE #45: **Learn to negotiate.**

The term *negotiate* has been used increasingly over the past number of years in the fields of social psychology and human relations, while previously it was used primarily in the fields of business and politics. In the context of human relations, it simply connotes **a constructive process for reconciling differences.** There are some connotations to the word *negotiate* that are important for couples, like *orderliness, civility* and *having manners.* These concepts will be discussed in detail below.

One of the biggest problems regarding negotiation is that people don't do enough of it. So often, partners withhold their feelings of dissatisfaction or concern, letting them build over a long period of time. By the time they begin to talk, they have such a head of steam that it makes orderliness and civility that much more difficult. Sometimes they wait so long that good feelings for one another vanish completely. **Both parties in a relationship need to use their voices and begin the process of negotiation. Having a good tool for negotiating increases the willingness to use it.**

> *Speak up and begin the process.*

Orderliness **means proceeding forward in a step-by-step fashion,** such as the steps described in Rule 46, "Have a road map for problem-solving." Negotiation often begins with planning and preparation. That means thinking about what to say and how to say it before actually talking. Orderliness also means having rules for negotiating. For example:

- Each party gets a "turn" to speak.
- When it is one person's turn to speak, the other person listens.
- Neither party gets to take too long of a "turn."

Orderliness can also mean putting thoughts in writing. It can help you remember what you want to say, particularly if you get anxious. Taking notes during a conversation can help to remember what was said. Writing down agreements can help create accountability. Writing things down should not be used as a weapon against your partner at a later time. It is for organizing thoughts, remembering and keeping track of what has been said.

- You can write an agenda.
- You can write down what you want to say.
- You can write down what your partner says.

You might think that this is a bit formal to actually be writing things down or planning what you are going to say—and I agree it is. Certainly such a formal process would be inappropriate for many of the decision that we have to make on a daily basis. However, when a thorny topic is being discussed, a more formal process may be helpful for negotiating successfully.

> *Be orderly when you are negotiating:*
> - *Each party gets a "turn" to speak.*
> - *When it is one person's turn to speak, the other person listens.*
> - *Neither party gets to take too long of a "turn."*
> - *Write things down if necessary.*

Manners are also a very important part of negotiation, for example:

- Be polite to your partner.
- Use tones of voice that are not too intense or loud.
- Don't interrupt when your partner is speaking.
- Have an appropriate physical space between you and your partner.
- Don't cross over into his space.
- Don't make threatening gestures.
- Don't name call or swear.
- Rebut only your partner's ideas.
- Don't belittle her ideas.
- Don't attack your partner's character.
- Take the time to really understand your partner's point of view.
- Enter into the negotiation with a sense of good-will.

All of these manners are important for having a good conversation, and all are regularly (but not always) used in the business arena. If we can have manners in one place, we can have manners in another, even if it takes effort. We spend much of our childhood learning manners and how to act with civility in many different social settings. It is important to apply all of this learning when solving problems at an intimate level. If, for some reason, some of these acts of civility were not learned in childhood, they can be learned now.

The goal of negotiation is mutual understanding. Sometimes mutual understanding is achieved by just acknowledging each other's point of view. More often than not, it is achieved by making a joint decision. To make joint decisions well, you have to have the attitude that **if the decision that you reach isn't good for your partner, it isn't good for you, and vice versa. That requires that both you and your partner know your limitations and boundaries.** There is a difference between changing a boundary and exceeding a boundary. It is possible that you may have thought that you needed a decision to go one way, but after considering or trying other options, another direction turned out to be okay. In that case, you changed a boundary. On the other hand, after considering or trying other options, the new direction may continue to feel unacceptable. In that case, you are exceeding your boundary.

> *Be aware of your true limitations/boundaries when you are negotiating.*

When a decision is good for both parties, it is sometimes called a **win-win decision.** Negotiating for a win-win means that when there is a compromise, both parties have a sense of balance regarding what they have given up and neither party has exceeded his boundaries. However, if a boundary has been exceeded or the balance is very uneven, it is no longer a win-win compromise; it is a *win-lose* compromise. Win-lose compromises build resentment over time. And the follow-through on win-lose compromises is not nearly as good as follow-through on win-win compromises. The "losing" party rarely feels very good about the process of negotiation and she will be hesitant about trying to work things out in the future for fear of being on the losing side again. On the other hand, win-win feels good and encourages future negotiation. Often, a win-win can be reached without either party having to give up too much.

> ## Create win-win decisions.

When both parties use their creative thinking, they might find that there are solutions "outside the box" that they hadn't considered, which solve the problem without requiring compromise. These types of solutions are sometimes called *synergistic.* When this happens, it can be surprising and it feels great. It can occur when both parties are listening to each other, acknowledging each other's feelings and thoughts, and working hard to arrive at a solution or decision that is good for the "we" and not just the "me." It gives wonderful definition to the concept of *partnership.*

Jane has been home all day and wants to go out for dinner. John has been on the road for the past three days and has been eating at restaurants every night. He was really looking for a home-cooked meal. After talking about it, Jane and John decide to go on a picnic and that solves the problem for both of them.

> ## Seek synergistic solutions.

- *Speak up and begin the process.*
- *Be orderly when you are negotiating:*
    - *Each party gets a "turn" to speak.*
    - *When it is one person's turn to speak, the other person listens.*
    - *Neither party gets to take too long of a "turn."*
    - *Write things down if necessary.*
- *Have manners:*
    - *Be polite to your partner.*
    - *Use tones of voice that are not too intense or loud.*
    - *Don't interrupt when your partner is speaking.*
    - *Have an appropriate physical space between you and your partner.*
    - *Don't cross over into his space.*
    - *Don't make threatening gestures.*
    - *Don't name call or swear.*
    - *Rebut only your partner's ideas.*
    - *Don't belittle her ideas.*
    - *Don't attack your partner's character.*
    - *Take the time to really understand your partner's point of view.*
    - *Enter into the negotiation with a sense of good-will.*
- *The goal for negotiation is mutual understanding.*
- *If the decision that you reach isn't good for your partner, it isn't good for you, and vice versa.*
- *Be aware of your true limitations/boundaries when you are negotiating.*
- *Create "win-win" decisions.*
- *Seek synergistic solutions.*

EXERCISES FOR LEARNING TO NEGOTIATE:

1. Spend some time with your partner talking about this Rule. Talk to your partner about the concept of *negotiation*. Talk about whether or not it feels like you and your partner negotiate. Is there a sense of orderliness when you discuss a problem? Do you think you act with civility and have manners?

2. Do you and your partner negotiate with orderliness as described in the text or have other elements of orderliness? Do you ever write down ideas to discuss or your agreements? How do you feel about writing these things down?

3. Look at the list of manners. Do you and your partner observe these? Are there ones that you and your partner need to give special attention? Are there others that need to be added to this list?

4. Have you and your partner ever thought about resolutions as "mutual understandings?" Do you have mutual understandings?

5. Do you and your partner think that your mutual understandings are mostly win-win understandings? When there are compromises, do you think that there is a sense of balance? Do either of you exceed your boundaries just to get along? Do you see a difference between moving your boundaries and exceeding your boundaries?

6. Do you think that any of your current agreements are actually win-lose agreements? Do you think that you need to renegotiate any of these agreements?

7. Talk to your partner about synergistic solutions. Do you and your partner ever have a creative element to your negotiation such that a win-win decision is something neither of you thought of until you started negotiating? Is there anything that you and your partner can do to make this aspect of negotiation stronger?

RULE #46: **Have a road map for problem-solving.**

A road map is always useful in knowing where you are going and how to get there. Having a general sense of the kinds of problems that couples confront and a general strategy for solving those problems will help to lower anxiety and find solutions. This sequence of steps creates a constructive, goal-directed endeavor rather than an out-of-control venting and overreacting argument. Many of the following sections of this book will help to create rules and guidelines for how to be involved in this process of problem-solving more successfully. This section outlines the pathway.

The kinds of problems that couples discuss are quite varied. They include: personal grievances, concerns about interpersonal issues, concerns about partnership issues, plans for the future, and discussions of each others' views on a wide range of subjects from current events to community affairs, sports, what they are watching on TV, to the price of tea in China. Listed below are some of the most common topics of conversation couples have. There may be considerable difference in feelings from one topic to the next. In some cases there will be hurt and angry feelings associated with the topic. In other cases, feelings will be completely neutral. The strength of feeling will likely determine the need for conversation. Here are some of the kinds of problems that couples discuss:

Personal grievances – current:
  Hurt/angry feelings.
  Complaints/Negative Feedback.
  Broken agreements.
  Broken rules.
  Unmet expectations.

Personal grievances – past.

Concerns about interpersonal issues:
  Communication.
  Problem-solving.
  Time together / time apart.
  Shared and unshared interests.

Bothersome patterns of behavior.
Sexuality.

Concerns about partnership issues:
  Co-habitation.
  Family/children.
  Spirituality/religious practices.
  Finances.
  Friends and extended family.
  Employment/jobs.
  Community service.

Planning for the future.

Discussion of world views.

A ROAD MAP FOR PROBLEM-SOLVING

I. Defining the problem:

1. Think about the problem.
2. Present the problem.
3. Acknowledge the presentation.
4. Confirm that there is understanding.
5. Seek or add clarification or additional information.
6. Acknowledge misunderstandings or lack of information.
7. Look for circumstantial non-relational explanations.
8. Acknowledge circumstantial non-relational explanations.
9. Apologize for mistakes.

Problem resolutions
(Steps 1 – 9)

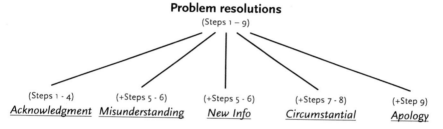

(Steps 1 - 4)	(+Steps 5 - 6)	(+Steps 5 - 6)	(+Steps 7 - 8)	(+Step 9)
Acknowledgment	*Misunderstanding*	*New Info*	*Circumstantial*	*Apology*

10. Agree that there is an unsolved problem.

II. Finding a Solution:

1. Both parties present possible solutions.
2. Both parties discuss the pros and cons.
3. Both parties consider the possible solutions.
4. Both parties make efforts to reach consensus.
5. Compromises are made if necessary.
6. Both parties mutually agree on a solution.
7. Verbal statements are made outlining the agreed-upon solution.

Unresolved Problems
(Steps 1 – 7)

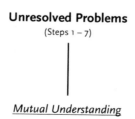

Mutual Understanding

8. If consensus is not reached, the issue is tabled for future discussion.

STEPS FOR PROBLEM-SOLVING.

The following is a sequence of steps for problem-solving. This problem-solving process may take a short time or a long time, depending on the importance and the difficulty of the issue that is being discussed. Some problems lend themselves to quick fixes while others may take repeated conversations over several days or longer. Nonetheless, the process remains about the same.

For the purposes of this presentation, I have used the following designations:

Person who Presents the problem = **P** (Pat).

Person who Responds to the problem = **R** (Ron).

I. Defining the problem:

1. **P thinks about the problem.**
   a. has an "open mind" attitude
   b. develops a verbal script

   Pat: "I'm not sure why Ron is late for dinner but I've been waiting for a half hour. I don't like it and I want to let him know that I don't want him to make a habit of this."

2. **P presents the problem (not the solution) stating thoughts and feelings.**
   a. has a calm attitude
   b. uses "I" language
   c. states her feelings and describes the problem

   Pat: "Ron, I'm upset that you were a half hour late for dinner and I just don't want you to make a habit of this."

3. **R acknowledges the presentation.**
   a. listens with interest and compassion
   b. reflects the presentation
   c. asks for confirmation of his/her reflections

   Ron: "Pat, I understand that you're upset and don't want this to repeat itself."

4. **P confirms understanding** or clarifies the problem if necessary.
   Pat: "Yes, that's right."
   R further acknowledges the problem until there is confirmation by P.
   Ron: "Okay."
   Pat: "Thanks. I just wanted you to hear me."

> # RESOLUTION 1: *P states that she **only wanted acknowledgement** of her thoughts and feelings and thanks R for listening.*

5. R thinks about whether or not there might be a lack of information.
   R seeks additional information if needed.
   Ron: "What time did you think I said I'd be home?"
   P gives additional information if needed.
   Pat: "Six p.m."
   R adds clarification.
   a. has a calm and non-defensive attitude
   b. clarifies misunderstandings should they exist
   c. gives added information
   Ron: "I thought I told you I wouldn't be home till 6:30 because I had a late meeting. Did I just think I told you and didn't?"

6. **P acknowledges a misunderstanding.**
   Pat: "No, you told me. But I thought you said 6:00, not 6:30."
   Ron: "Perhaps it was just a misunderstanding."
   Pat: "I'm okay with that. Let's hurry up and eat. I was going to get together with some friends after dinner."

> # RESOLUTION 2: *Both parties agree that there was a misunderstanding.*

P acknowledges that there was a lack of information.
Ron: "I didn't realize you had plans or I would have tried to be home sooner."
Pat: "I guess I didn't tell you. Let's just hurry up and eat. It will be okay."

> # RESOLUTION 3: *Both parties agree that there was a lack of information.*

7. R suggests a circumstantial or non-relational explanation.
    a. has a calm and non-defensive attitude.
    b. uses "I" language.
    c. suggests a non-relational perspective

Ron: "Honey, it is 6:00 p.m. right now. The clock in the kitchen wasn't reset after the power outage yesterday."

8. **P acknowledges that the problem is circumstantial or non-relational.**
    Pat: "Oh, my mistake. Sorry."

RESOLUTION 4: *Parties agree that it is a circumstantial non-relational problem.*

---

9. **R admits making a mistake and apologizes.**
    Ron: "I know that I messed up and I'm sorry. I realize that I frustrated you and I feel bad I didn't call and just kept you waiting, particularly when you had other plans. Is there anything that I can do make this better?"

    P listens to the apology and accepts it if it feels like it is solving the problem.

    Pat: "I appreciate you apologizing. I'd like you to clean up the kitchen because I need to get going and I'd like you to really try to not be so late in the future."

RESOLUTION 5: *Admit a mistake and apologize.*

These 5 problem resolutions are:

---

1. *Acknowledgement*
2. *Misunderstanding*
3. *New Information*
4. *Circumstantial or Non-relational*
5. *Apology*

If none of them work to resolve the problem, then:

10. **R responds to P's presentation agreeing that they have a problem.**
   a. has a calm and non-defensive attitude
   b. agrees that a problem does exist for the relationship
   c. states his own feelings and gives his perspective

   Ron: "I understand that you are upset that I got home at 6:30 thinking that I would be home at 6:00. And I also understand that you are upset because you have other plans. However, I ran into a very difficult situation at work and I couldn't leave. I really don't see how I could have been home any sooner."

P acknowledges R's reaction:

   Pat: "I understand that you feel like you couldn't have done anything to get home sooner. This just happens way to frequently and I would like to try to figure out a solution."

Both parties continue to discuss thoughts and feelings about the problem as needed and go to the solution phase.

II. Finding a solution for unresolved problems:

1. **Both parties present possible solutions.**

   Pat: "How about you just coming home when you say you are."

   Ron: "That's not always possible because my boss sometimes makes me stay late. How about I just call and let you know?"

2. **Both parties discuss the pros and cons.**

   Pat: "But I'm trying to put dinner on the table. Hearing from you fifteen minutes before you get home doesn't work for me."

   Ron: "Most of the time I know at least an hour in advance if not more. I will call you as soon as I know if I am going to be late."

3. **Both parties consider the possible solutions. (If needed, a break from the discussion is taken.)**

4. **Both parties make efforts to reach consensus.**

5. **Compromises are made if necessary.**

   Pat: "Okay, we can try that but you can't forget. And, you have to agree that you don't come home late just because your work is piling up. And we will have to reevaluate in a month and talk about whether or not your job has too much of a priority over your family."

   Ron: "Okay, I can go along with that; but I may want to discuss how we handle this in our busiest times of the year."

6. **Both parties mutually agree on a solution.**

> Pat: "Okay."
>
> Ron: "Okay."

RESOLUTION 6: *Both parties mutually agree on a solution.*

---

7. **Verbal statements are made outlining the agreed upon solution (with the option of putting it in writing).**

> Pat: "Okay, so our agreement is that you will be home by 6:00 p.m. for dinner unless your boss tells you that you have to stay late in which case you will call me immediately. You're also agreeing to not come home late because your work is piling up. And we will reevaluate how this is all working in a month."
>
> Ron: "I agree."

If consensus is not reached, the issue is tabled for future discussion.

Review the six kinds of resolutions:

1. Acknowledgement only.

2. Both parties agree that there is a misunderstanding.

3. Both parties agree that there was a lack of information.

4. Parties agree that it is a circumstantial non-relational problem.

5. An apology is made.

6. Both parties agree on a solution.

These steps are a guideline and not something to which one has to rigidly adhere. During the discussion of the problem, couples may go back and forth multiple times in an effort to create an understanding of each other's point of view. Acknowledging your partner's thoughts and feelings reduces the need to restate them over and over with increasingly greater intensity. When discussing solutions, try to be open and creative in finding a win-win.

EXERCISES FOR HAVING A ROAD MAP FOR PROBLEM-SOLVING:

1. Make two copies of the graphic in this section for you and your partner to use when you are having a difficult conversation.

2. Spend some time with your partner and review the kinds of problems that couples have. Discuss some of the kinds of problems that you have in your relationship to see if they fall into any of the categories that are listed. If not, make up a new category and add that to the list.

3. With your partner, review the series of steps for problem-solving. Go over them in detail to see if you can both understand the different steps and the different type of problem resolutions. If you want to individualize this series of steps for yourselves, please make additions or subtractions as it suits you.

4. Over the next several months use this graphic as needed when you are talking about something difficult. During any of those conversations you can take a moment to look at the road map to get a better sense as to where you are and to steer yourself back on track.

RULE #47: **Table the conversation if stuck.**

When problems are presented with strong feelings, just getting through the acknowledgement part of problem-solving can be difficult because of the triggering aspect of those strong feelings. Actually, solving the problem when it first comes up may be too much to ask. So couples may need to take a break from the conversation. Many people find that in the heat of the moment they feel defensive and adversarial, but after some reflection, they are more agreeable or willing to compromise. That is why taking a break is often exceedingly useful.

In formal group meetings this is called *tabling the discussion*. Commonly used rules permit a request for tabling to occur at any time, followed immediately by a vote. A simple majority is all that is required to put the discussion on hold. It has long been recognized in group meetings that people can become entrenched or in need of more information and this break then becomes very useful. The same is true for couples. However, for a couple, it only requires the request of one person to table a conversation. **If one person can't continue, the couple can't continue.**

Tabling a conversation and resuming it at a later time can have very positive results. When feelings are strong, our mind can be impacted and our thinking may not be as clear until we are alone. It is not uncommon that problems seem to get resolved much easier a day or two later. Sleeping on it also gives us time to come up with other options and other solutions so that a synergistic outcome may be more easily attained.

Asking to take a break needs to be done with good manners and an effort needs to be made to schedule a time to resume the conversation. Here are some examples of how to say it:

- "Hey, look. I'm getting pretty frazzled here and I don't think I can go on much further in this conversation. Can we take a break and get back to it sometime tomorrow?"
- "I think I need to take a time out. I'm getting overwhelmed. How about let's continue this in a couple of hours."
- "I really don't think that we can continue until we get more information. How about both of us trying to get more information on the subject and get together again in a couple of days?"

- "I'm feeling stuck and I just want to think about this by myself for a while. Can we figure out a time to get back to this later?"

- "I'm exhausted from talking. Can we get back to this later? When?"

- *Take a time-out from conversation if you need it.*

- *Time-outs only require one person.*

- *Set a time to talk later.*

EXERCISES FOR TABLING THE CONVERSATION:

1. Spend some time talking to your partner about the idea of tabling a conversation. Can you both agree that it is sometimes necessary? See if you can create a guideline for how this is supposed to work for the two of you.

2. What kind of language can you agree to use for tabling a conversation?

3. What is the best way to go about making sure that you return to the conversation at a later time?

RULE #48: **Use good listening skills.**

One of the most important skills for problem-solving is good listening. **The objective of good listening is understanding the thoughts and feelings of one's partner.** This can be difficult when the listener has strong feelings about the issues that are being raised. Strong feelings can lead to misinterpretations or distortions of what was said; coupled with emotional reactivity, this can inflame conflict. Thus, **the challenge becomes focusing on your partner's thoughts and feelings while quieting your own thoughts and feelings.**

> *Listen by focusing on your partner's thoughts and feelings.*

Good listening is *accurate* listening. Acknowledging the thoughts and feelings of our partner **is essential for establishing listening accuracy. One of the best ways to do this is simply by** restating the original expression without interpretation or expansion. This is called reflective listening.

- "Let me see, what I heard you say was..."
- "Here is what I think you have said to me..."
- "Here is my understanding of what you just said..."
- "I'd like to tell you what I just heard..."

It can be helpful to get confirmation that you have heard correctly by simply asking:

- "Did I understand you correctly?"
- "Did I get that right?"
- "Am I hearing what you said?"

Because accurate listening is so important, repetition may be necessary for understanding. Both parties need to agree that repetition is okay and to not become judgmental or irritable. It is *not* useful to say things like:

- "I don't have any idea what you are saying," or
- "Well, that's because you never listen."

Instead say:

- "I guess I didn't hear you. Do you mind saying it again? I want to understand," or simply,
- "Sure."

Reflection continues until there is confirmation.

Use reflective listening.

Using reflective listening and confirmation skills may feel awkward and unnatural at first. However, like any new skill, once it is learned it will feel more natural. Most of our daily conversations don't require the use of reflective listening and confirmation, unless they are going sideways. Reflective listening skills are important to use in conversations with strong feelings. Those are the conversations that give couples difficulty. "Please pass the salt and pepper" is typically not the problem.

There are two parts to listening: intellectual listening and emotional listening. *Intellectual listening* is hearing all of the words and the concepts being expressed. *Emotional listening* is making a feeling connection to our partner by the feelings he expresses and by his body language. Part of good listening is empathizing, particularly when there are strong feelings. So in addition to being an accurate listener, it is important to be an empathic listener. (See Rule 21, "Acknowledge feelings and be compassionate.") Part of being a good listener is letting your partner know that you understand the feelings that he has. You can't achieve this unless you care about what he is saying. Have caring, show caring, be compassionate and be empathic to your partner's feelings.

Listen empathetically.

Showing interest is another part of good listening. So in addition to being an accurate listener and an empathic listener, be an *interested* listener. (See Rule 22, "Be interested in your partner's thoughts and ideas.") Part of being a good listener is letting your partner know that you are interested in what she has to say to you. You can't achieve this if you are bored with what she is saying. Be interested, develop interest if you don't initially have it, and show interest in her thoughts and ideas.

Listen with interest.

When you're not feeling understood, it is useful to develop an agreed-upon way to ask for understanding.

"I'm really not feeling like you are getting what I am saying. Could you reflect back what you have heard?"

"I'm not feeling understood and I really want to know that you are getting what I am saying. Can you tell me what you think you have heard?"

Develop an agreed upon way to ask for understanding.

"So, I guess you don't want to spend time with me."

"No, I just have too much work to do today."

"I don't think you even care that my brother is sick."

"I do care. I just don't think I'm that good at expressing it."

No matter what you think you heard from your partner, when he disagrees regarding his own thoughts and feelings, defer to him and acknowledge him as your default. (See Rule 37, "Your partner knows their thoughts and feelings better than you.") **While it is possible (not probable) that he is intentionally or unintentionally obscuring the truth, first try to recognize and acknowledge a simple lack of understanding on your part, your own sensitivities, or your possible laps of memory. If you hold your ground and argue about what was previously said or that what is being said is untrue, then the conflict will become further inflamed.** You hold the claim to your own thoughts and feelings, and your partner holds the claim to his own thoughts and feelings. **It is your job to understand his thoughts and feelings as well as you can.**

Each person holds the claim to their own thoughts and feelings.

Now it is possible for your partner to **change what she said** from what was said previously. It just doesn't do any good to argue about it, particularly if she stands her ground. You can gently tell her that you heard her say something different before; however, in most cases you will have to discuss the most recent iteration of what she said, because that is what is current. Sometimes this can be quite disruptive, because many of the thoughts and feelings that you currently have could have been based on what you heard previously. This is another reason why getting confirmation by your partner at the time she stated her thoughts and feelings can be so important. On the other hand, if your partner tries to change a previously agreed-upon agreement, that's another matter, and what was disruptive can become dysfunctional (See Rule 38, "Expectations and agreements"). Agreements shouldn't be confused with expression of thoughts and feelings.

> ## Don't get into a fight about what was previously said.

A more subtle but equally difficult problem is **if a partner is truly out of touch or not admitting his real feelings.** This often happens when someone is upset or angry but is uncomfortable exposing those feelings. He might be afraid that admitting anger might lead to a fight or cause him to lose control. There is a multitude of reasons why people have difficulty acknowledging their own feelings, including not knowing how they feel. If your partner seems angry and is gently told so based on his facial expressions, raised voice or intense manner, it might help. However, again, if he holds his ground, it usually won't do any good to argue. Do your best to continue discussing whatever there is to discuss, although sometimes if your partner is very upset and won't admit it, you just won't be able to continue the conversation.

> ## Don't get into a fight about what you think your partner feels.

While there are many different behaviors that interfere with good listening, there are two that I would like to give special attention: interruption and overreacting. The one that occurs most frequently in my office is interrupting. I am constantly hearing comments like, *Hey, I'm speaking! Will you stop interrupting me? I'm talking now! I listened when you were talking; will you please listen to me now? Will you just let me say what I want to say before jumping in?* These are not comments that I hear just every once in a while. These are comments that I hear many times throughout a week of work. While it is true that some couples seem to be happy with a style of talking in which they talk over each other, most of the people I see find it disruptive in all types of conversations, not just arguments. Most of us want to be able to express our full thought and don't want to be cut off by an interruption. **Particularly** when we have disagreements, we want to be able to get our point across. There can be a lot of mental and emotional energy that is associated with that effort and when it is thwarted, it can be stifling and frustrating. Time and time again, I have observed couples who have a mildly frustrating issue and become increasingly upset because how they are talking becomes so difficult. Interrupting is one of the biggest culprits.

Interruptions can be verbal or nonverbal. Verbal interruptions are probably the worst, because it can be very difficult to continue talking when someone else is talking at the same time. But nonverbal gestures and facial expressions can be difficult, even though it is not the same as a verbal interruption. Interruption usually occurs as a result of uncontrolled impulsive verbal behavior; or, in plainer language, not stopping oneself from blurting out something. Good listening *does* require self-control. Managing our tendency to interrupt is one of the most important types of self-control in conversation. Sometimes people tell me that if they don't interrupt, they are going to forget what they have to say. Usually if a person forgets what he is going to say, it comes back to him later. If, in the unusual case, the thought doesn't come back, then it has to be sacrificed in the service of good listening.

On occasion I have observed interruptions happening as a result of someone's partner talking for too long or jumping from one topic to the next without giving the other person a chance to speak. If this occurs in your relationship, it needs to be addressed. However, that is not the usual reason interrupting occurs.

In one of the exercises below, you will be asked to talk to your partner about whether interrupting is a problem in your relationship. If it is, try to develop a consciousness about your own tendency to interrupt. See if you can develop a signal or a way to ask each other to not interrupt that is acceptable to both of you. Perhaps it will just be holding up a finger. Whatever the signal is, as soon as it is given, the person who is interrupting needs to immediately back down, say he's sorry, and allow the other person to finish what she is saying.

> ### Don't interrupt.

The second behavior that requires self-control is the tendency to overreact. While listening patiently is laudable, listening with a two-by-four is not (figuratively speaking, of course). Managing our emotions is a requirement for good listening. *But, I have a right to feel the way I do.* Everyone has the "right" to feel the way they do, but that's not an excuse for conversational overreaction. While we are part of the animal kingdom, one thing that distinguishes us from nonhuman species is the conscious, self-reflective, willful management of our emotional/behavior responses. **We have the capacity to inhibit responses, and that capacity must be exercised for good listening and overall civility.** I can't tell you exactly what it should look like for you and your partner, because that is an individual matter. It is up to you and your partner to determine what reactions are "over" reactions. In Rule 53, "Rules of engagement," I ask you to establish rules of engagement for yourself and your partner. A number of these rules speak to what constitutes an overreaction for you. However, as part of the exercise in this section, I ask you to begin the discussion because of the hugely disruptive problem this creates for good listening.

Don't over-react.

- *Listen by focusing on your partner's thoughts and feelings.*
- *Use reflective listening.*
- *Get confirmation that what you heard is correct.*
- *Listen empathetically.*
- *Listen with interest.*
- *Develop an agreed upon way to ask for understanding.*
- *Each person holds the claim to their own thoughts and feelings.*
- *Don't get into a fight about what was previously said.*
- *Don't get into a fight about what you think your partner feels.*
- *Don't interrupt.*
- *Don't overreact.*

EXERCISES FOR DEVELOPING GOOD LISTENING SKILLS:

1. Spend some time by yourself and write down examples of language that you would like to use for reflective listening. After writing them down, try to memorize the statements and practice saying them out loud.

2. Also write down some examples of language that you would like to use for confirming that what you heard was correct. After writing them down, try to memorize the statements and practice saying them out loud.

3. Spend some time with your partner and practice the statements that you have memorized.

4. Talk to your partner about how to ask each other to use reflective listening skills, if you are not feeling understood.

5. Over the next couple of months, before beginning any conversations of substance, talk to your partner about using good listening skills.

6. Have a conversation with your partner about any difficulties the two of you might experience in confirming an understanding of each other. Discuss whether feelings are perceived differently than they are stated. Discuss the concept of "each of us holding claim to our own thoughts and feelings."

7. Talk about whether or not interrupting is a problem in your relationship. If so, try to agree on a "please don't interrupt me," signal. Talk about what you would like to happen when this signal is given.

8. Talk to your partner about overreactions and whether you think they occur in your relationship. See if the two of you can agree on what constitutes an overreaction.

RULE #49: **Lower your defenses.**

Good listening is acknowledging your partner's thoughts and feelings by using reflection, getting confirmation of your understanding, and *not becoming defensive.*

Being defensive is taking action to protect ourselves. If we try to block someone from physically hitting us or if we run away, it is obviously a defensive action. What isn't so obvious is **what constitutes defensiveness to verbal behavior.** Understanding the answers to these three questions will be helpful:

1. *What* is being defended?
2. *Why* is it being defended?
3. *How* is it being defended?

What is being defended can be broken down into two parts: the *physiological* **and the** *psychological.*

People defend their **physiological** well-being from a verbal attack for the same reason they defend themselves from a physical attack. It physiologically hurts or they anticipate that it will hurt. Yelling loudly can hurt a person's ears, generating defensiveness. However, if someone quietly threatens another person physically or threatens her family or her property, that can also generate defensiveness. This type of defensiveness can be automatic and activate a **"fight-or-flight" (FOF)** response. This is part of our nervous system that evolved to protect us from physical harm. The fight-or-flight response is activated like an on-off, all-or-none switch that causes the individual to stand and fight or run away. It's difficult to listen when FOF is activated.

> *It is difficult to listen if your fight-or-flight physiology is activated.*

Some things that people defend **psychologically** are:

- their behavior
- their overall view of themselves
- their beliefs, values, rights and feelings
- their overall view of the world and people in the world
- their most basic constructs for how things are supposed to work

This assortment of thoughts and feelings is often called the **self**.

Why is it important to defend our self? It is important because the internal and external self is our operating system. These are the structures that allow us to get a glass of water, pan for gold, ride a horse, arrange a bouquet of flowers, cook a delicious dinner, develop relationships, have fun, connect with the universe, or do whatever we want. **Perceived challenges to these structures can disrupt what we think is needed to interface successfully with the world, thus creating anxiety.**

From the time we take our first breath of air, we are writing this personal operating system in the neural physiology of our brains. Like a computer, some parts of our operating system control many functions and some control only a few functions. Threats that challenge major parts of our operating system tend to be more disruptive than challenges to minor parts. The greater the disruption, the higher the possibility for defensiveness. If we perceive a verbal challenge to a major part of our self, like how we manage our money, we are likely to be become more anxious and defensive than a verbal challenge to something less major, like how we peel a banana.

Unlike today's computers, one of the most interesting characteristics of our self is the capacity for self-modulation, or change from within. **The less we are able to change, the greater is our need to be defensive.**

> *The easier it is for you to change, the lower your defensiveness will be.*

Defensiveness refers to both internal defensiveness and to defensive behavior. Internal defensiveness primarily serves the purpose of avoiding disruptions of the internal self that are anxiety-producing. Being internally defensive is an effort at reducing that disruption. There is a close link between how people defend themselves internally and externally, because often both are triggered simultaneously.

Some internal defenses are:

- not hearing the words that have been spoken
- internally changing what has been said
- quickly rejecting internally whatever has been said
- thinking about counter arguments.
- going blank

Defensive behavior also attempts to avoid disruption that is anxiety producing.
In conversation, we may be defensive by attempting to block what is being said,
by justifying our behavior, or by making a counter attack. *How* people defend
themselves behaviorally is endless. Most of these behaviors interfere with
communication and understanding.

Some behavioral defenses are:

- interrupting
- finishing the other person's sentences
- getting mad
- rejecting what was said
- exaggerating what was said
- changing what was said
- belittling what was said
- using sarcasm
- disputing the facts
- disputing the conclusions
- disputing the associated feelings
- justifying one's own behavior
- acting like an authority
- getting bossy
- using the silent treatment

***Not* becoming defensive means first recognizing that you *are* being defensive.**
This may be easier said than done. There have been many occasions in my
office in which a marriage partner has denied what appeared to be defensiveness. It's not uncommon for people to be defensive about being defensive.
Nonetheless, as with other feelings, the default ultimately remains with the
individual as the spokesperson for her own feelings. A person may say that
she is just explaining herself. And that might be true. An explanation of our
behavior is not necessarily defensive. The difference between an explanation
and defensive behavior is in the attitude and the intensity of the behavior. If a
partner is calm and is open to specific negative feedback, and if she feel like
she would be okay if the feedback were true, she may not be acting defensively.

As with other feelings, if a partner is in denial about being defensive, gently being made aware of her intensity may help, but there is not an easy solution.

> ***Providing an explanation for one's behavior is not necessarily defensive.***

One of the tests for knowing if you are feeling defensive is by being aware of feelings of agitation or anxiety, and the intensity of your response. Sometimes it is easier to recognize anxiety than defensiveness. Disturbances to the intra-psychic self typically cause anxiety just before defensive feelings and behavior are activated. The behavior may also be more intense than normal. So, **if you can be aware of your anxiety and your intensity, it may be easier for you to become aware of your defensiveness.**

> ***Anxiety and intensity is often evident when there is defensiveness.***

If you can become aware of your defensive feelings and behavior, the best approach for reducing defensiveness is by trying to reduce the underlying anxiety causing the defensiveness. **One big contributing factor to being anxious is a lack of self-confidence.** Typically, the more self-confident you are, the more sure you are that most things said to you don't have to disrupt the most important aspects of who you are as an individual such as:

- your behavior
- your overall view of yourself
- your beliefs, values, rights and feelings
- your overall view of the world and people in the world
- your most basic constructs for how things are supposed to work

If you are self-confident, you realize that changes you make may produce mild discomfort, but you know that it is manageable. If you are able to be confident, your anxiety will be less.

> ***More self-confidence = less anxiety***
> ***Less anxiety = less defensiveness***

The following are some things that you can do to be less anxious and less defensive in difficult conversations:

1. **Be mindful of staying calm.**

   Before you sit down, remind yourself that getting upset is likely going to derail the conversation. It will also increase the likelihood of your being defensive. Remind yourself that you can't listen if you are not calm or are overly angry. You do not want to work yourself up into a frenzy. When appropriate, tell yourself that there is likely no real risk of being physically hurt. Since your breathing is the only autonomic nervous system function over which you have immediate control, managing your breathing can be very helpful in staying calm and keeping yourself from slipping into the FOF response.

2. **Be mindful that urgency is not likely.**

   Also before you sit down, remind yourself that the greatest likelihood is that whatever your partner wants to discuss is not urgent. A resolution to the problem doesn't have to be achieved immediately. There is a window of uncertainty (Rule 51, "Stay in the window of uncertainty") in which you can discuss your partner's thoughts and feelings that gives you plenty of time to consider whatever it is that he is saying. You are not required to immediately agree or disagree with him. You get to think about what your partner has to say. You can take your time.

3. **Begin listening with a sense of self-confidence and openness.**

   Remind yourself that you are an okay person, and that whatever you hear doesn't have to bring about any massive changes in who you are as a person. Remind yourself that whatever you hear is just your partner's point of view, and it might not necessarily be correct or right. You are a player in the process of communication, and your thoughts and feelings are also important. Remind yourself that you are capable of making changes, should it come to that.

4. **Use your reflective listening techniques.**

   By using reflective listening, you will gain a better perspective on what is being said. This will also serve to decrease assumptions and interpretations that may make you anxious and defensive.

5. **Seek more information by asking questions.**

   This will extend your partner's explanation, blocking your own defensive reactions. Also, the more information you have, the greater likelihood for decreasing anxiety-provoking assumptions and misinformation.

6. **Listen to your partner's feelings and point of view first and foremost.**

   You have a choice to accept or not accept your partner's perspective. Remind yourself that your partner is talking because of her **feelings.** Those feelings arise in your partner's body, not in your behavior. If she didn't care or didn't have a sensitivity to your behavior, you wouldn't be hearing about it. **So the problem starts with your partner, who is making the complaint, and if you can put your attention on her feelings and her reasons for feeling that way, you will likely be less defensive.**

7. **Remind yourself to not "turn your shortcomings into sins."**

   If you are constantly dumping on yourself and having "I'm not good enough" thoughts when someone gives you feedback, you are going to go right into a dark hole. Being defensive will likely happen before you know it in an effort to get out of that hole. You *do* mess up sometimes, and if you are just able to admit it and make an apology, you can move on (Rule 15. "Don't turn your shortcomings into sins"). Continue to remind yourself that you remain a decent individual, no matter what your partner is saying. Practice the Rule about "relative right and wrong (Rule 36)," reminding yourself that your partner's concern is likely relative to her and not a violation of some community or moral standard. Thus you don't have to think that you can't do anything right. It is just a matter of working it out with your partner, understanding that what you did wasn't right for her.

8. **If you have made a mistake, admit it.**

   If you do accept what your partner is saying about you, recognize that it doesn't mean that you have to do a full-scale remake of yourself. Whatever changes you make to accommodate your partner are not going to be that huge. Her complaint can be contained within the context of who you are. So if you made a mistake, just admit it. It doesn't have to be such a big deal. Making mistakes in human interactions is one of the most common occurrences between all people, and the more you stand on pride that you don't make mistakes, the more defensive you will become and the more difficult it will be for you to even begin to work things out with your partner.

- *It is difficult to listen if your fight-or-flight physiology is activated.*

- *The easier it is for you to change, the lower will be your defensiveness.*

- *Providing an explanation for one's behavior is not necessarily defensive.*

- *Anxiety and intensity is often evident when there is defensiveness.*

- *More self-confidence = less anxiety.*
  Less anxiety = less defensiveness.

- *To be less anxious and less defensive:*

  - *Be mindful of staying calm.*

  - *Urgency is not likely.*

  - *Begin listening with a sense of self-confidence and openness.*

  - *Use your reflective listening techniques.*

  - *Seek more information by asking questions.*

  - *Listen to your partner's feelings and point of view first and foremost.*

  - *Remind yourself to not "turn your shortcomings into sins."*

  - *If you have made a mistake, admit it.*

EXERCISES FOR LOWERING YOUR DEFENSES:

1. Spend some time alone to see if you can figure out ways you are defensive both internally and externally. Refer to the lists above to help you. Write them down. Think about why you are being defensive and what you are defending, and write down your explanations.

2. Spend some time with your partner talking about the ways you both act defensively. Try to be descriptive about the behavior of defensiveness and give both your verbal and nonverbal observations of your partner's behavior. Try not to be defensive to your partner's feedback. Write down what your partner has to say.

3. Think about ways you can try to lower your anxieties associated with your defensiveness. Refer to the methods that have been suggested above, and in Rule 14, "Let go of useless worry." Write them down. Also think about behavioral things that you can do to act less defensively. Write them down.

4. Meditate about the suggestions you made for yourself above. Read them over to yourself and just think about them. Rehearse new thoughts and try to visualize yourself behaving differently. Concentrate on your breathing.

5. Practice mindfulness of your defensiveness in conversations with your partner. Try to be aware of the anxiety that is associated with defensiveness, defensive feelings and defensive behavior. See if you can implement some of the suggestions that you have made for yourself in Exercises 3 and 4.

RULE #50: **Introduce a concern by calmly stating the problem not the solution.**

Most of the time, when we bring up a problem, we want improvement. It turns out that the tone used in the first few seconds can have a huge impact on the success or failure of the conversation. If we start with all piss and vinegar, it probably isn't going to go very well. A loud voice and a high level of intensity can be very activating for our partner and, as a result, defensiveness will often occur. If that defensiveness takes the form of even greater intensity or withdrawal, the original concern might be quickly lost to an escalating process. **The more aggressive our entry, the less likely it is that a good problem-solving discussion will follow.**

If you start loud you will likely end loud.

If a topic is calmly introduced with an attitude of wanting to work something out, things will likely go better. If consideration is given to a concern prior to talking, including the possible language that is going to be used, the conversation can more easily get off to a good start.

Think about what you want to say before you say it.

If someone jumps right into a solution before ever mentioning the problem, she might find that her partner begins to formulate an opposing position before ever understanding the problem. On the other hand, if a problem is understood, there may be no opposition. But the possibility of generating a quick agreement may be lost if the listener jumps to a solution before the importance of the problem is ever mentioned.

Start with the problem, not the solution.

RULE
#50   Introduce a concern by calming stating the problem not the solution.

Examples:

"Why don't you just do what I told you to do instead of the screwed up way you are going about it?" *What an ass.*

As opposed to: "Hey, I'm feeling irritated and want to talk to you about something. I'm really upset about how you are doing that, and I'd like to see if it can be done differently."

Or: "Will you please pick up your damn clothes. You are such a slob."
As opposed to: "I am really getting tired of picking up your clothes. Can't we figure out something that will work better?"

You probably notice that in the first examples, the approaches are blaming, use the word *you*, and use intense language like swearing. The second approaches state a feeling without accusation and invite problem-solving. **The first statements are destructive, while the second statements are constructive.**

The way you approach your partner can make such a difference. Sometimes a couple comes into my office with such a head of steam and with such intense and accusatory language that it takes most of the hour just to calm things down. I might not intervene the first time this occurs, just to see what happens, and inevitably things go from bad to worse. It may be instructive to let the fighting go on one time, but after that, I interrupt an aggressive entry, because the resulting argument wastes time and wears everyone down. And that is in my office. When people are in their own homes, they report that it is far worse. These are the kinds of conflicts that couples try to avoid, and for good reason—they feel so bad. If this happens to you, I'm sure you would like to try to avoid this pattern of behavior also.

If your partner gets off on the wrong foot, can you agree on a way to tell her to start over with softer and easier language? I have sometimes asked couples to hold up a finger when this occurs and that is a sufficient cue for starting over. If you are the one starting to voice the concern and your partner holds up one finger, you have to guard yourself from getting upset with him and just start over using calmer tones.

Signal your partner to ask for softer and easier language.

This is the Rule that says that you have to get started on the right foot. See if you can find a way to make this Rule help you in this most critical stage of voicing a concern.

- *If you start loud you will likely end loud.*
- *Think about what you want to say before you say it.*
- *Start with the problem, not the solution.*
- *Signal your partner to ask for softer and easier language.*

EXERCISES FOR STARTING OFF ON THE RIGHT FOOT:

1. Spend some time with yourself and write down five examples of how you could begin to voice a concern to your partner in a constructive fashion. Memorize your examples and practice them out loud.

2. Spend some time with your partner talking about this Rule. Give feedback to your partner concerning whether you have had difficulty with the way he has begun to voice concerns and vice versa. Discuss this calmly.

3. After this discussion, review both examples of how to begin voicing a concern. Make sure that your tone of voice and what you have to say works for your partner. Practice making these statements with one another.

4. Talk to your partner about a way to tell him to start over using softer and less intense language or agree on a signal to use. Talk about how you will avoid being defensive or exasperated when this signal is used.

5. In the future, if your partner opens a conversation in a rough manner, request that she start over using softer language and tones, or use the signal that you have agreed upon.

6. Within a couple of weeks, check in with each other to see if there has been improvement.

RULE #51: **Stay in the window of uncertainty.**

One reason that interpersonal problem-solving can be so difficult is because it is so different from individual problem-solving. Our entire childhood is spent learning to solve problems individually, and by the time we are adults, we are pretty good at it. Unconscious habits are developed for reducing the tension of a problem by quickly attempting to find a solution. Most people don't want to remain in the tension of a problem for very long, so the quicker a problem can be solved, the better it is.

Couples can't operate the same way. They need to stay in the tension long enough to create a joint solution. There's a need for *collaboration*. Many people are inexperienced in solving problems this way, so it may feel uncomfortable at first. I call this slowed down approach "staying in the window of uncertainty."
It means:

- **not attempting to resolve the problem too quickly**
- **taking the time to really listen to one another**
- **discussing feelings until they are understood**
- **going through the necessary steps for problem-solving**
- **taking a break if needed and coming back to the discussion later**

It means asking questions like:

- **"Could you please explain your feelings about your concern a little better?"**
- **"How strongly to you feel about it?"**
- **"How do you feel about what I am saying?"**
- **"What are your thoughts about what I am saying?"**
- **"What is your explanation about what occurred?"**
- **"Is there information I don't have?"**
- **"Could there have been a misunderstanding?"**
- **"What do you think is a good solution?"**
- **"What are your thoughts and feelings about my proposal?"**
- **"On a scale from one to ten, how strongly do you feel about doing things the way you proposed?"**
- **"What do you think about our taking a break and getting back to this later?"**

> ### *Ask informational questions when you're in the window of uncertainty.*

The best methods of interpersonal problem-solving are not fast. It takes time to clarify concerns, acknowledge and confirm thoughts and feelings of both parties, figure out possible options, present pros and cons, and come to a mutual understanding.

> ### *Slow down.*

Many people have difficulty with the feelings of tension that are associated with the window of uncertainty. Groups often use rules like Robert's Rules of Order to create procedures for problem-solving and a set of guidelines for acceptable and unacceptable behavior when dealing with this tension. Couples also need rules that serve this same purpose (like Rule 46, "Have a road map for problem-solving"). When there is a sense of order to decision-making and problem-solving, the tension is less. Golden's Rules can help. (Rule 53, "Rules of engagement," is particularly important.) Once the Rules are mastered, the process of problem-solving may feel very satisfying.

> ### *Use rules of engagement to ease any tensions associated with uncertainty.*

People often try to resolve their difficulties too quickly. If we've had past experiences in which disagreements have lead to a fight, we may want to just get it over with, so we quickly present a solution. If we have feelings of urgency, any resistance to our solution may be met with bull headedness. This can lead to the very fight that we wished to avoid by pushing too hard and too fast. Arguments can easily escalate with both people asserting that their solution is best and "right." Each person may think the other person is belligerent, demanding, rigid, unyielding, power tripping, controlling, or just a pain in the rear.

If you or your partner seem to be moving too fast, ask her to slow down:

- "Can we just take things a little slower?"
- "It feels like we are acting like this is urgent. Is it?"
- "Can we just go back a couple of steps in the process? I'm not even sure why this is important to you."

- "Could we slow down and listen to each other a little better? I think we are getting all riled up, and I'm not sure we really understand how each other is feeling."
- "Could we take a little more time to brainstorm for solutions before making a decision too fast?"
- "I think that we have enough time to slow down. What do you think?"

> *Ask your partner to slow down if the conversation is moving too fast.*

- *Ask informational questions when you're in the window of uncertainty.*
- *Slow down.*
- *Use rules of engagement to ease any tensions associated with uncertainty.*
- *Ask your partner to slow down if the conversation is moving too fast.*

EXERCISES FOR STAYING IN THE WINDOW OF UNCERTAINTY:

1. Spend some time alone and write down questions that you can use to seek more information from your partner when he brings up a concern. Practice these questions out loud to yourself.

2. Write down questions that you can use to ask your partner to slow down if your conversation is going too fast. Practice these questions out loud to yourself.

3. Spend some time with your partner reviewing the kinds of questions each of you has written.

4. Next time you are in a conversation with your partner, announce that you wish to practice staying in the window of uncertainty. Try seeking additional information while you are in that conversation. Try to stay mindful of staying in the window of uncertainty for subsequent conversations.

RULE #52: Be open to your partner's explanation.

Staying in the window of uncertainty can be hard, particularly when we are hurt or angry. The strong feelings often seem justified. Certainty can feel more correct than uncertainty, and that can create a problem for the relationship. It is not uncommon to have strong feelings, only to find out later that there was a misunderstanding, misinformation or some other explanation that reduced the strength of those feelings. **Without listening to an explanation, angry and hurt feelings may unnecessarily fester.** Some of the best resolutions for hurt feelings are possible only by means of an explanation, and that requires openness and a calm conversation.

If you are feeling hurt or angry, it may not be the easiest conversation for you to have. It works best if the conversation begins with your feelings and the reasons for your feeling (see Rule 46, "Have a road map"). Hopefully your partner will use good listening skills. Perhaps he will agree with you and apologize. On the other hand, he might want to offer an explanation. Your job is to be open to his explanation. **You don't have to agree with him, but you do have to consider his point of view. Be open to the possibility that by hearing his explanation, you may feel differently.** You may come to understand that what occurred between the two of you was the result of:

1. **Misunderstanding or poor communication.** Misunderstandings frequently occur in relationships, and those misunderstandings can lead to hurt or angry feelings. A misunderstanding, by definition, means that there is no culpability on either person's part and thus no penalties. Acceptance of an explanation of misunderstanding can help to shift the focus away from feeling hurt to letting go of the hurt feelings and improving communication.

> *If there has been a misunderstanding, let go of the anger.*

2. **Lack of information.** Misinformation is also a frequent occurrence. New information may give a new insight into the circumstances that gave rise to the hurt and/or angry feelings. When viewed from a new perspective, the situation may appear different thus resulting in a change in those feelings.

| Be open to changing your feelings based on new information. |

3. **Circumstantial explanation.** Feelings of anger can quickly change upon hearing particular circumstantial explanations. For example, if it appears that someone simply forgot her appointment, the person who has been stood up might be angry. However, if it turns out that not showing up was the result of an automobile accident and the person is unconscious and in the hospital, the feelings might be quite different.

| Be open to circumstantial explanations. |

4. **Over sensitivity.** Sometimes hurt or angry feelings are the result of an over sensitivity like hunger, fatigue, illness, being hormonal or being irritable due to having a bad day. Be open to the possibility that your hurt feelings may have more to do with you than anything that your partner did.

| Be willing to consider that the problem may be an over sensitivity on your part. |

- *If there has been a misunderstanding, let go of the anger.*
- *Be open to changing your feelings based on new information.*
- *Be open to circumstantial explanations.*
- *Be willing to consider that the problem may be an over sensitivity on your part.*

EXERCISES FOR BEING OPEN TO OTHER EXPLANATIONS:

1. Spend some time with your partner and discuss the four alternative explanations: misunderstandings, lack of information, circumstantial explanations and over sensitivity. See if you can agree that these are valid reasons for letting go of hurt and angry feelings.

2. Discuss misunderstandings and whether you agree that neither party should pay a penalty for a misunderstanding.

3. Discuss some ways to improve communication to reduce the frequency of future misunderstandings.

RULE #53: **Develop rules of engagement, particularly around anger.**

Every society operates under some type of "rules of engagement." These rules help people manage their conduct and remain rational when emotions are intense. You also have some rules of engagement, even if you haven't thought about it, like: no hitting, no use of weapons, no spitting, no yelling in a restaurants, etc. This section is about formalizing these rules and adding others that you and your partner can agree upon. Some of the rules may come from the pages of this book (like from the discussion of orderliness and civility), and some will come from your own creation. During the Exercise portion of this section, I am going ask you to write them down.

One of the most important sets of rules is for the expression of anger. In a previous section on anger (Rule 11, "Let go of anger, blame and resentment"), anger was discussed from an individual perspective. Considerable time was spent discussing how to reduce angry feelings. In this section, anger will be discussed from the relationship perspective. Consequently, there will be an emphasis on the *expression* of anger; i.e., angry behavior. The term anger will be used in a generic sense to connote feelings and behavior that can range from irritation to rage.

When we are angry, we are usually angry at something or someone specific. **I like to say that anger seeks an object.** *Anger* often carries the notion of blame and injustice, the idea of being unduly wronged. *Frustration* is different. Frustration doesn't usually imply blame, nor does it seek an object in the same way. A person might be frustrated *with* a situation but angry *at* someone. Frustration usually connotes a feeling of dissatisfaction in not getting what is wanted, *without* the feeling that some basic right has been violated. Interpersonally, when someone describes a feeling of dissatisfaction as *frustration* rather than *anger,* the exchange is usually easier on the relationship because it doesn't imply blame and therefore it doesn't as easily evoke defensiveness. **Unfortunately, people often allow feelings of frustration to convert to anger expressions.** Try to distinguish feelings of frustration from feelings of anger by asking yourself these questions about your partner:

- *Has she done something wrong?*
- *Has she violated something previously agreed upon?*

Or:

- Did I not get what I wanted?
- Did things not work out the way I would have liked?

If feelings of anger can be converted to feelings of frustration, it may be very helpful to your relationship. The overall reduction of expressed anger in a relationship is usually beneficial.

One type of frustration that is particularly worth mentioning is frustration with circumstances or with people other than your partner. A common but destructive pattern of behavior is directing the frustrations that occur through-out the day at our partner. Since "anger seeks an object," when frustration converts to anger, a likely target becomes our partner. In psychological terms, this might be called *displacing anger*. In every-day language it is called "kicking the cat" (Rule 29, "Don't kick the cat"). It was put it in the section on creating closeness because it destroys a good mood and makes it difficult for closeness to emerge. It is one thing to come home and be in a bad mood because you had a rough day and need the support of your partner. It is another thing completely to come home and start screaming at your partner for something he did that was totally trivial, or for no reason at all. If this is something you do, see if you can be mindful about it, think about it on your way home from work, and find a way to express feelings of frustration with your day rather than anger at your partner.

> ## Don't let feelings of frustrations convert to anger.

Anger is a common human feeling. When couples want to establish intimacy, stuffing or repressing anger often generates resentment and a lack of closeness over time. So, if you are feeling angry with your partner, acknowledge the feelings to yourself and try to understand why you are feeling angry. If you are unable to let go of your anger, it might be time to let your partner know how you are feeling. *How* you do that can be very important. We have laws that regulate some of our expressions of anger, like being physically harmful to another person. However, even without a physical expression of anger, high-amplitude verbal anger with words that reflect hateful feelings can be very damaging. Some couples attack each other with anger that is so aggressive it destroys the very foundation of their relationship. I often suggest that couples **talk about what type of angry expressions are really troublesome to**

one another and come up with guidelines around the expression of anger that works for both of them. For example, couples may put in place rules about swearing or other angry expressions that agitate one another. I believe that this is a premarital and marital exercise that benefits all couples, and I highly recommend it.

What exact words are okay to use when you are angry?

- "I'm upset with you."
- "I'm pissed off at you!"
- "I'm ticked."
- "This really takes the cake."
- "This is the last straw!"

What words are not okay to use when you are angry?

- "You piss me off."
- "You are such a _____!"

How loud a voice is okay?

- You can hear it in the room next door.
- You can hear it several rooms over or on another floor.
- You can hear it standing outside the house.
- The neighbors can hear it next door.

Is it okay to make threats?

- "I'd like to bash your head in."
- "I'm going to rip your face off."
- "I'm going to scratch your eyes out."
- "I'm going to smash the car."

Is it okay to swear? If so, what words?

- Is it okay to call your partner names?
- "You are such an ass."
- "You're a pig."

Is it okay to characterize your partner?

- "You're a slob."
- "You're completely self-centered."
- "You're the dumbest thing since sliced bread."
- "You're mean."
- "You're nasty."
- "You're a tightwad."

Are there expressions that are off limits?

- "I hope you die."
- "Shut your mouth."
- "You are just like your mother/father."
- "I want a divorce."
- "You always...! You never...!"

What non-verbal behavior is and is not okay?

- Being within _____ feet from your partner
- Using threatening hand gestures
- Standing above your partner when they are sitting

Is it okay to be physical towards your partner?

- hitting
- slapping
- pushing
- holding
- throwing objects at him
- protecting oneself. If yes, how?

Is it okay to destroy property?

- throwing objects
- breaking objects
- ripping paper
- banging pots and pans

Is it okay to drive away angry?

What is the protocol for angry expressions?

- How long does the first partner get to speak?
- Does the respondent get to be heard without interruption?
- For how long?

What cues can be given that alert your partner that they are violating one of the rules?

- Time-out
- Point of order
- "Hold it. You're violating one of our rules."
- Holding up one finger?

Create rules for the expression of anger.

Rules for specific situations can also be helpful, like:
- when one is in the car (when it is difficult to get away)
- in the morning just before one goes to work
- when couples are in bed
- when one person is in the bathtub
- when the kids are around

Because these situations have built-in constraints, conflict may become intensified and thus they may need some special guidelines or rules. For example, some couples have the rule "no arguing in bed," or "no starting a controversial conversation just before someone goes out the door." Establishing times to talk when couples can fully express themselves is a good idea.

Create rules for specific situations.

Situational problems usually require situational solutions. However, sometimes a situational problem brings to mind irritations about a **pattern of behavior** (behaviors that are generalized across a variety of situations) and feelings about that pattern may be more intense than the irritations about the specific situation. This is a common problem for established relationships. Partners start talking about a specific problem that recently occurred, and the conversation quickly escalates into irritations about patterns of behavior. When that happens, the conversation often doesn't go very well unless the pattern of behavior was the focus of the conversation from the start. If there is irritation at a situational level, it usually works best to try to resolve it at that level first and save the discussion of the pattern of behavior until discussion of the situational problem is finished (see Rule 43, "Giving and receiving feedback"). When relationships are emerging, this problem doesn't occur because patterns of behavior have yet to be established. As couples age, this problems intensifies, particularly if they haven't addressed these patterns earlier in their relationship.

Stay focused on the situation that is creating the difficulty.

It is common for patterns of behavior to become a topic of conversation. Because patterns of behavior and characterizations of a person are closely linked, sensitivity and defensiveness can be easily triggered. Thus guidelines or rules are useful. For example:

Don't drift into characterizations of the person as being bad or inadequate.
- "I don't know how anyone else could put up with you."

Don't make degrading comments.
- "You act like a three-year-old."

Don't make assumptions about your partner's thoughts and feelings.
- "You don't care how this house looks."
- "You make me wait just to piss me off."

Don't use psychological jargon.
- "You are so passive-aggressive."
- "You are anal retentive."

Don't use extreme language like "always" and "never."
- "You are never on time."
- "You are always thinking of yourself first."

Don't compare your partner to others.
- "None of your siblings act that way."
- "Why don't you try to be more like Bill?"

Don't tell your partner what is normal and that they are abnormal.
- "You're not normal."
- "You're weird."

Create guidelines for discussing patterns of behavior.

Sometimes, one thing leads to another so quickly that partners start yelling at each other about anything that irritates them about the other's behavior. Nothing constructive can ever happen at this point because it is just a free-for-all, with partners just bringing up one thing after another with derogatory comments and angry epitaphs. Blame, judgments and negative characterizations take over. Some people call this "throwing in the kitchen sink." It's destructive. This is a type of argument that needs to stop and both people need to cool down.

Don't throw in the kitchen sink.

Often conflict just becomes too intense for one person or the other. Having a rule for taking a break from one another until such time that both partners feel like they have better control is a good idea. The key to taking this break is to not stonewall the other person and to resume the conversation at a later time. If one party just walks off in an angry disrespectful fashion, it doesn't work as well. Sometimes couples establish a code word, like, "I need to take a time-out," that signals the other party that the conversation has become too difficult. It is helpful if the person who disengages makes it her responsibility to reengage in some fashion within twenty-four hours.

> ## *Have a time-out rule.*

Sensitive **topics** of conversation may need to be handled differently from other topics. They might include:

- one's upbringing
- one's extended family
- a situation that carries shame
- a topic of insecurity
- very personal or private topic like sexuality
- illness
- getting fired
- unemployment
- encounters with the police
- divorce

> ## *Have rules about specific topics of conversation.*

One contributing factor that can create huge difficulties for couples is alcohol. Alcohol is a disinhibitor, and negative feelings may be activated when a person is drinking that otherwise don't get activated to the same degree. That's why fights break out more easily in bars. Statistics on domestic violence show that alcohol often plays a role. **Trying to resolve problems while drinking is typically a terrible idea that invites disaster.** It may help to create rules of engagement concerning alcohol.

- Are there any controversial topics that are okay to discuss when drinking?
- Is there a quantity of alcohol beyond which controversial conversation should not occur?
- Are there types of alcohol that should create a boundary on conversation?
- What is the best way to cue one another about not wanting to have a controversial conversation if drinking has occurred?

- What should happen if one person wants to stop the conversation and the other one doesn't want to, and alcohol is involved?

> ## *Have rules of engagement as it concerns alcohol.*

Social situations seem to bring up a variety of unpleasant feelings, including: embarrassment, abandonment, guilt and insecurity. Rules for social situations can be helpful.

- What topics are not okay to bring up in social situations?
- What behaviors are embarrassing to your partner?
- How do you know when it is time to go home?
- When is it important to stay together and when is it okay to separate?
- If you separate, how long before you need to try to reconnect?
- How do rules about alcohol apply in these circumstances?
- Should your conduct be different if children are there?

> ## *Have rules for social situations.*

While most of this section has been written on rules of engagement concerning anger, it can be useful to add a broader list of rules for the over-all well-being of your relationship. Exercise 16 will help you to do this.

- *Don't let feelings of frustrations convert to anger.*
- **Create rules for the expression of anger.**
- *Create rules for specific situations.*
- *Stay focused on the situation that is creating the difficulty.*
- *Create guidelines for discussing patterns of behavior.*
  - *Don't drift into characterizations of your partner as being bad or inadequate.*
  - *Don't make degrading comments.*
  - *Don't make assumptions about your partner's thoughts and feelings.*
  - *Don't use psychological jargon.*
  - *Don't use extreme language like always and never.*
  - *Don't compare your partner to others.*
  - *Don't tell your partner what is normal and that she is abnormal.*
- *Don't throw in the kitchen sink.*
- *Have a time-out rule.*
- *Have rules about specific topics of conversation.*
- *Have rules of engagement as it concerns alcohol.*
- *Have rules for social situations.*

EXERCISES FOR DEVELOPING RULES OF ENGAGEMENT:

1. Spend some time with your partner and discuss the general concept of having rules of engagement. Write down some topics in which the two of you feel like you need to have some rules.

2. Talk about the difference between frustration and anger. See if you both can agree on the difference between them. Give examples of each. Use this Tool for discerning the difference:

   - Has he done something wrong?

   - Has he violated something previously agreed upon?

   Or

   - Did you not get what you wanted?

   - Did things not work out the way you would have liked?

3. Talk about whether you feel like either one of you "kicks the cat." If so, reread out loud to one another sections of Rule 29, "Kicking the cat," and do the appropriate exercises.

4. Talk about what types of angry expressions are really troublesome to each of you, and come up with some guidelines around expressions of anger that can work for you both. Use the question above as a template. Make a written list of these guidelines and make a copy for each of you. These guidelines should be reviewed on a regular basis and updated as needed.

5. Discuss situations that create difficulties when attempting to resolve conflict. See if you can agree on how to handle problems that arise in these situations.

6. Discuss the problem of not being able to stay on the topic with escalations into patterns of behavior. Talk about ways in which you can stay focused.

7. Have a conversation about how things go when you are discussing patterns of behavior. Read the list on "don'ts" out loud and ask each other if you use any of those verbal expressions. Discuss some better ways of saying things.

8. Discuss whether you have the problem of throwing in the kitchen sink. See if you can set up some guidelines for handling this problem, should it occur.

9. See if the two of you can agree on a time-out rule. Talk about how it can be implemented, with what language, and how you will return to the conversation later.

10. See if specific topics of conversation need greater sensitivity. Write them down. See if you want to set up any guidelines specific to those topics of conversation.

11. Discuss alcohol. Do you need to be handling alcohol differently? If so, use the set of questions above as a guideline for talking about alcohol. Write down your answers.

12. Talk about social situations and whether you need to have some guidelines there. If so, you can use the questions above as guidelines. Write down your answers.

13. At the end of the body of this section, I have given you a somewhat random list of rules of engagement. Some may think that it is fairly robust, while others may think that it isn't long enough. I would like you to first review this list by yourself and check off rules that you think are particularly important to the wellbeing of your relationship. Some of these rules will have sections in this book written on them. You might note on the page what that section is.

14. Later, I would like you to discuss your list with your partner to see if you can come to an agreement about which rules are important for the well-being of your relationship. Discuss which rules are important for you both to work on now, and see if you can prioritize the top five for immediate work. If there are sections in this book that are written on those topics, refer to them for help.

15. This list of rules of engagement is not *your* list; it is my list from this book. Try to think together if there are other rules that you think should be in *your* list of rules of engagement and write them down. See if any of those rules need to be added to your top five that need to be worked on.

16. Come up with two lists. The first list is a list of general rules of engagement that could be posted and shared between the two of you. The second list is the list of rules that you believe need the most attention now. Have them written up in a form that is clear and shows accountability for progress.

Sample rules of engagement

- Each party gets a turn to speak.
- When it is one person's turn to speak, the other person listens.
- Neither party gets to take too long a turn.
- Be polite to your partner.
- Use tones of voice that are not too intense or loud.
- Don't use provocative body language.
- No interrupting.
- Do not finish your partner's sentences.
- Do not reject your partner's feelings.
- Do not exaggerate what your partner said.
- Do not change what your partner said.
- Do not use sarcasm.
- Explain, don't justify.
- Don't act like an authority.
- Don't talk in extremes and absolutes.
- Don't be bossy.
- Don't use the silent treatment.
- Have appropriate physical space between you and your partner.
- Do not cross over into your partner's space.
- Do not make threatening gestures.
- Do not name-call or swear.
- Rebut only your partner's ideas.
- Do not belittle your partner's ideas.
- Do not attack your partner's character.
- Don't make assumptions about your partner's thoughts and feelings.
- Take the time to really understand your partner's point of view.
- Enter into negotiation with a sense of goodwill.
- Acknowledge your partner's thoughts and feelings.
- Get confirmation that your understanding is correct.

- Introduce a concern by calmly stating the problem not the solution.
- Be mindful of what you are going to say before your say it.
- Stay in the window of uncertainty.
- Use only expressions of anger that are agreeable to both parties.
- Turn down the volume.
- Don't use the kitchen-sink approach.
- Don't attack your partner's family.
- Don't overreact.
- Don't fight in sacred places.
- Don't embarrass your partner in public.
- Don't tread on your partner's sensitivities.
- Take a break when needed (but return later to the discussion).
- Don't drink too much alcohol.

RULE #54: **Turn down the volume.**

I hear this a lot. The reason that I hear it a lot is because we often have difficulty with loud voices. We get agitated and activated. It's basic to human physiology. The volume goes up, the heart rate goes up, rational thinking deteriorates, and things go out of control. **One of the surest ways for conflict to go south is for loud yelling to begin.**

This is the third section in this book that I have devoted primarily to anger and anger management. This is because of the importance of this topic to the overall health of relationships. **Turning down the volume is one of the simplest and most straightforward ways to immediately improve the outcome when partners are angry at each other.** There have been exercises in previous chapters on the topic of anger, and you may have already established some rules about the volume of anger. One of the reasons for getting more technical is because couples often have a difference of opinion regarding what constitutes "yelling." What may be a strong firm voice for one person is yelling for another. Addressing volume specifically is one way to break up this log-jam. Exercise 1 below asks you to calibrate excessive volume by thinking in terms of whether or not your voices could be heard: in your room, in the room next door, several rooms over or on another floor, outside the house, or in the house next door.

Volume is not something that can go unmonitored. This is another one of those topics in which process (*how* you are talking) can overshadow content (*what* you are talking about). It really doesn't matter what you are talking about or how important it is, if you are screaming at one another the conversation will likely deteriorate and nothing will be accomplished. This can be frustrating particularly when there is something important to discuss. People monitor their volume all the time in the workplace but not at home (Rule 29, "Your home is not your castle"). **By using workplace restraint on volume in one's home, angry disagreements may go much better.**

> *Volume needs to be monitored.*

But what about the importance of getting it off my chest? High volume is rarely needed, even though many people believe that "getting it off one's chest" and yelling are one in the same. For them, letting off steam isn't followed by calm; it is followed by an explosion. **Feelings can be expressed respectfully while still producing a feeling of unburdening oneself.** Volume may result in things being said that shouldn't be said, threatening postures, and for some, escalations into physical violence. These escalations hurt relationships, and partners invested in their partnerships will personally suffer as a result of those expressions. Perhaps one of the worst situations involves unmonitored expression of anger while drinking. This is just a recipe for disaster.

High volume puts relationships at risk.

All in all, it is far better to express feelings with words rather than with volume. It takes a lot less time to get back to a calm and loving place with your partner from a four on the volume scale than from a nine. See if you and your partner can figure out the best volume for your relationship and how to manage yourselves to achieve that goal.

Use your words.

If you want to turn down the volume, the first step is developing awareness. Having awareness of the appropriate volume can sometimes be difficult, because we can lose our sense of proportion when we are angry. Being able to notice ourselves takes practice. Practicing first when you are alone helps develop awareness when you are with your partner. Some techniques are:

- **sitting down in a relaxed posture**
- **closing your eyes**
- **focusing on breathing**
- **counting to ten off and on**
- **noticing sensory input**
- **noticing feelings**
- **noticing two states at the same time, like breathing and anger or counting and seeing**
- **noticing multiple feelings simultaneously like anger and sadness, or shame, or fear or self-doubt**

Develop awareness when alone.

Before talking:

- **Think about what you are going to say.**
- **Think about how you are going to say it.**
- **Think about how your partner might receive it.**
- **Think about your partner's thoughts and feelings.**
- **Maintain an open mind.**

That will likely lower your righteous indignation, which will, in turn, lower the intensity of your anger and the volume of your expression.

> *Think about what you want to say before talking and maintain an open mind.*

When beginning to talk:

- **Sit down with a conciliatory posture.**
- **Fold your hands in front of you.**
- **Close your eyes momentarily.**
- **Focus momentarily on your breathing.**
- **Count to five.**
- **Try to be mindful of your feelings and your body language at the same time.**

> *Use non-aggressive body language.*

When beginning to talk:

- **Start with a soft tone of voice.**
- **Use feeling language with appropriate volume.**
- **Choose words that express meaning.**
- **Don't choose words that are simply inflammatory and will agitate you.**
- **Talk slowly.**

> *Use non-aggressive verbal language.*

While you are talking:

- **Stay aware of your existing volume.**
- **Stay aware of the appropriate volume.**

Both you and your partner need to be monitoring volume while you are talking. You also need to develop some way to alert your partner, and vice versa, should either of you start getting too loud.

> *Develop a way to cue your partner and vice versa for turning down the volume.*

Suggestions for turning down the volume:

- *Develop various states of awareness when alone.*
- *Before talking, focus on why you are angry.*
- *Before talking, be open to other explanations.*
- *Think about your partner and how he might receive what you have to say.*
- *Think about what you want to say before you talk to your partner.*
- *Sit down with a conciliatory posture.*
- *Fold your hands in front of you.*
- *Close your eyes momentarily.*
- *Focus momentarily on your breathing.*
- *Count to five.*
- *Try to not have only a singular focus on your anger.*
- *Try to be mindful of your feelings and your body language at the same time.*
- *Try to be aware of any additional feelings like sadness, shame, fear or self-doubt.*
- *Start with a soft tone of voice.*
- *Use feeling language with appropriate volume.*
- *Choose words that express meaning.*
- *Don't choose words that are simply inflammatory and that will agitate you.*
- *Talk slowly.*
- *Acknowledge your partner's point of view.*
- *Stay aware of your existing volume.*
- *Stay aware of the appropriate volume.*
- *Consciously speak softer if your volume is too high.*
- *Develop a way to cue your partner and vice versa for turning down the volume.*

EXERCISES FOR TURNING DOWN THE VOLUME:

1. Spend some time with your partner to determine what it means to be talking too loud. Talk about what yelling is for each of you. One method of calibrating loudness is to use the following scale. Could you be heard:

In our room only?	In the room next door?	Several rooms over or on another floor?	Outside the house?	By the neighbors next door?

2. Review all of the suggestions for turning down the volume on the previous page. Talk over with your partner what suggestions are most important for you. Add any other suggestions that you think might be helpful. Write down a few of the most important suggestions for yourself on an index card.

3. Create a way to tell your partner to turn down the volume should it get too loud while he is talking.

4. Keep the index card in your pocket for the next couple of weeks and glance at it several times throughout the day. Rehearse in your mind the suggestions. Practice the awareness-strengthening techniques as needed.

5. If you are angry and you want to talk to your partner, compose your thoughts before you talk to her. Write it down if you need to.

6. When you are talking to your partner, take out your index card and put it right in front of you while you are talking. Use all of the techniques that you have practiced and developed for turning down the volume.

RULE #55: **Make yourself the "default."**

This Rule means that when you are trying to fix an interpersonal problem, think first about the changes *you* have to make in order to fix the problem. I call that the "default" position, the baseline, or how to begin thinking about interpersonal change. Rule 12, "You have more power to change yourself than to change others," is very similar but written from the personal rather than the interpersonal problem-solving perspective. Making yourself the 'default' when it comes to problem-solving is opposite the way in which most people approach interpersonal problems. Most of us start by thinking that the other person has to change. I am asking you to consider entering into a discussion with your partner with a different mindset. It is the mindset that, while both of you may have to try to see things differently and while both of you may have to change, the only changes you can control are your own. **Making yourself the default is an attitudinal shift, but it isn't a plan of action (POA). A POA has specifics regarding the goals, strategies and outcome desired for personal changes.** If you are in a conflict with your partner, think about what you can do to make the situation better.

> *Think about what **you** can do to improve the situation.*

When tension is experienced with others, it often feels like the tension is being caused by them. Thus getting rid of the tension means that others have to do something different. It is common and usual to think this way. It's our biology, and it works pretty well with most things other than humans, varmints and the weather. Consequently, to be successful in our human interactions, we have to learn to do some things that aren't automatic. Making ourselves the "default" is one of the things that we can do to achieve that objective.

> *Make yourself the "default."*

This Rule does not mean that you should take the blame for your partner's errors, or that you shouldn't use interpersonal methods for solving problems. When there is a problem between yourself and another person, sometimes the onus of change will be on him, sometimes it will be on you, and most of the time it will be on both of you. When couples get stuck, it is not uncommon that each person thinks that it is because the other person isn't doing enough to change. Making yourself the default is a way to solve that conundrum. **Having the willingness to really look at what you can do to resolve a dispute is a conceptual shift that has far-reaching ramifications.**

- *Think about what **you** can do to improve the situation.*

- *Make yourself the "default."*

EXERCISES FOR MAKING YOURSELF THE "DEFAULT":

1. If you haven't already done so, do the exercises for the Rule 12, "You have more power to change yourself than to change others."

2. Think about several situations in which you have a complaint about your partner. Spend some time thinking about what your partner does that upsets you. Write down some specific things that you can do that might improve the situation.

3. Try implementing the changes that you suggested making by creating a plan of action. Hold yourself accountable for several weeks while you are making these changes and note whether the changes that you made created a change in your feelings towards your partner.

RULE #56: **Learn how to apologize.**

Making an apology is widely accepted as a healing response to someone who feels hurt, offended or wronged. The hurt party typically wants her feelings understood, an admission of guilt, and a verbal statement using the words, "I'm sorry." The following six steps are discussed for making an apology. Each behavioral step needs to be supported by the appropriate attitude.

As you go through these steps bear in mind that there are degrees of wrongdoing. Our justice system recognizes this by giving out stiffer punishments for more severe offenses. One of the chief criteria for judging the severity of an offense is how much harm has been caused. If a great deal of harm has been caused, it may be difficult to repair the damage, particularly if there is a total loss of trust based on the perception that there is a character trait that won't change. However, if a person sincerely believes that she can change and if she truly understands the impact of her behavior, apologizing is a step in the right direction. When there is substantial harm, apologizing may need to be repeated over weeks or even months.

1. **Listen to your partner's feelings.** This is the first step, and it can't be short changed. You have to make available all the time that is necessary for your partner to tell you how he feels. Your partner is trying to process what has happened to him and part of that processing is telling you how he feels. If you cut him off by saying something like, "I know, I get it!" you may be piling more harm on top of the other. Your partner likely needs to tell you how he feels, maybe repeatedly. If you want to apologize, then it is necessary to truly understand the amount of your partner's hurt and harm. Try not to get distracted from listening by being defensive, wanting to give an explanation, thinking about what you are going to say, or even by your feelings of remorse. While it may be uncomfortable, the first step is listening to your partner's feelings.

---

1. Listen to your partner's feelings.

---

2. **Be empathic to your partner's feelings, and communicate it.** If you want to apologize, listen with your feelings and not just your intellect. To have a deep understanding of your partner's feelings, try to step into your

partner's shoes and empathize with how she feels about what you did. You have to detach from your own feelings, including your guilt, long enough that you can have feelings for what is going on for her. Remember, this is a person that you love and she feels hurt. If someone other than you hurt your partner, you'd be upset for her. It might be hard, but try to empathize as deeply as you might if it were not you that caused the problem. Then communicate that understanding to your partner: "I understand your feelings. You are hurt because I.... This is why you are so upset. I get it." Your partner will typically want to know that you understand how hurt she is by whatever you did. Communicate that understanding as best you can. You will likely have to do it more than once.

2. Show empathy to your partner's feelings.

3. **Admit your mistake.** If you are going to apologize to your partner, recognize that what you did was not okay. It certainly was not okay for her and it may also have been a violation of a code of conduct that the two of you had previously established. It also may have been a violation of a community standard or a violation of the law. The admission of your mistake acknowledges to your partner that your own behavior was out of line, hurtful, or wrong. It may need to include recognition of the degree of wrongdoing. While there may be an important explanation regarding what happened, this explanation is secondary to the primary acknowledgement that was done was not okay Trying to justify one's actions poisons an apology because it nullifies an acknowledgement of culpability. If your partner begins to hear your explanation as a justification, immediately stop and resume acknowledging your mistake. You may need to do this multiple times, each time being unequivocal in your admission.

Some people have difficulty admitting that they've made a mistake or are wrong. Do you have this difficulty? Some people are unaware of it. Being able to admit that you made a mistake is essential for making an apology and for the overall health of a relationship. If you have this difficulty, you may want to review Rule 15, "Don't turn your shortcomings into sins."

That may be part of the problem. If you don't work to correct this problem, you will forever be defensive and unable to accept negative feedback. You also won't be able to make a sincere apology.

One of the most common defenses is the "I didn't mean to do it" defense. I've heard it hundreds of times: *It was an accident. I didn't do it on purpose. I didn't intend to do it.* Perhaps you have said this yourself. If you are intentionally hurting your partner, you have a much bigger problem than your situational problem. However, it's not likely; most people don't intentionally hurt their partners, and you probably don't, either. If your partner is hurt, he probably isn't even thinking about your intentions; he is thinking about his hurt. **If the first thing to say to your partner after he tells you that he is hurt is that you didn't mean to do it, he probably isn't going to feel like you are taking responsibility for what you did.** Whether you meant it or not, the results are still the same: your partner got hurt.

I remember one time when I was driving, a woman rear-ended me while I was parked at a stop sign. I got out of the car to assess the damage, and she got out, too. She was pretty agitated. "I didn't mean to hit you," she said. I said I really didn't think that she meant to hit me, either, and added, "That's why they call these things automobile *accidents*." There was actually hardly any damage, so I told it would be fine and I didn't even take her name or phone number. I got back into my car smiling to myself about just how ludicrous the "I didn't mean to do it" defense is.

---

3. Admit your mistake.

---

4. **Show contrition.** You can't show contrition without feeling bad about what you did, without being empathic to your partner's feelings, and without believing that what you did was not okay. Feeling bad for what you did is commonly thought of as the sincere part of a sincere apology. This is what conscience is all about. This is about feeling bad that you caused harm to another human being, particularly one that you love. It may be expressed as feelings of remorse. You need to say that you are sorry. Your partner wants to know that you *feel* sorry, and it makes a big difference to him if you do. It will help him believe that Step 6 is possible. Even when showing contrition, the focus of attention needs to be on your partner's hurt, and not on your guilt. While it's important for your partner to know that you feel bad for what you did, the apology is not about you.

---

4. Show contrition.

---

5. **Be willing to make restitution.** If you have caused harm, it is your responsibility to try to repair any resulting damage. If you broke something, replace it. If you hurt someone and they have to go to the doctor, pay the doctor's bill. If you hurt someone's feelings, the way to make restitution may not be clear; however, you can always ask if there is anything else that you can do to make things right. If you have hurt your partner, think about what you can do to make things right and talk to her about it. Let her know that you are willing to do what you can to make things better.

---

5. Be willing to make restitution.

---

6. **Commit to your intention to not reoffend.** Make a commitment to your partner that you will do everything that you can to not repeat the mistake that you made. "I promise to work hard to never do it again." "I commit to you may intention to never do this again." "It is one of my highest priorities to regain your trust and not repeat what I have done." But just saying it or just thinking about not reoffending a couple of times is not likely to be sufficient. You have to put some effort into it. That means having a specific plan of action for not reoffending. You might employ some of the strategies in other parts of this book to help you. Working on not reoffending means keeping what you need to do conscious so it won't happen again. You may have to spend some time thinking about it and give yourself reminders. An old-school technique is the written apology. A written apology is useful because it gets you thinking about what you did at a time that is not so proximal to the situation itself. Also, writing an apology at a later time more fully reinforces your intentions to change. A written apology is a *beginning* effort in working on not reoffending, not the last effort. If you make a copy of your written apology and read it to yourself several times over the next weeks or months, it will further reinforce your intentions. The other benefit of a written apology is that it can communicate the depth of your sincerity to your partner, and it demonstrates that you are really willing to put some effort into trying to not repeat what you did.

---

6. Commit to your intention to not reoffend.

You have likely noticed that I have stated this sixth step in conditional language, it is your *intention* to not reoffend rather than you will not reoffend. This is because it may be difficult for you to guarantee that you won't reoffend in the future. A promise to "never to it again" introduces the additional problem of having "broken your promise," should you reoffend. The broken promise can be a distraction from the larger issue of the offense happening again. Being accountable for reoffending is the most important issue. It is up to the offended party to decide if she is going to give her partner another chance. There are more important considerations than whether or not a promise was made. Reoffending is a very serious matter and should not be taken lightly, particularly when there is an apology. The best strategy is to just not repeat the problem.

In the next section, I will talk about forgiveness and letting go. **Letting go or forgiveness doesn't happen immediately upon your making an apology, even if the apology is very sincere.** It might take your partner a little while to get through her feelings of hurt, depending on the severity. Empathizing with your partner also means understanding that it takes time to heal angry and hurt feelings. Don't be one of those people that says, *I've said I'm sorry, why don't you get over it already?* If you feel that way, you're not working hard enough at being apologetic. And if you say those things, you will make matters worse. **Feeling apologetic is not something that happens for just a few minutes.** If one is truly feeling apologetic, the feelings associated with being apologetic will last for a while. Experience those feelings, communicate them to your partner, and give it time. Apology is a healing balm.

> **Your partner needs time to heal.**

---

1. *Listen to your partner's feelings.*

2. *Show empathy to your partner's feelings.*

3. *Admit your mistake.*

4. *Show contrition.*

5. *Be willing to make restitution.*

6. *Commit to your intention to not reoffend.*

Your partner needs time to heal.

EXERCISES FOR MAKING AN APOLOGY:

1. Spend some time by yourself and write down the six steps to making an apology. Commit the steps to memory and say them out loud to yourself several times. Try doing the same thing tomorrow to see if you can remember the six steps without looking.

2. Think about something you have apologized for in the last year. Go through the steps for making an apology and ask yourself if you did all of these steps. If not, think about how you could have done a better job.

3. Think about something that you have apologized for and whether you committed to your intention to not reoffend. Did you reoffend? How are you working on not reoffending? Write down the action plan that you are using to keep yourself focused, so that whatever you did, you won't do it again.

4. Spend some time talking to your partner about making apologies. Discuss these six steps with him. Discuss whether or not either of you seem to have difficulty in admitting your mistakes. If either of you do, the person who has this difficulty should try to explain to the other person why he thinks he has this difficulty.

RULE #57: Be forgiving. Let go. Don't hold a grudge.

Forgiveness and *letting go* both require time and both require an active process of changing the way you feel. They are a little different from one another. **Forgiveness has an external focus** while letting go has an internal focus.

- You forgive somebody.
- Forgiveness has a focus on a specific act or specific acts with parameters.
- You forgive others for what they did to you.
- It means that you no longer require them to make restitution to you.
- You no longer wish for them to be punished.
- It means you no longer want them to show contrition or make apologies.
- You no longer want to get back at them or have them make retribution for what they have done.
- Forgiveness means no longer holding on to angry feelings towards the person who harmed you for what they did to you.

Forgiveness does not necessarily mean that the feelings of hurt or sadness are gone. It does not mean that the hurtful act is now condoned. It is not the same as *reconciliation*. We can forgive somebody and reject her at the same time, if our feelings about her have changed as a result of what she did. However, if the offender is your partner and you still want to have a relationship with her, then reconciliation is pretty important. You can forgive your partner and you can reconcile with your partner while still remembering what has occurred. What happened may continue to have an impact on your relationship, even if you we have forgiven her. **Forgiveness is principally a change in feelings of anger and revenge towards someone who has been hurtful and a change in a desire for retribution.** Those changes can be very cleansing and healing for the forgiver. While an apology is not required for forgiveness, it makes it a lot easier.

You forgive a person.

Letting go **has a more internal focus.** I think of letting go as how a person gets over her hurt and anger, particularly if there is no apology. For many people, being forgiving is difficult if there is no apology. Nonetheless, we may not want to continue to feel angry and hurt, and the alternative to forgiveness is "letting go." Unlike forgiveness, when we let go of our strong feelings of hurt and anger we still may retain the desire for justice to be served on the perpetrator. It is probably going to be difficult to reconcile with the person who hurt us if we still want retribution. If there is no apology, reconciliation may not be possible because of fears of being hurt again in the same way. While "letting go" is an alternative for helping oneself, without forgiveness, it doesn't do much for helping a couple reconcile. However, "letting go" can be a step towards forgiveness and reconciliation if a couple is willing to continue to work on the problem.

You "let go" of feelings.

As I mentioned in the section on making apologies, there are degrees of wrongdoing, and for most people, **there is a relationship between the ease of forgiveness and the degree of wrongdoing.** It is possible that we may have been hurt too deeply or we may think that what was done to us was so horrible that we don't want to be forgiving. If that is the case, you are not likely to be able to reconcile with the person who hurt you, particularly if you also want him to be punished. It is also possible that you may not be sure if you want to be forgiving. That may depend on your partner and whether or not he chooses to apologize. You may feel like your partner has to earn your forgiveness and, once again, that may depend on the degree of hurt you suffered. I would like to say that is not a matter of either giving or not giving forgiveness. It is a process, something that happens over time. **Becoming forgiving may involve:**

- the degree of wrongdoing
- the sincerity and strength of your partner's apology
- whether they remain apologetic over time
- the explanation of their wrongdoing
- whether or not the same thing has occurred previously
- their efforts to repair the damage
- your belief in their love for you
- how much you trust your partner

- the history of your partnership
- your willingness to let go of anger
- the overall strength of your relationship
- your desire to remain coupled

> ## *Make consideration of forgiveness an active process.*

If the hurt is not very big, the apology may not have to be big. In fact, you may not even require an apology. You may be able to let go and be forgiving because it isn't that big a deal. **It is only when the hurt is bigger that the strength of the apology becomes more important. If your partner has difficulty admitting her mistakes, it might be difficult to be forgiving.** That is why learning to make an apology is so important.

If you are the one that has been hurt, it can become very challenging to know what to do if your partner doesn't apologize.

- You do need to give it time.
- If you and your partner are able, continue to discuss what occurred.
- In time, your partner may come to take more responsibility and apologize.
- In time, your partner's explanation may make more sense.
- Your initial feelings of hurt may decrease over time.

Apology and forgiveness take time and conversation to figure out. If a partner is stonewalling, it's not going to go so well, in part because **the longer the stonewalling goes on, the greater hurt from being stonewalled becomes, adding to the previous hurt.** On the contrary, there is a need for engagement. This is not to suggest a constant rehashing of the problem; just a willingness to talk even if it is difficult. **In all likelihood, the deeper the hurt, the greater will be the need for conversation.**

> ## *Give it time and try to stay connected.*

If your partner's position doesn't change over time and she doesn't apologize, and if you continue to feel violated, the severity of the violation has to be considered. You may find yourself considering whether or not your partner's behavior constitutes grounds for separation, particularly since there has been no apology. **If you decide that you want to stay together, then you have to begin the process of trying to "let go," because living with hurt and anger will be burdensome to you and harmful to the relationship.** You run the risk of just piling one hurt feeling on top of another until you are depressed and miserable. *Acceptance* **is ultimately the pathway for letting go of hurt and angry feelings, if no apology is given.**

- It is accepting that whatever occurred is now past.
- It is accepting that your partner disagrees that an apology is warranted or that she has difficulty in making an apology.
- It is being more accepting of your partner's point of view.
- It is decreasing the degree of importance that you originally placed on the situation.

Accepting some of these things may not be pleasant for you, but that is what it is going to take in order to let go of your hurt and angry feelings. However, as I have said before, if you let go of anger and hurt feelings and still retain a desire for retribution, it is going to be difficult to reconcile with your partner. **So in the service of your relationship, letting go has to ultimately turn into forgiveness for the best healing to occur.**

> ### *Acceptance is the pathway for letting-go of feelings.*

Two aspects of forgiveness are important to remember at this point:

1. **Forgiveness is for past discrete acts or activities in which there are some parameters.**
2. **Forgiveness doesn't erase the memory of what has occurred.**

Forgiveness isn't a panacea. Forgiveness doesn't roll forward. Forgiveness is not for character traits or for patterns of behavior past and future. If your partner was unfaithful, you may decide to forgive one act of infidelity, or even two acts of infidelity, but you are not choosing to forgive all acts of infidelity past or future. Having forgiven your partner for one act of infidelity doesn't erase the memory of the pain that it caused. Thus, if your partner is unfaithful a second time, you might not be so forgiving. You have likely heard the expression, "First time, shame on you; second time, shame on me."

No expression gets to say how many times you are supposed to be forgiving for similar actions. It is individual and based of different circumstances and situations. So maybe "shame on me" takes a second, third, or fourth time. That is ultimately up to you to decide based on all the variables.

I'll give you example: If a man has been unfaithful to his wife by having an affair with a woman at his office and it is later discovered that he has had lunch with a different woman at the office without telling his wife, this may or may not be considered another act of infidelity by his wife. It well may feel like another breach of trust to his wife, and it may bring up the old feelings, even if his wife forgave him for the affair. His wife may come to the conclusion that this represents a character flaw, and that he is just starting up the same old thing again. Or she may conclude that this was a business meeting and while she was initially concerned because of his past act of infidelity, this was not the same, and that her husband just failed to tell her. You can see by this example that it isn't always easy to sort these things out. What is clear is that forgiveness doesn't roll forward, and that the memory of the past has an influence on whether or not one wants to be forgiving in the future.

> ### *Forgiveness is not a panacea.*

When a person continues to have angry feelings about something that has happened to her in the past, this is called *carrying a grudge*. Often these feelings are coupled with a desire for revenge. If you find that you have a need to continue to remind your partner about something that he did months or years ago, long after the processing has ceased and long after apologies have been made, you might be holding a grudge. Holding a grudge has to do with the feelings that you are continuing to have. Only you can know that. If the feelings are angry and intense about a specific event that occurred some time ago, you have to ask yourself if you have more work to do in letting go of those feelings. Sometimes people hold a grudge as protection against the possibility of some future hurt. If they stay angry and a little distant, they may not feel as vulnerable. I believe that it is, in part, a form of mistrust. Holding a grudge is destructive for relationships. It means that the relationship can never really heal from past difficulties. It also means that past wrongdoings may be used as weapons in some future disagreement with the same compliment of angry feelings that may have originally occurred.

Let's use the man who had an affair as an example of holding a grudge. The couple has reconciled and there have been verbal exchanges of apologies and forgiveness. It is now a year later. Whenever the husband glances in the direction of another woman, his wife angrily accuses him of unfaithful intentions. She tells him that he's just starting the whole thing up again, and she doesn't feel like having anything to do with him. She tells him that he never really suffered enough for the affair and stops talking to him for several days.

That's holding a grudge.

Holding a grudge is destructive for relationships.

On the other hand, if your memory of past events merely informs your current feelings, that is different. **The difference between holding a grudge and remembering the past has to do with the depth of the feelings, particularly the anger and revenge part of the feelings, and how great a stimulus it takes to activate those feelings.** If feelings of anger and revenge are easily activated in all kinds of situations, it may be grudge holding. If feelings of hurt are principally only activated in a situation similar to the original offense, then it may have more to do with remembering the past—albeit in a feeling way as well as an intellectual way. There may be feelings of anger, but they have more to do with the current situation and the fact that the same thing has occurred a second time.

Using the same example, if now the man has secretly gone out with another woman, his wife may be hurt and angry. She tells him she can't believe that he has done it again after his heartfelt apology and the way she worked to restore her faith in him. This is not holding grudge. This is remembering the past coupled with the feelings that are associated with the current situation.

Remembering the past is not the same as holding a grudge.

It is possible that in spite of your partner's apologies, she may continue to repeat the same offensive behavior again and again. If you have feelings about this repeating behavior, it is not the same thing as carrying a grudge. This is having **feelings about a pattern of behavior** that has occurred over time, and it is this pattern of behavior rather that any specific occurrence that is causing the difficulty. If this is how the past events reemerge for you, it is helpful to identify it as such to your partner, so that she doesn't simply say that you are holding a grudge and dismiss what you have to say.

Dealing with offensive patterns of behavior can be a very difficult matter for couples, and it is not the same thing as practicing forgiveness and letting go, as I have described it in this section. Again, only you can answer the question in your memory of whether the past represents concerns and feelings about a pattern of behavior in your partner that trouble you.

Once again, using the same example, if the man continues to exhibit flirtatious behavior with other women, is secretive about his activities with other women, is known to go to strip clubs, and is defensive about all of the above with his wife, his wife is quite likely to be angry and upset. This isn't holding a grudge. This is about a pattern of behavior that her husband has and the feelings she has as a result.

> *Feelings about "patterns of behavior" are not the same as holding a grudge.*

It is also possible that, after a wrongdoing and after apologies have been made and forgiveness has been given, **the person who has been hurt may be anxious about being hurt again.** This may manifest as suspiciousness or worry. There may be continued mistrust even though it might be diminishing over time.

If we again use the same example: If the man goes on a business trip, his wife might ask him to give her a detailed accounting of where he is going, what he is doing, and who he is doing it with. This is not holding a grudge. There is no increased activation of a similar current event by the past event, and there may not be any pattern of behavior to account for his wife's feelings. She is simply anxious because of how hurt she was, and it hasn't been long enough for her trust in her husband to be fully restored.

> *Having anxieties about what might occur is not the same as holding a grudge.*

Forgiveness is not an easy state of mind to achieve. And, even when we do, it is not a panacea for resolution of all the difficult feelings that are associated with being hurt. Nonetheless, it is one of the most important parts of the process of reconciliation between the offender and the offended. It helps both. It unburdens the offended from feelings of hurt, anger, and revenge. It helps to lift the guilt from the shoulders of the offender and offers a possible pathway back towards the offended. And it begins to heal a broken relationship and give it the potential to be loving once again.

- *Make consideration of forgiveness an active process.*

- *Give it time and try to stay connected.*

- *Acceptance is the pathway for letting-go of feelings.*

- *Forgiveness is not a panacea.*

- *Holding a grudge is destructive for relationships.*

- *Remembering the past is not the same as holding a grudge.*

- *Feelings about "patterns of behavior" are not the same as holding a grudge.*

- *Having anxieties about what might occur is not the same as holding a grudge.*

EXERCISES ON BEING FORGIVING AND NOT HOLDING A GRUDGE:

1. Spend some time with your partner. Have a discussion about what forgiveness is and is not. Have a discussion about what letting go is and is not.

2. Review the conditions for being forgiving. See if the two of you agree with those conditions. Are there others?

3. Talk about the distinctions between:

   - holding a grudge
   - remembering the past
   - having feelings about patterns of behavior
   - have anxious feelings about future infractions

4. Discuss whether or not either of you have feelings that you would characterize as falling into any of these four categories. See if you can differentiate the categories based on the kinds of feelings that you have.

5. Do either you or your partner feel like you would like to be forgiven for a past wrongdoing? Discuss what it is. Discuss whether or not forgiveness has been given. If one person says that it has been given and the other person doesn't feel like it has, discuss why it doesn't feel like it has. See if the forgiveness that has been given meets the definition that I have given above. If it does meet that definition, see if you can figure out why it doesn't feel like it. See if it has anything to do with remembering the past, feelings about patterns of behavior, or anxious feelings about future infractions.

**Make numbers an ally
not an enemy.**

Numbers and data can speak volumes. Numbers can give a picture of reality in a way nothing else can: how far it is from one place to another, how big a space is, or how many days it will be till an event. When numbers are reported accurately, they reveal honesty and they bring us closer to the truth, like whether a diet is working, whether one's debt is decreasing, or how much work has been completed. Numbers can help us know when to continue on the same course or alter our direction. They can help us know how much to spend, how much to eat and what time to go to bed. Numbers can help us check our feelings against reality, like when we feel cold on a hot day, or when it feels like forever until the food is served. Couples make many decisions that are data-dependant: how often they go out to dinner, how often they have family time and when, who walks the dog and when, what time the kids need to be in bed, what time they need to get up in the morning, how often snacks or sweets are allowed, how much time can be spent watching TV or being on the computer, what the temperature of the house can be in the winter time, how much of certain food items are okay to eat at any one time...

Numbers used in this fashion can be a useful way in which people run their lives. Numbers can be used as a way of noticing the kindnesses of one's partner and the habitual ways in which they add quality to their spouse's life. Another very important use of number is for talking about finances. I will discuss this separately in the next section.

Use numbers constructively.

But couples also use numbers in an aggressive and hostile fashion with one another. That is when numbers and fighting start working hand in hand. Here are some examples:

"Look at you. You must weigh over 200 pounds."

"Well, look at you; you must be tipping 250."

"In the last month you have told me only two times that you loved me."

"Well, how many times have you told me that you love me?"

"I've added it up and it turns out that your mother spends more time with the kids then you do."

"Well, I've added it up, and you spend more time talking on the telephone to your friends than you spend time talking to me."

"So this time you were forty-five minutes late."

"No, I was twenty minutes late."

"I spent an hour and a half just picking up the mess in the house."

"Well I spent two hours washing the cars. And by the way, you made the mess to begin with."

These are not helpful ways to use numbers. Often arguments just ensue about the numbers, and the real content of the conversation is lost. In my office I often find myself saying, "We aren't going to quibble about the numbers. See if you can express the same feeling without using the numbers." There is often some passion associated with the numbers, so it is also important to express that passion is a way that is acceptable to both parties. See if you can be conscious of when you might be using numbers as a weapon against the other person and when you are using numbers in the interest of the "we."

Don't use number destructively or as weapons.

Numbers can also be used to exaggerate, distort, or hide the truth. Since we are dependent on numbers to help reveal truth and accuracy, when they are used in an exaggerated fashion, it can be confusing and frustrating. Some people think that an exaggerated use of numbers is kind of cute and doesn't cause any harm, but that isn't my experience. I find couples getting frustrated when it happens, particularly when it pertains to a topic of importance: *I'm sure that the project will only take you a few minutes to complete*... but, in fact it takes two hours to complete. *I'm sure that it will only cost a couple of hundred dollars more to complete the landscaping on the other side of the house*... when, in fact, it cost and additional $600.

Be accurate when using numbers. Don't exaggerate.

People also use numbers to hide the truth: I only spent a little more than $100 on the shoes...when in fact it was almost $200. I only had a couple of drinks... when in fact there were four drinks and they were all doubles. Sometimes it can be difficult to distinguish a distortion from a lie, but in either case, over time it becomes increasingly harder to dismiss and it begins to erode trust.

> *Don't use numbers to hide the truth.*

Some people speak by distorting numbers when it would be better to speak in terms of feelings. For example a husband may say to his wife, "We haven't had alone time for the past three months," With frustration, his wife reminds him that they had alone time two weeks ago. It might be better if he said, "It *feels* like we haven't had alone time for a very long time." When she reminds him that they had alone time two weeks ago, he can easily say that two weeks seems like a long time for him. There is less frustration because an exaggerated use of numbers wasn't used to replace an expression of feelings.

> *Don't use numbers to express feelings.*

- *Use numbers constructively.*
- *Don't use numbers destructively or as weapons.*
- *Be accurate when using numbers. Don't exaggerate.*
- *Don't use numbers to hide the truth.*
- *Don't use numbers to express feelings.*

EXERCISES FOR MAKING NUMBERS YOUR ALLIES:

1. Spend some time with your partner and talk about how the two of you use numbers. Talk about whether you believe you use numbers in positive or negative ways. Discuss whether or not you use numbers:

   - constructively

   - destructively or as weapons

   - accurate or to exaggerate

   - to hide the truth

   - to express feelings

2. If you misuse numbers in any of the ways above, write down what occurs. See if you can find different ways to express whatever you are trying to express without misusing numbers.

3. Review what you have written over the next couple of months to see if you can make positive changes so that you don't continue to use numbers in these ways.

RULE #59: **Have a financial plan.**

This book addresses primarily issues that are *process*-oriented; that is, *how* a subject is discussed. *What* we talk about or the subject matter of conversation is called the *content*. Some specific topics couples often talk about are so important to the well-being of a relationship that I am going to give them special attention. One of these topics is finances.

The first Rule in this chapter on problem-solving is about not avoiding important conversations. This is true in spades when it comes to talking about money. Some topics of conversation that are avoided cause small problems, and some topics of conversation that are avoided cause big problems. **This is one topic of conversation that, if avoided, can cause two big problems.**

1. **For most people, desired uses for money exceed their supply of money. Consequently, needs, wants and desires, as they relate to money, are often not fulfilled.** If these NWDs are not discussed, resentments can grow and become very intense. Basic survival needs such as food, shelter, clothing, supplies, transportation and health care can be jeopardized. Big-ticket items for which money needs to be saved may be totally unaffordable because there is no savings plan. Future survival can be jeopardized without financial planning.

2. Because the desired uses for money exceed the supply of money, without a budget, **spending can ultimately outstrip income and debt will accumulate to a point that it can no longer be serviced.** A couple may then attempt to close the barn door, but the horse will already be gone.

> *Problems can occur when the desired use of money exceeds the supply of money and when there is too much accumulated debt.*

Financial issues are a little like the weather—they are going to keep coming at you whether you discuss them or not. You can be prepared or just take your chances that a financial storm will never come. But, like the weather, if you have a plan and if you are prepared, you will mitigate any damages. That plan is:

1. a short-term budget
2. a long-term budget
3. a savings plan

The savings plan may include some type of investments. All of this takes planning and conversation.

Finances are one of the areas in which talking about numbers is essential. Two important numbers are the amount of money coming into the house and the amount of money that is going out; that is, *total income* and *total expenses*. If total income is bigger than total expenses, if both people feel like their priority monetary needs, wants and desires are being met, and as long as a savings plan is in place that is satisfactory to both parties, the couple is in pretty good shape. However, if this is not the case, then there needs to be conversation about these numbers. Determining the various amounts of money that are being spent on different things can further refine this conversation. This is a basic budget. Some couples have less detailed budgets and some couples have more detailed budgets that work for them. **Having a conversation about these numbers is the rudimentary financial conversation that most couples need to have to keep them out of trouble.** While it might seem basic, it is the conversation that many couples with financial difficulties do not have.

> ## Talking about finances means talking about numbers.

Some topics that couples can discuss include:

- ongoing income
- ongoing weekly or monthly spending
- savings for big-ticket items
- savings for a "rainy day"
- savings for vacations
- savings for education
- savings for retirement
- debt. What kind and how much?

These are hard topics to discuss. When discussing finances, often the devil is in the details, so particulars matter. **Conversations about finances often require more information than conversations about most other topics. Consequently, it is very important to hold emotions in tow until all of the information is gathered and shared.** Financial decisions are hard decisions because couples are dealing with what they want and what they may not be able to have. This stirs up emotions. Couples have to be extra careful to not start blaming, judging or ridiculing each other during these conversations, or they will just fall apart. Managing emotions is a very high priority when having financial conversations.

> ### You need to stay calm when discussing finances.

It may be useful to utilize tried-and-true materials that have been developed by others that can assist you in having good conversations about finances. There are tons of resources available, many on the internet. There are also professionals that can help you discuss these important matters. Be prepared to have multiple conversations over several weeks or even months, for the purpose of getting your financial house in order. Also, be prepared to have maintenance conversations about finances that need to occur on a regular basis.

> - **Problems can occur when the desired use of money exceeds the supply of money and when there is too much accumulated debt.**
> - **Talking about finances means talking about numbers.**
> - **You need to stay calm when discussing finances.**

EXERCISES FOR HAVING A FINANCIAL PLAN:

1. Spend some time with your partner discussing whether either of you are concerned about how money is being spent or whether you have too much debt. Try to be specific about your concerns and talk about numbers. Be calm.

2. Have a conversation about the topics listed above to see if you have concerns and acceptable plans regarding ongoing income, ongoing weekly or monthly spending, savings for big-ticket items, savings for a rainy day, savings for vacations; savings for education; savings for retirement; debt. What kind and how much? Again, talk about numbers. Be calm.

3. If you have concerns, see if you can create budgets that address those concerns. Divide up responsibilities for gathering any materials that you might need to assist you.

RULE #60: **Create agreements on standards and "by-whens."**

This is another *content*-oriented topic. One topic that comes up again and again when I am talking to couples is who does what around the house, and whether it actually gets done. I call this a **distribution of responsibilities** or a **division of labor** topic. It applies to all domestic responsibilities: cooking, cleaning, shopping, laundry, yard work, bill paying, child care, etc. Many couples that I see have never had a discussion about this. They tell me that it just sort of evolved over time. They may fight about who does what in a sort of piecemeal fashion, but they rarely look at the big picture, and they rarely discuss how it might work best for both of them. It's work figuring this all out. Many couples don't want to take the time, don't know how to talk about it, and are concerned it will just lead to a big fight. So they are passive and frustrated.

To solve the problems associated with the distribution of responsibilities in the household, several ongoing conversations are needed to reach agreements. Significant changes in circumstances create a need for renegotiation of those agreements. **I have discovered two major areas of difficulty when it comes to division of labor: "standards" and "by-whens."**

Standards **are the criteria for determining what constitutes a completed job.** Standards can be detailed; for example, determining how clean is clean. There are often differences between couples regarding standards, and there can be misunderstandings regarding what constitutes completion, if this isn't discussed. I often say that **the person with the higher standards wears the vulnerability.** What I mean is that along with higher standards, there are more NWDs. The more NWDs you have, the more vulnerable you are to not having them met and being frustrated. That's because "You can't always get what you want," Rule 8. In a partnership, the person with the higher standards may end up having to do more work and be frustrated by that. There can be a lot of feelings in the person who has the higher standards, and this can make for increased tension in the relationship. Consequently, this is a high-priority topic for conversation and negotiation.

To lower frustrations, agree on criteria for the completion of tasks.

By-whens are the deadlines for job completion. For the couples that I see, by-whens rarely get discussed, but they cause a lot of trouble when one partner's anticipated completion time doesn't fit with the other partner's anticipated completion time. The person who wants something completed in a more timely fashion can have a lot of frustration when it doesn't happen. If this is a pattern of behavior in the relationship, it can cause a lot of difficulty.

> *To lower frustrations, agree on deadlines for the completion of tasks.*

Having an honest discussion about standards and by-whens allows both parties to realistically express their NWDs, feelings, constraints and limitations. Many of the Rules that you have previously learned in this book will be useful when having this discussion. Resolution of division of responsibility issues, standards and by-whens may be reached through negotiation and resulting agreements. **These agreements are important, as they help bridge differences and settle what can be highly charged topics. Therefore, lack of follow-through on these agreements can be very disruptive.** Agreements should not be made unless both parties have confidence that there *will* be follow-through. Couples are far better off when the parties under-promise and over-deliver than vice versa. If either party is unsure of his ability to complete a task by the time being discussed, it should be stated and discussed.

> *Follow through on your agreements regarding division of responsibilities to avoid disruption to your relationship.*

> - *To lower frustrations, agree on criteria for the completion of tasks.*
> - *To lower frustrations, agree on deadlines for the completion of tasks.*
> - *Follow through on your agreements regarding division of responsibilities to avoid disruption to your relationship.*

EXERCISES FOR CREATING AGREEMENTS ON STANDARDS AND BY-WHENS:

1. Both you and your partner spend time alone making a list of your domestic responsibilities.

2. While alone, think about the issues of standards and by-whens. Ask yourself if you have any concerns about either of these two issues regarding any of the domestic responsibilities that you have, that your partner has, or that are shared by both of you. Write down your concerns.

3. Have a conversation with your partner and review the lists. See if you have discrepancies. Are there domestic responsibilities that aren't on either of your lists? Write them down. See if you can come to an agreement regarding what the current situation actually is, whether you agree with the division of responsibilities or not.

4. Share with your partner any of the concerns that you have written down about standards or by-whens.

5. See if you can resolve any differences regarding standards and by-whens. Try to be realistic. Write down any agreements that you reach.

   Exercises 4 and 5 may require more than one conversation. If you reach an impasse, set up another meeting that is no more than a week away to see if you can arrive at a mutual understanding.

6. Think about whether you need to renegotiate your division of responsibilities. If you do, see if you can reach some new agreements and write them down.

RULE #61: **Have a reset button and use it.**

So is this really the last Rule in the last chapter of this book? For now, it is. I guess I've just about run out of Rules. This is a good one, though, and it's called "Use a reset button." I actually got this idea from several of the electronic devices that I own. **I noticed that when one of these devices became frozen and nothing would work, all I had to do was press the "reset" button. It sort of cleared the deck of any current electronic difficulties.** I started talking about this idea of a "reset button" with some of the couples that I was seeing and I asked them if they had any "reset buttons" already. Many couples responded that they already had them, but not by that name. If a couple had none, I asked them to develop some. It has been fun finding the "reset buttons" for many couples.

> *A reset button is used when an electronic device is frozen.*

Here is why a reset button may be useful for you: If we use the electronic language from above, I could say that **you might sometimes get "frozen" when dealing with some difficulty with your partner.** You might get stuck. You might not always be able to reach a mutual understanding when you are trying to resolve a conflict. After you have been at it for a while with your partner, attempting to resolve a problem, you might want to take a break.

- Perhaps you have both expressed your feelings and thoughts and feel pretty confident that each of you have been understood.
- You may have gone through other steps of problem-solving and tried out some of the other approaches mentioned in this book.
- You may be tired from talking about your concerns, but you know you are not done and that you need to get back to the conversation at a later time. You may have conversation fatigue.

You may still be emotionally keyed up with some of the feelings that you had coming into the conversation, and you may have new feelings as a result of the conversation. You are not so keyed up that either of you want to take a time-out from each other; you just want to take a time-out from the conversation. **Consequently, you want the negative feelings to go away so you can enjoy each**

other's company. You just want to turn the page. That's when it's nice to have a reset button.

> *A reset button can help you get unstuck from negative feelings*
> *so you can move on to positive feelings.*

A reset button is a way to change the subject or a way to do something else that will be incompatible with the mood and physiological state in which you find yourself at the moment. It breaks the mood; it changes the focus of attention; it enlarges the psychic space for other more positive feelings and thoughts. It could be:

- walking the dog together
- reading something funny to one another
- turning on enjoyable music
- getting something to eat
- going for a ride
- watching a funny movie
- doing some gardening together
- exercising together
- getting together with some friends
- making love
- doing a host of other activities that you come up with on your own

> *Pleasant activities can serve as a reset button.*

See if you can figure out some of these options in advance, and write them down on your "reset button" list. Then when you are feeling a bit befuddled from your conflict, you can hazily go over to your list and with your partner's help, select one of the reset activities, and go do it. You might have low energy to proceed forward at first. You may even find that you are a bit resistant because you are still upset and having a hard time letting go. **If you become self-righteous about being upset, it may be difficult.** *I have a right to be angry, and if I stop being angry my partner is going to think that everything is okay. And everything isn't okay!* That's the decision point. You're feeling angry but you are unsure if you want to continue being angry. Like I have previously said, your anger isn't on autopilot as if you don't have any control over it. You *can* decide to turn down the volume, if you want. And if you do want, the reset button can help. If you are on the fence, I'd suggest that you go ahead and hit the "reset button." **You will typically find that it feels great to move on to something else, and you can get back to whatever made you angry at a later time.** You will likely do a better job in resolving the issue at a later time anyway, because you will likely not be as angry. In the meantime you can find your way back to the lifeblood of your partnership, enjoyment of life and enjoyment of one another's company.

- *A reset button can help you get unstuck from negative feelings so you can move on to positive feelings.*
- *Pleasant activities can serve as a reset button.*

EXERCISES FOR FINDING A RESET BUTTON AND USING IT:

1. Talk to your partner about the concept of a reset button. See if she can agree that it might be a good idea to use some time. Try to figure out some guidelines for using a reset button.

   - What are some of the circumstances?
   - At what point in a conversation is it okay to use?
   - How do you know if the suggestion to use a reset button is really because of argument fatigue or if it is simply to avoid conflict?
   - Do you both have to agree?
   - What if you don't both agree?
   - How soon after someone suggests the idea should you begin to try to disengage from the argument and reengage in the new activity?
   - Should you spend a few minutes by yourselves in between the two activities?

2. With your partner, make a list of activities that would serve as a reset button. Write the list down where it can be readily accessible to both of you. Talk about whether or not you need different reset buttons for different situations.

Conclusion

RULE #62: **Have presence with your partner's best qualities.**

When I was in my mid thirties something happened to me that was life changing. I was in the final months of my job at the Oregon Health Sciences University where I had been working for seven years and I was going into full time private practice. My father was dying of cancer. My wife and I had a two year old and she was pregnant with twins. She had gone into early labor and was under doctor's orders to be in bed. Now, I should tell you that I'm one of those, do-it-yourself kind of guys and doing it myself was beginning to be my undoing. I had my hands full and then some. And about the time that I was about to burst apart at the seams, extraordinary things began to happen. People started pouring out of the woodwork to give us help. A dinner brigade was formed and several times a week dinner appeared on our front porch. People would come over to help clean, spend time with my wife and help with child care. Some of the help came from people I didn't even know. Our community stood up for me and for my family. As long as I live, I will never forget what was done for us. As you can imagine, I had enormous gratitude.

But something else happened and that is why I am telling you this story in the conclusion of this book. What happened is that I learned, more accurately, relearned, that without question there is a great deal of good in other people. Many of the people who helped us were not our good friends. They were just regular people who saw a need and wanted to respond. I experienced a community spirit in others when I was first growing up because we knew our neighbors, we played outside together and we helped one another if a tree feel down or if the snow had to be cleared. We walked to school, to the playground and to most all of our extracurricular activities so we knew our neighborhood. Many service providers came to the house including the milkman who came to deliver our milk along with vegetables that he grew in his garden. We had a connection with people in our community and while there were squabbles, we could feel a positive spirit in others.

With all the moving around that I did in my twenties and early thirties, my sense of community began to wane. The Vietnam War had created an awful polarization and the media pounded my senses with stories of humans at their worst. Life was sort of pushing away what I had learned in my childhood, that is, most people want to do the right thing and have good hearts. When the community stepped up for my wife and I, my faith in humanity was renewed and it has never left. This faith brings me great comfort and gives me confidence to reach out and make connections with people everywhere.

In the introduction to this book, I said that there were many themes that overlapped one another in the sixty-two Rules and various Tools that I have given you. One overriding theme for having healthy relationships is the theme of having a positive external focus, whether it be in the form of being open to your partner's point of view; being interested in what he has to say; having compassion for how she feels; being appreciative; giving him support; accepting her influence; or thinking in terms of "we" and not just me. Couples often get stuck because one or both parties cannot defocus on themselves; on their own point of view and on how they themselves feel. So having a positive external focus, in and of itself, accomplishes a lot in the human relations department.

Also in the Introduction, I expressed that it would be nice if there could be just one Rule or just a few Rules that could steer us towards good relationships with others. I still think that the Golden Rule is a wonderful effort in that direction as is One for Another. So, in conclusion, I would like to offer up just one more Rule for creating a healthy relationship that I think covers a lot of ground.

Have presence with your partner's best qualities.

People are basically good hearted and so is your partner. We are living in difficult times with a world-wide recession and global warming that is just beginning to wreck havoc on our weather. Many challenges lay in front of us, and the stresses from those challenges are right on our front stair steps. You are facing these challenges with your partner. More than ever, a solid team is important. When you look at your partner and notice his/her finest qualities, your partnership will grow stronger. Let your heart and your consciousness be filled with the many wonderful attributes that your partner has and all the rest will be much easier.

Glossary of terms

as they are used in this book

Absolutist thinking: Black and white thinking; being totally and completely sure of oneself.

Acceptance: Letting go of the desire to make things different from how they are right now.

Acknowledge: To recognize; to validate as real.

Acute: Rapid onset and short duration.

Addiction: A physical/psychological compulsion that is habit forming.

Agreement: A promise to do something; a contract.

Alienation: A state of being withdrawn or estranged.

Ally: A friend.

Anger: A generic feeling that ranges from irritation to rage.

Anxiety: A feeling of unsettledness, unease, and/or stress.

Apology: Accepting blame and having regret and contrition for an offense.

Appreciation: An expression of thanks or gratitude.

Arousal: A state of being stirred up.

Attitude: A state of mind; a disposition; a specific set of beliefs and feelings.

Attribution: Assigning causality to something or someone.

Awareness: A state of being cognizant; recognition.

Blame: A state of accepting responsibility for an occurrence; culpability.

Boundaries: The demarcation between acceptable and unacceptable behavior.

By-whens: Deadlines for job completion.

Care: A feeling of concern and a desire to fill another's needs.

Catalyst: An event that encourages a reaction.

Cathartic anger: Anger that is expressed to achieve a feeling of release.

Causality: An explanation that a specific effect has been produced by a specific stimulus.

Chronic: Lasting for a long time.

Circumstantial: Conditions that lie outside on one's personal control.

Civility: Proper behavior, ethical, reasonable and with consideration of others.

Collaboration: A joint cooperative effort.

Commission: An active, purposeful and overt act.

Commitment: Making a pledge or promise to do something.

Communication: The exchange of information, ideas and/or feelings.

Compassion: Care and concern for others that grows from a loving heart.

Complaint: An expression of dissatisfaction; a grievance.

Compulsion: A singular preoccupation with a behavior or behaviors.

Conciliatory: A willingness to make concessions to another person.

Confirmation: Verifying the correctness of one's understanding.

Conflict: A state of disharmony, disagreement, or controversy.

Connection: The blending of two people's experiences.

Conscience: Feeling compelled to act within the boundaries of right and wrong.

Consciousness: Awareness of oneself, one's state of mind, one's situation.

Consensus: An agreement that is reached by all parties.

Containment: To hold feelings and behavior within some bounds and limits.

Content: The subject matter.

Continuum: A continuous series.

Contrition: Sincere remorse for wrongdoing.

Courtship: Seeking the affections of another.

Cover-up: An attempt to conceal a wrongdoing.

Criticism: Making unfavorable judgments.

Curiosity: A desire to learn or know.

Customs: A set of behaviors followed by people of a particular group or region.

Default: The baseline setting.

Defense: A psychological mechanism for reducing anxiety or a perceived threat.

Differences: A condition of dissimilarity.

Differentiation: A process that brings about separateness.

Dishonesty: Deceit; lack of truthfulness.

Disinhibited: Lack of restraint.

Division of labor: The distribution of responsibilities.

Double standard: Conditions that are divided unequally.

Egregious: Conspicuously offensive.

Empathy: Relating to someone else's feelings as if they were one's own feelings.

Entitlement: A state of feeling deserving.

Environment: All living and non-living surroundings.

Existential: Something that relates to existence.

Expectation: Anticipation of a probable occurrence.

Explanation: An accounting that attempts to answer questions of causality.

Eye contact: Meeting of the eyes between two people that expresses non-verbal meaning.

Fairness: Equitable treatment; free from bias or favoritism; impartiality; just.

Fantasy: A creation of the imagination.

Fear: An immediate state of distress with associated impulses to take action.

Feedback: An evaluative response regarding the impact of another person's behavior.

Fight or flight: An involuntary biochemical response to stress that readies a person to take action.

Financial budget: A systematic plan for expenditures.

Financial plan: A comprehensive plan for income, expenses, savings and investments.

Follow-through: Completing what was agreed upon.

Forgiveness: The act of excusing an offense.

Frustration: An emotional response to not getting one's needs met.

Generalization: The transfer of a response that is learned in one situation to another situation.

Generosity: A suspension of one's own needs in the service of another; a willingness to give.

Goodness: A quality of being kind and generous.

Gratitude: Feeling thankful and appreciative.

Grudge: A deep-seated feeling of resentment that lasts long after an offense occurred.

Guilt: A feeling of remorse for having done something wrong.

Habit: An unconscious and repetitious pattern of behavior.

Honesty: Being truthful.

Humanitarian: An ethic of kindness and service that extends to all human beings.

Imagination: The ability to form mental constructs for something that was not personally experienced.

Immutable: Unchangeable over time.

Individuation: The developmental process of differentiating from childhood into adulthood; separating from the protection of one's home and growing into oneself.

Infidelity: An act of sexual unfaithfulness.

Influence: Having an impact that brings about change in behavior, thinking or feelings.

Inhibition: Restraint of behavior or impulses.

Instrumental anger: Anger that is expressed to achieve a specific outcome.

Intention: A goal or purpose.

Interrupting: To break in or disrupt communication by injecting commentary.

Intimacy: Deeply personal and close.

Introspection: The examination of one's own mental and emotional states and processes.

Intra-psychic: The internal psychological processes of an individual.

Joy: Ecstatic happiness.

Judgment: The formation of an opinion that is based on right and wrong, good and bad.

Justification: A statement that attempts to show that an action was necessary or reasonable.

Kindness: Considerate, generous, warmhearted, humane.

Letting go: The act of releasing or eliminating troublesome feelings.

Lies: False, deceptive and misleading information.

Listening: To perceive what is being said.

Loving kindness: A feeling of care and concern for fellow human beings, animals or the planet without regard to getting something in return.

Manners: A socially correct way of behaving.

Misrepresentation: A misleading falsehood.

Mores: The accepted traditional customs and manners of a particular social group.

Mutual understanding: A shared decision or opinion.

Mutuality: Something shared in common.

Needs, Wants, Desires (NWDs): A state of dissatisfaction in which it feels like something is lacking.

Negative feedback: A negative evaluative response.

Negotiation: A dialogue for resolving differences.

Non-disclosure: Information that is not shared.

Obligation: A duty to act.

Obsession: A preoccupation with a single thought or set of thoughts.

Omission: Something that is left out.

Orderliness: Adhering to a method or system.

Over-reacting: An excessive or exaggerated response.

Panacea: All encompassing.

Pattern of behavior: The same behavior that repeats itself in a variety of situations.

Perception: A person's personal interpretation of stimuli, what he senses.

Perseverative: A specific thought or behavior that repeats itself like a broken record.

Physiology: Functions of the physical body.

Plan of Action (POA): A comprehensive plan that has goals, internal and external strategies, and desired outcomes.

Pleaser: A person whose main priority is to meet the needs of others.

Presence: Being mindful of the present moment.

Priorities: Those things that are most important.

Problem-solving: The process of finding solutions to problems.

Process: A series of steps; how to go about doing something.

Projection: The attribution of one's own attitudes, feelings, or suppositions to others.

Promise: A commitment to do something.

Psychic: Relating to the human mind.

Psychology: The study of mental processes and behavior in humans.

Psychotherapy: The treatment of mental health difficulties.

Rationality: The use of reason, logic and common sense.

Reactivity: Easy emotional activation by a stimulus.

Reconciliation: Reestablishing a relationship after a quarrel or disruption.

Reflective listening: A listening process that mirrors back what has been said.

Relationship: A connection between two people.

Relative thinking: Formulating ideas relative to how others are thinking, feeling, and behaving.

Re-offend: Repeating an offense.

Reset button: A mechanism that reestablishes the baseline settings.

Response: A behavior that follows and is impacted by a stimulus.

Responsibility: Having prescribed duties or obligations to something or someone.

Restitution: To restore to a previous state as compensation for damages.

Restraint: To exercise control over one's behavior.

Retribution: A punishment for wrongdoing.

Revenge: To retaliate through an act of vengeance.

Romance: An amorous connection; a strong feeling of attraction between two people.

Rule: A generally accepted guide or principal for regulating conduct.

Rumination: Going over and over the same anxious thoughts to oneself.

Self: One's individuality; the totality of distinct characteristics that define a person; a person's unique separateness.

Self-centered: A preoccupation with oneself.

Self-confidence: Belief and trust in oneself.

Self-discipline: Getting yourself to do something for self improvement that you don't feel like doing.

Sensitivity: An easily activated feeling response.

Sociology: The study of human social behavior.

Spread: To distribute widely; to extend to a larger area.

Standards: The criteria for completion.

Stimulus: A behavior or a condition that precedes and has an impact on the response.

Stuffing feelings: Feelings that are pushed aside, are not immediately accessible but are still present.

Synergistic: "Outside the box" solutions.

Tabling: To postpone consideration; to shelve.

Tension: Mental or emotional strain; stress.

Time-together/time-apart ratios: The relationship between two people's separate desires to be with one another.

Tool: Something that has practical utility and is used to achieve an objective.

Uncertainty: Having doubt; not being sure.

Unconditional love: Love without conditions. Parental love.

Understanding: Recognizing and knowing how someone else thinks and feels.

Validate: To confirm or corroborate.

Victim: A person who is hurt or harmed by someone else.

Vulnerability: Being susceptible to emotional injury or harm.

Willingness to walk: The willingness to end a relationship if there is a lack of fit or a serious breach of boundaries.

Willpower: The strength of mind to carry out one's decisions.

Win-win: Decisions in which both parties feel satisfied.

Worry: An anxious or agitated concern about a future event.

CPSIA information can be obtained at www.ICGtesting.com
Printed in the USA
BVOW011945160113

310812BV00005B/10/P

9 780985 999308